Proudly Serving My Corporate Masters

Proudly Serving My Corporate Masters

What I Learned in Ten Years as a Microsoft Programmer

Adam Barr

Writers Club Press

San Jose New York Lincoln Shanghai

Proudly Serving My Corporate Masters
What I Learned in Ten Years as a Microsoft Programmer

Writers Club Press
an imprint of iUniverse.com, Inc.

For information address:
iUniverse.com, Inc.
5220 S 16th, Ste. 200
Lincoln, NE 68512
www.iuniverse.com

ISBN: 0-595-16128-6

Printed in the United States of America

To my parents, Michael and Marcia Barr.

Contents

Acknowledgments

This book wouldn't have happened without the help of many people.

My greatest thanks are to my wife, Maura, for listening to me rant about how I should write a book, encouraging me to write the book, and offering support (and watching the kids) while I actually wrote the book. Without you none of this would have been possible. I love you!

My children, Zachary, Madeline, and Keenan, didn't have much to do with producing the book, but they are so darn cute I had to mention them. Daddy should be spending less time in the den now.

My parents, Michael and Marcia Barr, read draft after draft and filled them with comments. Plus they gave birth to me, raised me, and are the greatest parents ever. Would you believe that my father wrote a program for the UNIVAC computer at the University of Pennsylvania way back in 1956? And that my mother took a job writing BASIC programs to help pay for me to go to college? No wonder I turned out the way I did.

My sister, Becky, who by fortuitous circumstance is a professional editor, edited the whole original mess that I claimed was a complete draft. Her comments were much appreciated, as were her lessons on how to use the editing toolbar in Microsoft Word. All in all we are now even for her having stolen my pacifier when I was an infant.

My brother, Joe, read most of the book and provided encouragement in his own inimitable way. I should mention that my brother is a different person from "Papa Joe" Barr who is a contributing editor at *LinuxWorld*.

My uncle, Tony (whose given name was Alan), was the first person I ever knew who actually worked as a computer programmer. I always enjoyed the time he spent with me in his home office, introducing me to the computer game "Adventure" or waxing philosophical on the virtues of 8-inch floppy drives. Tony died too young on February 16, 1999.

My brother-in-law, Gerard Varni, who is a better writer than I am, read several early drafts of the book and gave me lots of advice and encouragement.

My editor, Bob Drews, did a fantastic job beating my alleged final draft into the smooth-flowing read you have before you. Julie Pignataro, John Robbins, and June Sanns-Kaylor proofread the result to perfection.

Various people deserve mention for their help on the book, some of it unintentional: Buzz Aagaard, A.J. Agarwal, Avi Belinsky, Val Bercovici, David Byrne, Peter Cherna, Tim Cherna, Alan Deutschman, k. Margaret Grossman, Leslie and Matt Holle, Margaret Landon, Elaine Law, Alice Leiner, Doug Lovejoy, Becca and Ken Moss, Eric Nace, Toula Poletti, Bernie Ryan, Michael Scott, Sean Selitrennikoff, Kate Varni, and Patrice Varni. I'd also like to say howdy to the members of the Princeton Writing electronic mailing list.

Thanks to this lovely new invention called the Internet, I was able to do a lot of the fact checking for the book from the comfort of my own home. Who knew that so many people spent their free time maintaining websites full of computer history? I would especially like to note sites maintained by Tom Carlson, Alexios Chouchoulas, Troy Fisher, Paul Grebenc, Ron Heuse, Dan Landiss, Chris Owen, Ken Polsson, Donald A. Thomas, Jr., David Wyatt, and Steve Zeigler.

Finally, I'd like to thank all my co-workers during my years at Microsoft. Without you there would be no book, so you can pat yourselves on the back for that.

Introduction

When I started working at Microsoft back in March 1990, it was just another software company. Like most people, I had no idea it would become the company it has—one of the most talked about, feared, admired, hated, loved companies in the world. Microsoft is everywhere these days. The company sells over 100 software and hardware products, in virtually every segment of the market. A search on the Web for "Microsoft" returns over 20 million hits. Microsoft appears in late-night comedy routines, in advice columns, in business school studies. Everybody in the world, it seems, has heard of Microsoft and has an opinion about it. Microsoft affects everybody who uses a computer, and pretty much everybody uses a computer.

The value of Microsoft's stock has soared: $10,000 invested on the day I started would have been worth, at its peak, almost $800,000. The company's chairman and CEO, Bill Gates, has become one of the richest men in the world, and not coincidentally, one of the best known.

Many books have been written about the company, but none that capture the experience I had there. I was a developer, in many ways the key position at Microsoft. Developers are the programmers who are responsible for actually writing the software that is shipped out to millions of people. By the time I left in April 2000, I had my own ideas about the company, which didn't always match popular opinion.

As I worked on various projects, I saw first-hand how Microsoft works internally: the relationships between development teams and the rest of the company; how Microsoft recruits and interviews people; the sacrifices that are made to get software done; what it is like to be sued by your own government; and of course, the lure of stock option wealth.

This book is a view from the bottom of the programmer pile. In 10 years at Microsoft I never rose above first-level management, never had more than two people working for me. I was never interviewed for any magazine articles, never had a press release mention my accomplishments, never participated in a meeting with Bill Gates. The story told here is not the one of high-profile meetings between powerful industry titans. It is the outsider's view, my own personal opinion on why the company has succeeded, what it does well and what it does badly, and what it needs to do in the future.

Back in the late 1980s, some employees felt that Microsoft was getting too bureaucratic. They distributed buttons at the annual company meeting, emblazoned with the phrase "Proudly Serving My Corporate Masters." The meaning was half ironic; they certainly were proud to be associated with Microsoft, but at the same time they didn't want management to think that its decisions would be accepted without question. This book was written in the same spirit.

The book is part history, part narrative, part analysis. It talks about how Microsoft recruits employees, then relates the events from my stint at Softimage, a company Microsoft owned. I will explain the history and significance of evangelism, one of Microsoft's great strengths. Linux is considered for a bit, as well as Microsoft's various image problems and legal foibles. Finally I discuss Microsoft's future prospects. Mixed in are some flashbacks to the early days of personal computing, to provide some perspective on the present.

The book is not about the specifics of how Microsoft writes software. Nonetheless there are several technical topics that I felt needed a little more explanation than you typically find in a business book. Scattered among the chapters are three short "Technical Digressions" in which I delve a little deeper into these subjects. I encourage you to read these no matter what your technical level; they will help you understand some of the issues I discuss. If your eyes start to glaze over, you can consult the glossary in the back for the 10-second version.

As a matter of full disclosure, I will mention that I have an investment in a company that a friend of mine started, which is working on Linux-based home computing appliances. On the other hand, as a former employee I also own a good chunk of Microsoft stock. So I figure those two balance out, leaving me reasonably unbiased.

Please feel free to contact me at adam@proudlyserving.com. Enjoy!

1

Feeding the Engine

On October 26, 1999, it was announced that Microsoft would be one of four new components in the 30 stocks that make up the Dow Jones Industrial Average. This was a long-overdue recognition of the role of technology in the U.S. economy, and in particular of Microsoft's central place in the industry.

But Microsoft was different from the other three newcomers. It has no computer chip manufacturing plants like Intel, no chain of retail stores like Home Depot, no network of phone lines like SBC Communications. Indeed, it's not "industrial" at all. Its product is software; its assembly line the brainpower of its employees. And while companies across America would naturally say their employees are vital to their success, for Microsoft in a large sense the employees *are* the company.

And that makes Microsoft very particular about who it hires.

In high school I read Tracy Kidder's *The Soul of a New Machine*, the Pulitzer-Prize-winning book about the race to develop a new minicomputer at a company called Data General. The company had set two teams competing against each other; one team had a large budget and all the elite engineers, and the other got some office space and a pat on the back. The

story followed this second team as its members worked crazy hours, sacri-
ficed their personal lives, and took assorted engineering risks to produce a
computer, soundly trouncing the "A" team. As I whiled away my college
nights in the computer lab at Princeton University, I thought of the Data
General employees who had spent their nights working in their own lab.
When I began my job search in anticipation of my graduation in 1988, I
was eager to abuse myself by working on one of these crazy projects.

Unfortunately, all I got were dull, tedious interviews that left me with
corresponding impressions of the companies.

I thought AT&T would be cool. At school I used the Unix operating
system, designed at AT&T. Some of my professors were AT&T engineers
teaching at Princeton for a semester or two, who regaled us with stories of
Bell Labs hi-jinks. AT&T had massive office buildings scattered throughout New Jersey, and I knew that somewhere inside them there were cool
people working on cool projects.

In my first AT&T interview I didn't go anywhere near those people. I
talked to four or five people who all worked on the same piece of equipment. Each of them spent the first half-hour describing it in great detail (I
still remember—how could I forget?—that it was a fancy handset that
could be plugged into a phone line to diagnose problems). The rest of the
interview consisted of us discussing nothing in particular. I had to make
small talk to avoid embarrassing pauses in the conversation. Then it was
on to the next interview, for more of the same. Luckily I had recently broken my finger playing hockey, so the cast on my hand gave us *something* to
talk about (I recommend a cast as a great ice-breaker for anyone doing
interviews).

The highlight of the day, such as it was, was lunch. The building had a
sit-down restaurant, normally off-limits to peon-level employees relegated
to the cafeteria. But an interview lunch allowed everyone who was going
to meet with the candidate to eat in the restaurant. So I had lunch with six
other people, all of whom were more excited to be there than I was. The

other thing I remember is that there were monitors in the hallways that constantly displayed the AT&T stock price.

Somewhat alarmed that the food had been the best thing about the place, I came away determined never to work there. It seemed full of bored employees working on boring tasks under a bureaucracy that reached to the sky. I asked one of the employees if he ever worked late, and he said, "Oh, once in a while I have to work until 6." To me, coming out of college, with *The Soul of a New Machine* ringing in my head, this was exactly the opposite of what I wanted to hear. I wonder if AT&T knew how badly it came across to a gung-ho college kid like me.

I tried interviewing at another AT&T site, but it was the same dreary agenda minus the fancy restaurant. The one unusual interview I had was with a fellow Princeton graduate. He spent the whole interview telling me what a great place AT&T was. Why? Because you didn't work hard and got paid well. Great! This guy also told me that he interviewed with other companies all the time, presumably to make sure there wasn't someplace else paying even more for less work.

After I ultimately accepted a job at a small startup near Princeton, I continued to do some interviews. Sure, I had no intention of working at any of these places, but you got free food, maybe a hotel, a plane ticket if the company was far enough away—more than enough to ease any moral qualms. One of these was at Hewlett-Packard in sunny Silicon Valley. California! I was hopeful because the HP employee who had done my on-campus interview had been pretty hip, which boosted HP several notches in my ranking of companies. Unfortunately the corporate interview was awful. The building I interviewed in was a maze of cubicles. The big conceptual breakthrough was that every employee had a certain type of chair, based on his or her level in the management hierarchy. All managers were then given a visitor's chair that matched the next level below them on the chain. Thus, when you went to talk to your boss, you would be spared the discomforting sensation of sitting in a chair that was a different design from the one you sat in at your own desk.

Hewlett-Packard did do me one favor—they didn't offer me a job, so I never had to feel guilty about flying out there under false pretenses. They also cured me of my "Why not?" attitude toward interviews. Someone from another division within HP, who either didn't know or didn't care that I had already been turned down after my first interview, called to offer me another trip to California for another set of interviews. In fact she tracked me down at my parents' house in Montreal during a vacation. With my Mom in the room I just couldn't bring myself to agree to fly out.

IBM, of all places, managed to create a decent impression. Weeks before my interview, someone in Human Resources sent me a release form to sign stating that by law IBM had to notify me that I was going to be given a standardized test. Impressive, but unfortunately the entire evaluation consisted of that test. The rest of the day was one giant schmooze-fest. Give IBM people credit, they managed to make this seem more palatable than AT&T or HP, despite the fact that the job they were discussing sounded even more mind-numbingly boring than the AT&T one. I actually considered working there! I could imagine the people I talked to singing songs from the IBM songbook, without it seeming corny (this was in 1988, when IBM was near its historic high in employment; now, with the company three-quarters its former size, and having endured painful rounds of layoffs in the early 1990s, this noble feeling may have dissipated).

The most amazing thing IBM did for me was to give me money for dinner, in cash, *before I left in the late afternoon*. Furthermore it was some ungodly sum, like $16, far more than I could ever spend at McDonald's—and I could keep the extra! The recruiter also said IBM would pay for another night in my hotel if I didn't want to drive back to school in the snowstorm that had developed, but somehow it was the trust embodied in that $16 that got to me. Who said college graduates are hard to impress…but it still wasn't enough to get me to work there.

By the time I graduated from college, I had been using an IBM PC with Microsoft software for almost 6 years. Microsoft was the first company I interviewed with, and the one I desperately wanted to work for. I knew in advance which day the sign-up sheet for Microsoft interviews was going to be posted, and I was the first one on the list.

Microsoft came out to Princeton in force, with a recruiter and four interviewers. They further impressed me by taking some of the candidates out to dinner the night before the on-campus interviews. I managed to snag an invite to this through someone who had been an intern there the previous summer. They took us out to Lahiere's, the toniest restaurant in town. I debated over whether to order caviar, wondering if it would show up on my interview report. One of the interviewers was Nathan Myhrvold, who later became known both as Chief Technology Officer of Microsoft and as a noted gourmet. Nathan solved my dilemma by ordering caviar for the whole table.

The interviews at Career Services the next day were the final proof that Microsoft was the place for me. Instead of going over my resume and making small talk, the Microsoft recruiter jumped right in and started asking me programming questions. And the on-campus interview is merely a preview of the interview you do when you fly back to Redmond.

Microsoft interviews in Redmond for technical positions are structured the same now as they were then. You first meet with a recruiter, who explains how your day is going to go. Next come interviews, typically with three people in the group you are going to work with, then your potential future boss, and then perhaps his or her boss. Whichever of these interviews falls around lunchtime will be turned into a slightly longer lunch interview. If things are going well, you meet with the person up the chain who has the actual authority to hire you; he or she is known as the "as-appropriate" because the meeting only happens if it is appropriate to do so, meaning that there is a chance you are going to get a job offer. After all this you meet with the recruiter again for a wrap-up.

The recruiter probably already knows whether you are going to get an offer, but usually keeps mum at that point.

As the pool of people who have worked at Microsoft, interviewed at Microsoft, or read about Microsoft interviews has grown, people have started to have expectations about the significance of the number of interviews they do. The more the better—"three interviews and out" is a very bad sign.

The key thing about all the interviews is that they are "technical."

After some introductory small talk and maybe some discussion about items from the resume, the real fun begins. The candidate is asked between one and three "Microsoft questions"—the kind that earned Microsoft its interviewing reputation. The specifics can vary widely. Logic problems are common. Developers, as programmers are referred to at Microsoft, are almost always asked to code up the solution to a small programming problem on the office whiteboard. (Developers at Microsoft actually have the lofty title of Software Design Engineer, commonly referred to as SDE, but I won't bother with that.) Program managers, who among other things work on determining the appearance of the software, are often asked questions related to user interface design. Testers (officially called Software Test Engineers) are asked how they would test a hypothetical piece of code if it were handed to them. Real answers are expected, but the process by which they are arrived at is also watched. Candidates are expected to ask their own questions to clarify the interviewer's question, think before talking or scribbling, and be prepared to convince the interviewer that a solution is correct.

The interviewer asks the candidate whatever he or she feels like asking that day. Some interviewers will ask the same question of all candidates. Sometimes they will hear of a question that another candidate has been asked and decide to try it out on their own candidates.

My interview with Microsoft went well, in my opinion, except they didn't offer me a job. I had prepared for the interview by working all night on a school assignment, then heading to the airport the next day still not having slept. After a day off in Seattle courtesy of Microsoft, which I was supposed to spend exploring the city but spent most of sleeping, I did the interview at Microsoft, flew home, and immediately went back to the lab at school, pulled another all-nighter, handed in the assignment the next afternoon, then crawled back to my room to sleep. An hour later the phone rang: it was the Microsoft recruiter, telling me they had turned me down.

I probably should have been tipped off to what was coming by my interview dinner. Every candidate got taken out to dinner by a Microsoft person who knew how the interview went but who wasn't supposed to say anything about it. Of course if you wanted to impress someone, you drove him or her across the lake to Seattle for dinner at an expensive restaurant. I got taken to dinner at a Thai restaurant a mile from campus, where a grand total of $20 was spent on me, my gracious dinner host, and two friends that he brought along for backup. He spent most of dinner describing what a great time he had had at a steakhouse with a friend of mine from Princeton, who had interviewed a few weeks before and gotten an offer. He made a point of telling me that they had eaten so much that the two of them exceeded the $75 limit that Microsoft would cover for interview dinners.

Getting hosed just made me want to work there even more. To a candidate coming out of college, a Microsoft interview is a breath of fresh air—stressful, but fun. You come away from the interview thinking, "Wow, if they only hire people who make it through this, I bet there are some pretty smart people working here." This is similar to the strategy described in *The Soul of a New Machine*, in which the head of the project explains how they wrapped up their interviews with candidates they liked: "We tell him that we only let in the best. Then we let him in."

*   *   *

The company I wound up working for right after college was a small startup called Dendrite International, headquartered 45 minutes north of Princeton. Dendrite wrote territory management software for pharmaceutical salesmen, the representatives of large drug companies who make presentations to doctors and hospitals. Dendrite seemed to have accidentally hit on the prototype for the Microsoft interview. The guy who interviewed me on campus was a recent Princeton alum named Dennis Moore. Dendrite had only about 30 employees at the time and no official college recruiting program. Dennis had decided on his own to interview at a few schools and had done the necessary paperwork himself.

He spent the interview drinking Diet Coke and trying to stay awake. He explained that he had been up all night at work and had driven straight to Princeton from there. He looked like hell. All I could think was, "Where do I sign?"

Dendrite wanted me to come in for more interviews. It didn't occur to anyone to offer to rent me a car, and it didn't occur to me to ask, so I borrowed a friend's car and drove up. I met Michael Mee, my future boss, who handed me two pieces of paper with some code on them, then left me alone for a while with instructions to figure out what they did. Then I wandered around and met all the programmers (there were fewer than 10). The whole process was very haphazard but also very compelling. A few days later, Michael called and offered me a job.

When I started at Dendrite, everyone was working insane hours to meet unattainable deadlines—just like in *The Soul of a New Machine*! I loved it, of course—my own personal death march. The saying was, "Work at Dendrite, lose your girlfriend," although this was mostly wishful thinking since it presupposed a girlfriend being there for the losing. Upper management had no idea what was going on down in the trenches, but this fostered a great "us vs. them" feeling that bound all the programmers into the closest-knit team I have ever been on.

The strange thing in retrospect was that it really was fun. We would work together all day, then go out to dinner together, and then often as not come back to work together. It helped that we were all young, single, and mostly unencumbered with external social lives. It was interesting work, and with so few programmers you got to dabble in everything.

Looking back it is impressive that management was able to get us to work as much as we did. They didn't know much about what specifically we did all day (and night), but they sure knew how many hours we spent doing it, because everybody there had to fill out timecards. Dendrite wasn't paying us for overtime—they just wanted to be able to bill clients for it. A rumor went around that a report was prepared each month detailing how much free labor the company was getting from the programmers, but even that didn't do much to dampen our enthusiasm. Years later I was talking to Dennis about why we all worked so much and he said, "I don't know, I guess we all just liked Michael." This really is the key—if you want programmers to work crazy hours for you, they need to like what they are doing.

Unfortunately the company was growing quickly. Soon Michael and Dennis left, and a more corporate manager was brought in to run the programming department. This pushed the boundary of the clueless zone a little too close to home—programmers hate being second-guessed by management. Despite a core of quality people who remained, the fun atmosphere was gone. In the summer of 1989, a friend of mine got a job at Microsoft as an intern; I went to visit him and wound up interviewing for a job. It was similar to my interview as a student, with a different cast of characters and a different outcome—a job offer. I was about to resign from Dendrite when they announced they wanted to send me to Japan for 3 months. I postponed accepting the Microsoft job and went off to Osaka, but when I got back nothing much had changed at Dendrite. I called back my recruiter and found that the job offer was still open.

Microsoft flew me out for a "sell trip," which is similar to an interview trip except that since you already have an offer, each interview is a low-pressure sales pitch on why you should work for Microsoft. Unfortunately, if you put two programmers in a room with explicit instructions *not* to discuss technical questions, the result is pretty dull. I persevered to my final interview with Brian Valentine, the as-appropriate, at the time the head of the networking division. As soon as I sat down in his office, Brian crossed his arms, stared at me, and said, "So are you going to work here or not?"

A friend had advised me to ask for more stock options, but instead I meekly settled for a $2,000 signing bonus. In March 1990 I moved out to Seattle to start working for Bill Gates.

*   *   *

At Microsoft I got to see recruiting from the other side. It is impossible to overestimate how important interviewing and hiring are to Microsoft. The company is not long on process and training. The approach sometimes referred to as "masses of asses"—achieving results with large numbers of merely adequate people—is nonexistent. Microsoft's past and future success depends entirely on hiring very talented people.

I interviewed my first candidate about four months after I started working there. Microsoft intentionally puts recent hires on the interview schedule of incoming candidates. A lot of the candidates are college seniors and it impresses them to see Microsoft trusting someone just a few years older than them. Plus this fits in with the Microsoft philosophy that you learn by doing. To be on the safe side, interview schedules also include more experienced interviewers.

Microsoft is not very big on training of new employees in general, but it does offer interviewer training. I had signed up for this, but I was asked to do my first interview before the training happened. Nobody seemed too concerned about this, so I went ahead and winged it.

After each interview, the interviewer writes an email giving his or her feedback on how it went and sends it to a list of people that includes the recruiter, the as-appropriate, and all the other people on the interview schedule. So everyone sees everyone else's comments throughout the day. There is a rule in most groups that the first line of this feedback email should be either "hire" or "no hire," followed by a few paragraphs justifying the recommendation. This leads to "hire" and "no hire" being used as nouns when referring to candidates, as in "this guy is a definite no hire." Wishy-washy comments like "lukewarm hire" are not allowed. And saying, "Gosh, I didn't really get a good feel for this candidate, so I'm going to abstain from choosing," would get you nothing but grief and no more interviews.

When I finally attended interviewer training, the instructions handed out included examples of how to write the rest of the feedback, where the "hire"/"no hire" decision was expanded on. You need to be concise, mention what you talked about and what problems the candidate solved, defend your hiring decision, and be fair to the candidate. (In the networking group, you were explicitly prohibited from writing, "If you hire him, I quit.") Included were examples of "bad" feedback, such as this badly defended "hire":

```
Hire.
Bright, competent, articulate. He could be
a developer anywhere in the company. I was
unable to press him on his specialties,
since they are not mine, but his general
problem-solving skills were excellent.
```

It says hire, but it doesn't explain why in any detail. Get it? Here's a "no hire" that is also a little skimpy on specifics:

```
Until we started coding, I was impressed
with the dude, after flailing for almost 45
minutes on the code, the dudes a wash.
Strong No Hire.
```

In addition to committing the feedback faux pas of putting the recommendation *after* the feedback and embellishing it with a contraindicated adjective ("strong"), this doesn't explain what exactly happened. One of the reasons Microsoft wants good feedback is so it can defend itself if anyone ever sues after not being hired. Feedback like the previous one too easily hides biases on the interviewer's part. In this case the sample had email from the recruiter appended, pointing out the flaws and asking for a more complete summary.

Finally there was this classic of the genre:

```
Recommendation: hire

This guy is as green as grass and com-
pletely naive in the ways of the world, but
he seems smart enough and does seem like a
hard worker to boot.

Where has this guy spent his life? I took
him for lunch, and the menu fascinated him.
How do you pronounce "quiche" or "crois-
sant"? He'd heard of croissant, but had no
idea what either meant. I paid with a credit
card. Intriguing enough, but how was the tip
handled then? Well, you see, you can specify
on this line here...I mentioned that MS did
most of its sales outside of the US now, and
this seemed incredible. He's been to Europe
as a child (his father was in the military)
but his knowledge of the world is "I know
that when you are in the Orient, don't drink
the water."

He's fairly green computer-wise as well.
This was a non-technical lunch interview,
but when I asked him to describe a program
that he had written himself from scratch
```

that he was particularly proud of, it was a
struggle. On the other hand, he seems to
really dig at trying to find answers to problems, and I really like to see that. He has
a Z-80 computer at home with 48K of RAM, and
he was programming in assembly language and
he kept plugging away until he learned to
program interrupts. Then he realized that
debugging was going to be tricky with no OS
support, but he kept digging until he found
a way to do that too.

He don't know DOS, he don't know Intel, he
don't know networks, he don't know testing,
and he don't know life, but my impression is
that except for possibly the last category,
he'll learn fast. In other words, he'll fit
right in here!

Frankly I'm mystified as to why this was presented as bad feedback. It
certainly explains why the decision was "hire"! Maybe the candidate was
too much on the "huge potential" side of things and not enough on the
"could get something done within 12 months of starting work" side, but
you're supposed to be hiring for the long term, and anyway that is a
judgment call on the part of the interviewer. Sure, there is too much
space spent discussing what a rube the candidate was, but the result is
hilarious. In fact, the whole thing might not be actual interview feedback, but the result of someone trying to simulate bad feedback as an
example for others.

So the interviewer training provided these examples of how not to
write feedback (there are also examples of good feedback, too dull to
bother repeating). But these are useful only once you have made the
basic "hire" versus "no hire" decision. That is the tricky part. Sure there
are some candidates that just blow you away with their ability, and some

that are complete no-ops (a "no-op" is a computer instruction that intentionally does nothing, which is useful in some situations where you want to slow the computer down but not a compliment when applied to a person). The vast majority of candidates, however, fall somewhere between those two extremes. There were various tests suggested for resolving the borderline cases in your mind. Do you think the person could do your job? Would you be upset if he went to work for your competitor? But it all boils down to a personal feeling: "Should Microsoft hire this person?"

As I sat down to write my feedback after my first interview, I realized that I wasn't sure what to say. The person certainly seemed qualified, but I knew that most candidates who made it to an interview in Redmond seemed qualified. I realized that I had not been thinking during the interview of the eventual "hire"/"no-hire" decision I would have to make. I had asked him the standard stuff—about his previous job, some technical questions—but nothing stood out; there had been no sudden flash of inspiration. I had seen interview feedback before, and it seemed so self-assured. It was always obvious to the interviewer, and, by implication, to anyone with half a brain, that this candidate was either the greatest thing since sliced bread, or a complete idiot.

The problem was that I could justify either a "hire" or a "no hire." I could emphasize the positive parts of the interview and explain away the bad parts ("He got it wrong, but it was a tough question"), or I could play up the bad parts and criticize the good parts ("He got it right, but I think it was just a guess"). Luckily for me, I was not the first person to interview him that day; the previous interviewer had given him a "hire," so I followed suit and tailored the rest of my feedback to match. Eventually, every interviewer gave him a "hire" except for the as-appropriate. The candidate wound up coming in for more interviews, was hired, and worked at Microsoft for over eight years—which proves something, although I'm not sure what.

Because of indecisive lemmings like me, some groups at Microsoft have experimented with leaving out the hire/no hire decision, or simply not including the other interviewers in the feedback list—which is how many other companies handle things. Unfortunately if you don't see the previous feedback for a candidate you might talk about the same things the previous interviewer did—what we'll call the "AT&T handset syndrome." And leaving out the "hire" or "no hire" isn't much help because the rest of the feedback usually makes it obvious.

Even after I had a lot of interviewing experience I would often be extremely conflicted about whether to vote "hire" or "no hire." The general rule given is that if you have any doubt, you should vote "no hire." Unfortunately it can be hard to be hired at Microsoft if you have even one "no hire" on your feedback. This leads to "feedback inflation" where people vote "hire" because the previous feedback has all been "hire," and nobody wants to be the person who ruins the candidate's chances.

Despite the prohibition against it, people sometimes worked around this problem by writing feedback that is somewhere between "hire" and "no hire." Such as the following, taken from actual feedback I saw over the years: "I wouldn't give him a no hire, but I wouldn't be excited about having him"; "No Hire—this is really close, it's a fairly tough call"; "Hire (with reservations)"; "Weak no hire"; "As a hardnose I say no hire. As a nice guy I might say hire"; "I do not consider him to be a strong hire, but he does juuust pass the bar for me."

Translation: they didn't think the candidate was great, but they didn't want him or her to be tarred with the "no hire" brush. What they wanted to say was, "no hire, unless everyone else thinks hire, in which case don't let me be the person who stops him or her from being hired."

There's one more twist. When you were done interviewing a candidate, you needed to hand him or her off to the next interviewer, either by walking over to the appropriate office, or, more likely as the Microsoft campus grew, calling a shuttle to another building. You needed to give the next interviewer a quick summary of what your feedback was going to be, since you hadn't sent the email version yet. So you had to make a snap hire/no hire judgment right after the interview, before you had much time to think. This encouraged even more of a gut-feeling approach and less of a rational analysis. Sometimes you would tell the next interviewer one thing and on reflection, while you were typing the official feedback email, you would realize you had changed your mind. So you had a choice between sending feedback that justified your initial opinion, even if you no longer agreed with it—thus hardening the opinion into fact—or confusing the hell out of the next interviewer, and looking like a wishy-washy goofus to boot.

Technical Digression: Code

What do Microsoft employees do all day?

I was a programmer, a.k.a. developer, which means I wrote software. To understand Microsoft, you have to understand a bit about what programmers do, which means understanding a bit about software.

Software is written in a programming language. The result is often referred to as "code," and the process as "coding," although these terms do not mean that the code is encrypted in some way. People compare the variety of programming languages to the variety of human languages (English, French, Swahili, etc.), but this isn't really correct. All human languages are more or less equally expressive, whereas programming languages can vary widely. Human languages tend to have evolved over centuries. Programming languages are invented from scratch, usually by a few people. And in fact, most programming languages contain written snippets of a human language, almost always English.

Programming languages are more like the "languages" used for writing music down on paper. The most common one involves writing musical notes on horizontal lines, but there are also more specialized methods, such as the tablature form that describes guitar playing in

17

terms of which frets should be held and which strings should be played. Although musical languages have not proliferated as much as programming languages, it is easy to imagine others; you might write the notes down in English, in a form like "a-b-flat-c-sharp-quarter notes," or you could write down the wavelength and duration of the sounds produced at each point. Each of these might be more useful than basic musical notation for some specialized use, and—like programming languages—each might be debated and modified, championed and sneered at, and gain and lose adherents over time.

Written music and programming languages both have a defined starting point and an implied way to proceed. Written music also has separate notions of syntax and semantics. Syntax is the exact details of how the music appears on the paper—the time is written here, the notes go here, the words go here. Semantics is a higher-level concept involving the meaning of the music: "This music will cheer you up" or "Play this when the team is about to score a touchdown." People who can read music will be able to understand the syntax quickly, and if not, they can consult a book or other reference to help them understand it. Understanding the semantics by looking at the written music is an acquired skill, and sometimes it is necessary to play the piece to really grasp the semantics.

All this corresponds fairly closely to programming languages. Consider a snippet of code written in the programming language C:

```
int i;
printf("Let's count to 10!\n");
for (i = 1; i <= 10; i++) {
      printf("%d\n", i);
}
```

The syntax of C dictates the code's general appearance—the placement of semicolons and braces (which programmers usually call "squiggly brackets") and the rest. The parentheses do not indicate an explanatory comment; they are used purely as symbols with a meaning defined by the syntax of C. The location of the line breaks is not important and the code is formatted as shown only for ease of reading, although some languages do have rules about that. What matters in C is where the characters are in relation to each other—that the { comes before the }, that the ; is after the), that the word "for" is spelled correctly, and so on.

Most programming languages bear some resemblance to C. These are called "higher-level languages," as opposed to the language the computer actually understands, which is known as "machine language" and is simply a string of ones and zeroes. C looks essentially the same no matter what computer it is written for, whereas machine language is microprocessor-specific. Each microprocessor will have associated with it a language known as "assembly language," which is a human-readable form of machine language.

The semantics of this piece of code is to print out the numbers from 1 to 10. More specifically, it first prints out the line "Let's count to 10!", then on the next line prints the number 1, then on the line after that the number 2, and so on up to 10. The repetitive part of the code, where it prints out each number, is known as a "loop."

The first step in programming is to type the code into a file stored on the computer. This is known as a program. You then tell the computer to follow the instructions in the program, which is known as "running" or "executing" it. If you ran the program above, you would see "Let's count to 10!" and the numbers from one to 10 appear on the screen.

There are other ways to run programs. For example, some email contains programs that are run when the email is read—which can be an effective way for computer viruses to spread. A computer virus is a program like any other, but one whose code defines a set of malicious actions.

The first thing to understand about code is that right now, computers do what you tell them to do, not necessarily what you want them to do. For example, if your code looked like this:

```
int i;
printf("Let's count to 10!\n");
for (i = 1; i <= 20; i++) {
    printf("%d\n", i);
}
```

the computer, although first printing the message "Let's count to 10!", would actually count to 20. The difference from the previous bit of code is that "i <= 10" now reads "i <= 20". This result would be wrong from the point of view of a human watching, but would be right from the computer's point of view. A computer runs code like a soulless, perfect musician would play music—always playing exactly the notes that are written, and never noticing or caring if the music sounds beautiful or expressive.

The interface that computers present to users—the windows displayed on the screen, the word processor, the editor used to type in a program—is the result of programs that the computers are running. Those programs, although vastly more complicated than the short example shown above, are executed by the computer with the same "do exactly what the code tells you to do" accuracy. When a word processing program decides that you are writing a letter and pops up an offer to help, it is doing so because the code for the word processor itself has been written to do so, not because of any innate knowledge on the part of the computer. What computers don't have right now is "artificial intelligence"—the ability to figure out things on their own based on memory of past experience, the way humans do.

It is *likely* that the version of the code that printed "Let's count to 10" and then counted to 20 was wrong. That is, the programmer did not intend for the code to claim it was going to do one thing and instead do another. He made a mistake, maybe hit the wrong key when typing and didn't notice. A flaw like this is called a "bug."

The computer won't notice this bug, but the first person that sees this program run probably will. The programmer then has to figure out what exactly in the source code caused the bug to occur (a process known as "debugging") and decide how to fix the bug. This particular one is fairly obvious to anyone looking at the code. The programmer could either change the initial message to mention counting to 20, or change the loop so it only counts to 10 (the way the code looked in the first example). This example is contrived, but in a real-world case the code will have some specific task it is supposed to do, which will dictate how the bug should be fixed.

The fact that a computer does exactly what the code tells it to, without regard to whether that is what the programmer or user wants, is important in understanding why programs malfunction. Imagine a word processor that lets you make text boldface and also lets you underline it. Perhaps you highlight the text and then click a certain button to boldface, or click a different button to underline. You will assume that if you highlight the text and then click both buttons in succession, you will wind up with text that is boldfaced and underlined. That is almost certainly what will happen. But it will happen because a programmer put code in the word processor to make it happen. If the programmer ignored this situation for whatever reason, or made a mistake when writing the code to handle that case, then the program may do something unexpected when you attempt to both boldface and underline text. It may only boldface, or only underline, or do neither, or perhaps stop running and lose your file. The behavior of both boldfacing and underlining appears the most logical to the user, but the computer does not have any notion of one behavior being preferable to another. It does what the code tells it to do.

An example that impinged vividly on the public's consciousness was the Year 2000, or Y2K, problem. This involved computers that stored years using only their last two digits, and therefore could not tell the year 1900 from the year 2000 since both would be stored as 00.

Storing a date as two digits is not automatically a bug; the real question is what the code will do in this situation. One favorite example of Y2K alarmists was little computers that sat on power poles and monitored the flow of electricity. The theory was that when the date rolled around from 1999 to 2000, those power poles would decide that they had not been serviced in 100 years, and shut down the electricity. There were two levels of uncertainty. The first was whether the software would decide that the pole had not been serviced in 100 years. The programmer writing the code may have foreseen this and written the code such that it realized that the 1999 to 2000 rollover had happened but continued functioning normally. The second uncertainty was what the code would do if it decided it had not been serviced in 100 years. It might have been written to shut down immediately, or it might send out a signal saying, "Service me immediately." Without knowing exactly what code was stored in the computer, it was impossible to know how it would respond.

As it turned out, the electrical network—and the rest of civilization—survived the Year 2000 bug just fine. So at least one thing in the sequence required for failure—the computer storing dates as two digits, the decision based on that that it had not been serviced in 100 years, and the decision based on that to shut down—did not occur.

2

The Question

After doing interviews for a while, I started to wonder about the methodology. It is difficult to argue with the success Microsoft has achieved with the people hired over the years. Still Microsoft seems awfully strict in deciding whom to hire, and awfully random in deciding whom not to hire. The company is not under any obligation to hire every qualified candidate; it only has to hire enough to do the job. But "enough" keeps growing. When you have 3,000 employees, as Microsoft did in 1988, growing 10% means hiring 300 more; as Microsoft reaches 30,000 employees, you need to hire 3,000 more—a full 1988-era Microsoft each year. Microsoft's exponential growth has far outstripped any growth in the number of qualified workers and college graduates available. Microsoft at any given time has hundreds of open positions; projects are postponed or cancelled because they cannot be staffed, so not hiring folks who would have succeeded there becomes more and more of a loss.

Furthermore, as word of how Microsoft hires gets out, and more companies are staffed with Microsoft alums, the "Microsoft way" of interviewing is becoming more pervasive, and is being accepted as the proper way to do technical interviews, without being subjected to much scrutiny.

I have been to several Microsoft interviewer-training sessions. What you get is good information about the mechanics of an interview—what it is legal to ask, what can't be revealed, and what should be in feed-back—but not a lot of rules about how to decide whether a candidate is a "hire." It always comes down to a feeling you are supposed to get. I kept waiting for this feeling during interviews, but it rarely arrived. At the end of the interview, if you are lucky, you can make an educated guess. More typically, you are making a disturbingly uneducated guess. Sometimes in the training sessions, I sat there thinking, "Is it just me? Is everyone else a natural judge of talent? Or are they all nodding their heads, while inside they are thinking the same thing as I am?"

All employees at Microsoft are assigned a numerical "level," which corresponds to their skill set and determines the range of salary they will receive. Once during interview training, someone stood up and explained that they had a great system in his group. Each successive interviewer would ask a designated question. If the candidate got only the first question right, he or she would be hired as a level 10. Subsequent correct answers would result in a level 11 or 12 hire. The toughest question was for admittance to level 13—a question known as "Kanji backspace."

Kanji is a writing system used for Japanese. Storing Kanji on a computer is tricky because there are many thousands of unique Kanji characters, compared with only 52 characters in English (26 uppercase letters and 26 lowercase letters). A single byte of computer memory can hold 256 differ-ent values, so it is easy to store English text using one character per byte. For Kanji (and other similar systems), a storage method was invented known as "double-byte characters." Characters are stored as either one byte or two. Moving through the data in a forward direction, a program can look at each byte and tell if it is a single-byte character, or the first byte of a double-byte character. However, because of how the double-byte characters were defined, when going backwards—which is what you have to do, in a programming sense, when a user is editing double-byte character text and hits the backspace key—it is not obvious whether the byte right before the cursor is a single-byte character, or the second byte of a double-byte character. Figuring that out is the crux of "Kanji backspace." It's a good interview question because it is fairly easy to define and has a solution that is achievable, but still somewhat tricky.

Tricky, perhaps, but assuming that someone who could answer the question correctly was automatically a level 13 was a bit of a stretch. Level 13 implied that you were an expert in the company in some area, had impact across all phases of a project, had real experience shipping products, and so on. Answering the "Kanji backspace" problem correctly implied none of this. What I should have done, when confronted with this extreme example of level inflation, was to jump up and demand that this person immediately turn in his badge and resign, as penance for per-petrating a fraud on the interviewing process. Unfortunately I was a lit-tle too stunned at the time, so I contented myself with sending email later on to the recruiter who had been running the training, asking whether the concept of the "level 13 question" was correct interviewing practice? Her email response was, "You are entirely right. One technical question, especially the Kanji backspace, does not determine a level 13 hire." She also mentioned some "senior candidate interview training" that was being planned. I doubt that the "training" included the beating that they so richly deserved.

Some interviewers—not I—gain a reputation as "hard" interviews. If a candidate survives them that is a sure sign he or she will be a good Microsoft employee. Being a "hard" interview just means that you give more "no hires" than most people, and it's considered a badge of honor. Recruiters and hiring managers also tend to trust those "hard" interview-ers more. It's nice that some people are not being swept along in the tide of feedback inflation, but if everyone else gives a candidate a "hire" and you say "no hire," are you more demanding, or wrong? Of course, since you never know how candidates that get turned down would have done as employees, there is not much evidence that can be used against the "hard" interviewers.

At one interviewer training, one of the participants asked a question that pretty much summed this up. He said, "When I interview, I never feel certain either way. I wind up making a guess and then tailoring my feedback to match. And a lot of time, I think I am asking myself, 'Does this person remind me of myself?'" In all my years at Microsoft, he was the only guy who 'fessed up to feeling the same way I did.

The interviewer training I went to discussed only the overt, illegal reasons for turning someone down—race, gender, where he or she went to school, perceived sexual orientation. It ignored the subtle differences that can play in an interviewer's mind. The interviewer might be a very animated person, prone to jumping up on a chair and waving his or her arms about. Microsoft certainly has enough people like that. So how does that interviewer view a candidate who is quiet and reserved? Does this indicate the candidate's lack of belief in his or her own opinions, or is it just his or her personality? Clouding all this is the fact that there *are* some character traits that can make a career at Microsoft more difficult. There were a lot of arguments at Microsoft. People were expected to defend their ideas if they wanted to see them implemented. This can be viewed as a cultural problem for Microsoft—you shouldn't waste good ideas because only egomaniacs get heard. In fact, ideas were generally brought up in smaller, more decorous groups first, where they could pick up champions who could defend them more vociferously—so the "clash of ideas" view of Microsoft is somewhat overstated. Nonetheless that image weighs on the minds of interviewers as they make their feedback decisions. I saw more than one candidate given a "no hire" because it was felt that although they could do the work, they would not survive the culture.

When I started working at Microsoft in 1990, I was struck somewhat by the homogeneity of my group. In particular, it was mostly a bunch of white guys. Dendrite was a small company, having grown to about 25 programmers by the time I left, but it was much more racially diverse than Microsoft was (of course, New Jersey is also more racially diverse than Washington). The difference when I came to Microsoft was striking enough that I noticed it. I am 100% confident that this was not due to any outright racism on anyone's part. But if part of the interview is trying to determine whether someone is "like" you in a technical sense, it is hard to avoid some small bit of noticing whether he or she is like you in other ways. If you grew up in a culture where the way to get ahead was to yell and get noticed, and you feel Microsoft needs people like that, how do you handle people who grew up in a culture where that was frowned upon?

Around this time, the recruiting department noticed that it too was all white, and hired two minority recruiters. Now, 10 years later, I would say that Microsoft is at least as racially integrated as Dendrite was.

*   *   *

Early on in my career, I proudly described the interviewing process to my father, who is a mathematician. He snorted and said that any mathematician who interviewed at Microsoft would get turned down, though not because of lack of ability. Mathematics is similar to programming (except it is harder and pays worse), and many early computer scientists, who went to school before there were official computer science degrees, were trained as mathematicians. The concern my father had is that mathematicians don't jump up on their chair and wave their arms. They expect to be judged on the work they have done over the years, not one day of hour-long interviews.

This brings up one of the major aspects of Microsoft interviews, one that has both good and bad sides. Microsoft really does believe that it can judge a person through four or five one-hour interviews. The resume is used only as a starting point for discussions. An interviewer may discuss a previous job that is relevant to the actual work the candidate is being interviewed for, but may also ignore that and focus on something that looks interesting, or that the interviewer knows something about.

Microsoft is resolutely, defiantly proud of this, but pride and arrogance are not too far apart. Certainly it is very egalitarian not to prejudge candidates based on the reputation of a school or a previous company. I knew very successful developers who never attended college, or who majored in non-technical subjects, or who learned to program on their own while working at an unrelated job. Convincing Microsoft to interview you can be easier if your resume includes a degree from a well-known school, or job experience at a company that Microsoft knows well. But there are no specific attributes that you need to get an interview, no GPA or subject requirements. Once you get in the door, you are on an equal footing with every other candidate.

The downside of this complete reliance on the interview process is that it is hard to justify throwing out everything someone has done before. This can be true even for students fresh out of college, although they tend not to have worked on large-scale software projects. But Microsoft has recently been hiring more and more people directly into management positions. If someone has 5 or 10 years of experience at another company, there *is* some value in that besides providing fodder for an interview discussion. Microsoft's culture implicitly assumes that anyone who has worked at Microsoft for several years must be qualified, or they would have left or been forced out of the company. But the same assumption is not made about any competitors. Someone with a 10-year career at Oracle or Sun Microsystems can easily get a "no hire" in a Microsoft interview, and everyone winks about how competitors keep weak employees around.

The process reminds me of the Scholastic Aptitude Test, which is taken by high school seniors applying for admission to college. The SAT is a brief, very intense examination that attempts to distill four years of high school into one number. Although it is considered unlikely that someone will score well above their natural ability on the SAT, it is quite possible that they will score well below their natural ability for any number of reasons, including nervousness, their state of health, or—perhaps most distressingly—the fact that they may run out of time. Someone who might be able to double-check his or her answers and achieve a high score if the SAT were four hours long may get a much lower score in three hours. In statistical terms, it is weighted heavily toward excluding false positives, which inevitably increases the rate of false negatives.

The same is true of a Microsoft interview. It is unlikely that an unqualified candidate will get lucky and slip through, although more likely than in the case of the SAT (due to the extremely unscientific nature of Microsoft questions, and the far smaller number asked during a day of interviews). On the flip side, it is much more likely that a qualified candidate will not be hired. He or she may be unable to answer a question in 10 minutes, but able to answer it in 15—so failing to answer in 10 is not much of an indication of future potential.

Another example is the annual draft done by the National Football League. Virtually every player drafted has played football in college, but that only shows how that player performed against other college players. So teams bring in players for individual workouts. What they really need to know is how a player will perform against other professional players; what they wind up with instead is two approximations of that, the college career and the workout. Teams usually give more weight to the college career, but some players do so well in the workouts that they get drafted much higher than expected. These "workout warriors" also have a reputation for failing to live up to expectations. Yet by analogy, Microsoft ignores everything the candidate did in "college"—previous classes and jobs—and "drafts" people based solely on the "workout"—the job interview. It would seem that this emphasis on "interview warriors" would be prone to the same flaws as it is in the NFL.

The SAT comparison also brings up another concern, which is that knowledge about the interview process can have a distorting effect on the interview. Taking a preparatory course for the SAT will tend to raise someone's score, just from learning what the questions are like and how to guess if needed. A similar effect exists with Microsoft interviews. This was most clearly exposed when interviewing current Microsoft employees who were interested in transferring between groups. These folks knew the drill—that every question should first be probed a bit to get detail on the exact constraints, that this should then be followed by a few minutes of thought before blurting anything out, that you should appear confident but not cocky. These are the signs that interviewers were taught to watch for in candidates, tangentially to knowing the answer to the question, but they lose their value if the candidate also knows them. One time I interviewed a former intern for a full-time job. He wasn't doing very well at actually answering the questions, but I was still getting a good vibe about him. Eventually I mentally smacked myself and realized that I was being faked out by all the intangibles that he had going for him because of his knowledge of the process. Once I adjusted my opinion for that it turned into one of those rare situations when I was quite confident that a candidate was a "no hire."

Lunch interviews are even more prone to this flaw. In a lunch interview, you are not asked questions that involve writing down code (although the occasional scribbling on napkins was allowed). But you were still expected to confidently send hire/no hire feedback. The questions were more like the ones asked during interviews at most other companies: describe a typical day, what kind of work environment do you find challenging, how do you deal with a co-worker you don't get along with, blah, blah, blah. These questions are even more "spoofable" by someone who knows the "right" answers to them—the net effect is to penalize people who are honest and reward those who talk a good game. There are enough books on this subject that candidates know exactly what to say, how to admit the small weaknesses that give their answers a veneer of truth, while "accidentally" painting a glowing picture of themselves.

I remember during college interviews, companies often asked the question, "What is your biggest flaw?" The word going around was that you were supposed to provide a flaw that the company would see as a benefit, something corny like, "Sometimes I get too involved in my work and neglect my personal life." Did companies really think they had stumbled onto a university full of starry-eyed innocents who had never heard this question before? But they kept asking it, and if you reported an actual flaw, or said, "Gee, I never think about my flaws," it hurt your chances of getting to the next level of interviews. So student after student trooped into their interviews and, struggling to keep a straight face, explained their self-flagellatory tendencies to interviewer after interviewer.

*   *   *

Another example of the way in which interviews can be skewed concerns candidates from the University of Waterloo in Canada. Waterloo is considered the premier engineering school in Canada, and is most famous for its co-op program, in which students alternate school trimesters with work trimesters for five years. By the time they graduate, students have accumulated six different four-month work assignments. Some students wind up spending three or four of these co-op terms as Microsoft interns and then hire on full-time when they graduate. "Co-op" and "intern" mean the same thing in this case—one is the Waterloo term and one is the Microsoft term—but because of how the Waterloo schedule works, Waterloo co-ops will show up for Microsoft internships not only during the summer, but also from January to April and September to December.

Waterloo students have a reputation at Microsoft for being the crème de la crème among interns. In fact, for a while Waterloo interns were given special email addresses. While interns from all other schools had email addresses that started with "t-" (to visually distinguish them from full-time employees), Waterloo interns were given the unique prefix "w-". In the world of Microsoft that was high status indeed. Having grown up in Canada and knowing many people who went to Waterloo, I will state that there is nothing particularly magical about Waterloo students. Waterloo certainly does attract some of the best engineering students from all across Canada, but the admission standards are unquestionably lower than at the Ivy League universities, MIT and other top U.S. schools. Waterloo does a fine job of educating its students, but the curriculum is the same standard engineering courses offered elsewhere.

Despite this, Microsoft will happily turn down honors graduates from top U.S. schools, while drooling over Waterloo students. Why is this? It is because of the co-op program. But what is it about the co-op program? First of all, let's separate the students who did co-op terms at Microsoft, and lump them together with students from other universities who did internships at Microsoft. Those students *are* treated differently from others interviewing—Microsoft does recognize previous work experience *at Microsoft* as a valid input to the hiring process. One of the main goals of the whole internship program is to conduct extended, real-world evaluations for future full-time employment. If you have worked as an intern at Microsoft in the past and gotten good reviews from your boss, that is considered prima facie evidence that you will do well as a full-time employee and will factor into your interview after college. In fact it may become harder and harder for others to get full-time jobs at Microsoft, because hiring former interns carries so much less uncertainty.

But what about the students who have not interned at Microsoft before? Microsoft interviewers love to hear about specific tasks that were worked on by the candidate, with clear goals and results. Waterloo co-op jobs are great for this, so they give the students much more to talk about during interviews. This gives the Waterloo students a huge advantage over those from other schools, without indicating that they are likely to do any better once they are hired. The real ability they have is the ability to interview well at Microsoft.

I once asked a former Microsoft recruiter what she thought about Waterloo. Her first instinctive reaction was "a top school for technical candidates." But after thinking about it for a bit, she commented, "Outside of Microsoft, I've never heard of Waterloo."

Microsoft used to have a very bad attitude towards universities in general, viewing them merely as (imperfect) training grounds for students. Graduate degrees, with the exception of MBAs, were viewed as a waste of time. One senior manager, discussing recruiting students who were considering graduate school instead of Microsoft, once said, "We fully know how bogus [graduate school] is." This has improved recently (Microsoft now gives grants to schools without trying to dictate exactly what the money will be used for), but the bias against theoretical work and in favor of applied work still remains. Trying to figure out the relevance of a school project during an interview is hard—it is too dissimilar from the work done at Microsoft. Much easier to discuss co-op terms with a Waterloo candidate, and much less risk to recommend "hire" on one. So the myth of Waterloo persists.

*   *   *

In addition to being famous for the general style of its interviews, Microsoft is known for certain types of questions. Rather than ask candidates about where they see themselves in five years and what a typical day is like, Microsoft interviewers tend to ask unusual questions that require more mental agility. If you make an analogy between job interviewing and fraternity rush, other companies are asking people to talk about their major, while Microsoft is asking people what kind of vegetable they would be.

A few years ago my brother sent me email with a brainteaser in it. The email contained the following intro, typed by some anonymous forwarder:

> For those of you who like to solve prob-
> lems. Allegedly, this is one of the ques-
> tions for potential Microsoft employees. I
> must warn you, you can really get caught up
> trying to solve this problem.
>
> Reportedly, one guy solved it by writing a
> C program, although that took him 37 minutes
> to develop. Another guy solved it in three
> minutes. A group of 50, at Motorola, could-
> n't figure it out at all.
>
> See how long it takes you.

After the actual problem (which dealt with four people trying to cross a bridge at night with one flashlight), the email concluded:

> This is based on a question Microsoft
> gives to all prospective employees. Note:
> Microsoft expects you to answer this ques-
> tion in under 5 minutes.

This sounds like an urban legend, especially the part about the befuddled team of 50 at Motorola, and of course the bit about Microsoft is false. But it shows how the idea of the "Microsoft interview question" has entered the collective consciousness of us engineering types.

The most famous Microsoft question is, "Why are manhole covers round?" The "correct" answer—the answer expected from candidates—is that they are round because they can't fall in the hole that they cover (try it yourself if you don't believe me).

Now, I am sure that a long time ago some Microsoft person decided that manhole covers were round for this reason, and after congratulating himself or herself on his or her cleverness, went on to infect fellow interviewers with this question. The problem with this is that it is a "trick" question. In the world of logic puzzles, there are some questions which can be worked out with the mental equivalent of brute force, and others that require an "aha!" moment to get right. The manhole problem is in the "aha!" category.

This means there is no opportunity for the candidate to get the question half-right and perhaps work from that to a completely right answer with a little help; you either get it or you don't. If the candidate has made no progress after a while, the interviewer may start giving hints— "Think about the shape of the hole that it covers!"—and at that point a correct answer loses almost all value. Yet it is easy to spin this in feedback by saying, "The candidate got the answer with only a small hint."

A more basic flaw is that *nobody knows whether the expected answer is correct!* Although it has been passed down from interviewer's mouth to interviewer's ear for so long that it has achieved the status of truth, there is no convincing evidence that manhole covers are round because this prevents them from falling in the hole. There is another answer floating around, #1A if you will, which is that manhole covers are round because you can roll them on the ground to move them around.

The manhole cover question reminds me of those mental one-liners people used to ask in high school, where you were given a brief phrase and you had to figure out what happened. An example was, "The music stopped and he died." You were supposed to realize that the situation concerned a blind tightrope walker who was expecting the music to keep playing until he reached the opposite platform, so when the music stopped early he fell off the tightrope. Now ten years later those same smartasses are working for Microsoft, but that doesn't change the basic flaw in this type of question. Unfortunately many people accepted the manhole question as valid, because it was part of the unquestioned "Microsoft way" of interviewing.

When the writer and NPR commentator Andrei Codrescu spoke at Microsoft on April 28, 2000, he was asked why manhole covers were round. His reply was, "That's easy. In a fight, a round shield is better than a square one. The circle is also a symbol of infinity, which is why church domes are also round. The principle of 'as above as below' reminds pedestrians that they live in a divine world." Take that, Mr. Microsoft Interviewer! (To which the Microsoft Interviewer replies, "no hire"!)

The question eventually faded away. What killed it was familiarity. Magazine articles about Microsoft mentioned the question as an example of how hip and zany the interviews were. Word got around college campuses that this dopey question was being asked, and candidates showed up in the lobby yelling "So they won't fall in the hole!" before they had been asked anything. So it died a merciful death, albeit for the wrong reason.

Replacing it in the pantheon of dumb interview questions was a class of questions that I will call estimation questions. Examples of this are "How many gas stations are there in the United States?" "How much water flows by New Orleans in an hour?" and "What does the ice in a hockey rink weigh?" What the candidates are supposed to do is sit there and say, "Gosh, my hometown had 5 gas stations and 10,000 people, so let's assume there is one gas station per 2,000 people, and with 200 million people in the U.S., that works out to 100,000 gas stations." Or, "Well, let's say an ice rink is 200 feet long and 100 feet wide and the ice is an inch thick and a cubic centimeter of water weighs one gram, that works out to"—whatever the heck it works out to.

What they often did was stare at the interviewers as though they had lost their mind, and then wonder why their interview schedules ended right after lunch.

The real trick to these questions is that the actual answer doesn't matter. The method used to answer the question is the only important thing—the answer is ignored. Candidates are expected to come up with the estimation solution on their own, using numbers pulled out of thin air. If they do that, they get full credit, since the assumptions they make can't really be challenged. Even an arithmetic mistake in the final computation is excused. It's all in knowing how to go about the question, and if you know that, anybody can answer this. So this is another "aha!" thing that you either get or you don't, and who can tell if a candidate has been tipped off beforehand? Better yet, what if the candidate happens to have worked for the New Orleans water department or a hockey rink and just knows the answer to the question? Do you downgrade him or her for answering it too precisely? (For anyone who cares, an article in the June 1998 issue of *Car and Driver* stated, with no attribution given, that there were 187,892 gas stations in the U.S.)

This type of question seems to be dying off also, probably because information about it has also filtered out to candidates. They now know the expected method to use, and are able to spout wildly incorrect estimates at will. Which in general shows that if a question can be "spoiled" in this way, it's probably not a very good question.

There is another type of question that I have seen, particularly in program manager interviews. This is the "design" question. A design question will be something like, "If you were designing the controls for a VCR, how would you do it?" Keep in mind, Microsoft is not (to my knowledge) designing VCRs—the theory is that if a candidate can come up with a good VCR design, he or she will be able to come up with good software user interface designs.

This may not seem like a tough question, since everyone knows there is no "right" way to design a VCR—but wait! It turns out there is a right way to design a VCR. At least, from reading interview feedback where questions like this were asked, the interviewer certainly has an idea of the perfect VCR design, and candidates that don't arrive at it are considered lacking.

So you have an interviewer who has probably spent a lot of time thinking about VCR design, combined with enough arrogance to believe that his or her way is the one true way, asking someone else to come up with the same design in 10 minutes. Then Human Resources wonders why it is so hard to find people who do well in Microsoft program manager interviews.

With one program manager candidate whose feedback I saw, the opinions ranged from "A strong hire—I would go into sell mode with him" to "No hire—a bright guy, but a very poor fit for Microsoft." At the end of the day, the as-appropriate commented in his feedback, "I can hardly believe we all interviewed the same person!" Of course, to be on the safe side, the candidate was not hired.

On the other hand, the process can work to the advantage of an unusual candidate. One summer candidate had feedback from the as-appropriate that said, "There is not a shred of evidence from his past that he can drive issues that involve other people. I can see no examples from his resume, and he was utterly unable to produce any examples when pressed. Frankly, this is the greatest leap of faith I'm taking in recommending his hire as a PM [program manager]." Yet he summed up his feedback with, "Let's hire him—I'd like to give him a shot." The candidate was hired as a summer intern, came back as a full-time employee, and eventually became a group program manager.

Interview feedback for developer candidates can seem quite arbitrary too. When I saw some of the feedback, in particular some of the "no hire" feedback, it seemed the bar for "hire" was set improbably high—that interviewers would not hire themselves if they came in the door. At times like this it occurred to me, "Would I get hired again if I interviewed here?" I expect that if I interviewed repeatedly at Microsoft, I would probably get hired the majority of the times, but I am certain that I would also get turned down a fair bit. And I am at an advantage because I am familiar with the expectations for candidates! If I were able to interview repeatedly and somehow discard the knowledge I had picked up in the preceding interviews, I don't know if I my "hire" hit rate would exceed 50%.

I have done an unscientific version of this exact test, since I did interview twice, and was turned down once and hired once—exactly 50%, although the sample size is a little small. The strangest part is that I felt I did much better on the interview the first time around—I felt that I did well in all the interviews except for one in which I bombed miserably (I had claimed in my resume that I knew the programming language Forth, when in fact I had only a passing knowledge, and got nailed by an interviewer who was an expert and thought, "Oh great, someone to discuss Forth with!" Microsoft does do a good job of ferreting out such resume padding). The second time around, I felt I did sort of okay on all the interviews, with a lot of hand waving and "If you gave me five more minutes, I could give a better answer."

Someone who claimed to have seen my feedback from my first interview said that I was turned down due to inexperience. I doubt a year working at Dendrite was the experience they wanted. I assume I got turned down the first time due to the inherent randomness of the interview process, and I got hired the second time due to more randomness. The first time I surely got a strong "no hire" from the interview I bombed on, and maybe some strong "hires" from everyone else, and the second time I probably got a bunch of not-as-strong "hires" from everyone, and the second case is the one that results in a hire. But should you hire the generally above-average person or the one who excels in some areas and is weak in others?

My point is not to gripe about not being hired the first time. Working for another company for a year and a half before I came to Microsoft gave me a much better perspective and improved my career significantly. Still if we assume, based on my managing to stay employed by Microsoft for over 10 years, that I actually was a "hire," the question is, why was I turned down the first time? I came back a second time and got hired, but how many people do that? How many people that Microsoft should have hired are now working for competitors because they happened to wind up on the bad side of the draw the day they came to interview at Microsoft?

3

How Great Software Is Made

Interviewing job candidates was only a small part of what I did at Microsoft. I was hired as a developer, which meant writing code on a given software project—say the next version of Windows. A large project may have hundreds of developers working on it, but the tasks will have been divided and subdivided until you have a particular piece of functionality that is owned either entirely by you, or by you and a few other people that you work closely with.

Once all this has been clarified, you will want to plan out your algorithms (the logic you will use in the code to accomplish your task) and your data structures (the way your program stores information). After all this thinking, you may play a few games of Solitaire…but eventually you will get down to pounding out some source code.

Unlike most other engineering professions, there is not a lot of known methodology on how to solve specific software problems. There are various schools of thought on syntactical issues: how code should be formatted, or how functions should be named. Discussions about these issues are often called "religious wars," because there is no way to prove the argument. Should the { following an if() go on the same line or the line below, and if below, should it be indented? Should the function be called count(), counttoanynumber(), count_to_any_number(), or CountToAnyNumber()?

In the end it doesn't really matter, which is why such discussions can get heated. On semantic issues there is even less accepted wisdom to compare with, for example, the calculations civil engineers use to determine how much weight a bridge can support. When architecting software the accepted threshold is more like "seems reasonable to me" than any scientific proof of validity. Others may offer advice, but it will be along the lines of, "I did it this way once and it wasn't too bad." Effectively each new design is made up as you go along.

Because of this, programming can also be perceived as more of an art than some other engineering disciplines—in other words, there is a real craftsmanship to programming. Certainly programmers like to style themselves this way. Two different programmers might tackle the same task with radically different internal designs that nonetheless appear identical externally. A program such as a computer chess game will require some internal way to represent the location of the pieces on the board. What you want is a data structure that doesn't take up a lot of memory and lets the computer quickly play and analyze hypothetical future moves. There are a thousand ways to do this, but often a programmer needs to run through a series of failures before coming up with a design that works.

This lack of rigor also has a downside. I am reminded of a scene from one of the early Tintin graphic novels, the one where he travels to Russia. He is riding through the countryside when his car breaks down. He starts "debugging" by ripping out pieces of the engine and throwing them on the ground. He belatedly discovers that his problem is a flat tire, but once that is fixed, he still has his entire engine strewn around in little pieces. "Hmm, this looks complicated," he says to himself. Nonetheless he blithely starts tossing pieces of the engine back in, in no particular order and without attaching anything. Eventually the space under the hood is full, but he still has some pieces in his hand. He considers them for a while, and then tosses them aside. Naturally the car starts fine and off he rides. Some debugging and bug-fixing sessions for commercial software come frighteningly close to this scenario.

Another example of the reality of coding comes from an essay written by Jamie Zawinski, one of the early programmers at Netscape, a startup that was a pioneer in Internet software. In a piece entitled "The Netscape Dorm," about life back in the 1994 era of 24-hour coding binges, he writes, "I've just read over some of my diary for the last few months, and man, a lot of it is completely incoherent! It's full of incomplete sentences, made up words, random surreal imagery that I can't even understand let alone remember typing. Have I been typing in my sleep? I hope I don't sound like that in person. I wonder what my code must look like! Oh well, it seems to work." This is what coding is like—at Netscape, at Microsoft, and at a lot of other places. You may have doubts that you were even awake when you wrote it—but oh well, it seems to work. Ship it!

There are finer moments also. Coming up with an elegant, pleasing solution to a problem is one of the joys of programming. Sometimes you are wrestling with some detail of design, and suddenly you have a flash of insight and come up with a solution that seems so perfect, and so obvious in retrospect, that the actual writing of the code becomes a formality. Or you are wrestling with figuring out why a bug is occurring, and suddenly you realize you have crossed some threshold—maybe you haven't found the problem, but you know that you are *about* to find the problem. At moments like this you feel omnipotent, as if there is no programming problem you could not solve. A succession of these small tastes of nirvana is what got me hooked on programming.

*   *   *

To run source code, you need to turn it into "compiled" code, which means it has been translated from a human-readable language like C into machine language. These blobs of machine language are also called "binaries," since binary representation, also known as base 2, uses only the digits one and zero. Compiling is also known as "building," because you are building the binary files from the source code. This is not done by hand, but by a piece of code called a compiler.

Once code has been compiled you cannot go backwards to see the source code. If changes need to be made to the functionality of the software, or bug fixes need to be done, the source code is changed and new binaries are compiled. Thus, the source code is more important than the binaries because the binaries can be recreated from the source.

At Microsoft, as at most software companies, all the source code for a given project is saved on what is known as a "source control server." This is a central computer that holds all the master source files for a project. As a developer you will also have copies of the source files on your own computer, or at least the source files for the part of the project you are working on. The basic procedure is that you write new code, or modify existing code, until you have achieved the functionality you want. You do this on the copy of the source files that are sitting on your own machine, and use those to build new binaries to test the new functionality. At various points, you copy those source files back to the source control server, which lets other developers get access to them. This is known as "checking files in" or "doing a checkin."

The timing of when to do a checkin is the subject of some debate and angst at Microsoft. Once your code is checked in to the source control server, it will then be available to copy to other developers' machines. The first thing the other developers will do when they copy the latest source files to their own machines is to compile them, including your changes. Therefore the code you checked in has to be in reasonable shape; in the vernacular of developers, it can't be "broken."

There are two types of broken code. The first has syntax errors, and the second has semantic errors. It is very easy to put a semicolon in the wrong place and produce a source file that is not valid C code, which the compiler will complain about. This is known as a syntax error. Other times the code has valid syntax and will compile fine, but when it is run it doesn't do what it is supposed to do. This is a semantic error.

Developers need to compile their own code to test it, so how do syntax errors get checked in? One common reason is that the developer has modified several files in ways that depend on each other, and then forgotten to check in one of them. So the files on his or her machine will compile fine, but someone else who updates their source files from the source control server won't get the update of that one file, and the result won't build. Another way to break the build is by making a last minute change to a source file, and rather than taking the 30 seconds to run the compiler on it, you just check it in, and miss a syntax error you introduced. ("It was only a one-line change" is a famous non-excuse for checking in broken code.)

There will be one main build computer for the project. One person, or a team of people, periodically copies all the latest source files from the source control server to the main build computer and builds them (doing this daily is fairly common, although some projects, especially in the early stages, will do it less often). The result of this build is considered the daily (or weekly, or whateverly) build of the product, and when the product is finally declared complete, it will be the binaries built on the main build machine that get pressed on CDs and sent out in boxes.

When you break the master build, you are in for some excitement, such as a) a phone call from the build team telling you to fix it pronto, b) evil looks from your boss and co-workers, and c) a reputation as a build-breaker, which is the programming equivalent of bad body odor. Some groups take it even further, requiring that build breakers wear a dunce cap (no joke, this really happened), or assume responsibility for some odious task that nobody wants to do (such as helping the build team with their daily builds until some other poor sap breaks the build and relieves you).

It is a sad fact of life that on a big project, the build gets broken at least once every day, despite the best efforts of management, who go through despairing cycles of threats, begging, and appeals to developer pride in a doomed attempt to prevent it. Although virtually every build break in retrospect would have been preventable if the person doing the checkin had performed some simple task, it is not always the same simple task. Some groups attempt to come up with a complete list of actions that must be checked off before any checkin can be done, but the list of actions required to catch most build breaks is so onerous that developers ignore policies like that, leaving management to tear their hair even more. Or alternatively, people do follow the entire list of actions, but this cuts down on their productivity because checking in changes is such a hassle.

Once the build breaks have been resolved, the code can be tested and proceedings can move towards the discovery of the second type of bug, the semantic bug.

Semantic bugs happen only if you happen to run through the code with the bug in it, in such a way as to make the bug manifest itself. This makes them both better and worse than syntax errors that cause build breaks. They are better because if you check your code in with a semantic bug in it, and the other developers don't run through that piece of code, they won't care—as opposed to a build break, which will prevent them from doing anything because the code won't compile. On the other hand, semantic bugs are much more insidious, because they can exist in the code for a while before anyone notices them. In particular, they can exist in the product after it is declared done and shipped out to customers—the first person to notice a bug may be an end user, generally to his or her annoyance.

Semantic errors are viewed as more excusable than syntax errors, because programs are extremely interconnected and it is often difficult to figure out what the ripple effect of any coding change is. For example, you may be a developer on a word processor, trying to fix a bug about how, when the user chooses both boldface and underline, it doesn't do them properly, even though the two work separately. So you investigate and fix the source as you see fit, build new binaries, and try it out. Debugging is not a science; in some ways it is comparable to what a car mechanic does, except that the majority of bugs are a mysterious rattle that only occurs when the cars goes over a certain speed. You may have to do a couple of rounds of debugging; your first attempt at a fix might not work, or your first coding changes might only be extra code added to try to figure out what state the program is in when it misbehaves—what the data structures contained, how the algorithm was proceeding.

Once you think you have a fix, the first thing you will do is run the program and try boldface and underline together, to make sure that is fixed. Then you will probably try boldface and underline separately, to make sure that still works, that your fix to one area wasn't a step backwards in another area. Then perhaps you will try to print out boldface and underlined text, and so on, and so forth. Eventually you will decide, based on how much time you have available, how diligent you feel, and your own gauge of what features in the program were at risk of being affected by your change, that the bug is fixed and the fix doesn't seem to have hurt anything else. So you check the code in. But you can never be 100% sure that the fix didn't hurt something else. You may get a report a month later about a bug involving something apparently unrelated—saving a file to disk or something. But when you track that bug down, you discover that, gosh darn it, this new bug was caused by that change you made a month ago to fix boldface and underline together.

Developers always walk a fine line in deciding when to checkin a fix. Does your solution need to be more elegant? Did you test it enough? Should you hand it off to someone else to test, as a precaution? As you dither over this, other developers are changing the master source on a daily basis, so you might decide you need to grab the latest source files and rebuild your changes, causing even more delay. Eventually you decide to check it in, and then sit with blood pressure slightly raised until you feel it has been long enough—if your changes had broken anything important, someone would have been in your office by now.

*   *   *

This description of developers at Microsoft makes them seem more or less like free agents, writing code, fixing bugs, and doing checkins as they see fit. The actual process is more defined than that—although at times not a whole lot more defined.

There are three main groups of technical people at Microsoft: program managers, developers, and testers.

Program managers do *not* manage the other two. The title makes some cockeyed sense if you view them as managing the "program," where the "program" could mean either the project as a whole (as it is used in phrases like "the Apollo space program"), or else the code that winds up being shipped. I'm not sure how the phrase "program manager" was derived. Possibly someone was searching for a title that had "manager" in it, to create the *impression* that they managed the developers. Program managers are universally referred to as "PMs." Program managers are distinct from product managers, who are involved in marketing and are non-technical (or perhaps I should say, even less technical than the program managers).

What program managers do is write the specification (or spec) for a project, and then do whatever is necessary to ensure that the product winds up matching the spec.

Writing the spec (the noun "spec" has been verbed, although nobody is sure how to spell it) means defining what the product will do and what the user interface will look like. In order to spec a product that users will actually use when it is done, program managers spend time talking to users about the problems they are trying to solve, the programs they currently use, and what they would like to see in future versions. They keep track of what competitors have done and are planning to do (not by industrial espionage—they do what everyone else does, go to trade shows and read trade publications). This is similar to what sales and marketing people do, but the theory of program management is that the PMs will balance empathy for users with knowledge of what is technically feasible and come up with a spec for a product that will be doable technically, and sellable when the product is finally shipped, which for an operating system will typically be a year or two after the spec is written.

This balancing act is the real reason for the PMs' existence. Unfortunately, users tend to be sympathetic types who are just trying to run their hospital/bank/florist/whatever and are extremely gratified when someone from Microsoft takes the time to listen to their problems, and developers tend to be anti-social types who look annoyed every time a PM walks into their office. Developers' opinion of PMs is best summarized with a little story. Once I was in a large meeting with about a hundred developers. The presenter was having a bit of trouble getting what he saw on the computer screen in front of him to be displayed on the large projection screen behind him. Someone yelled out, "Is there a program manager in the house?" A comment like this is inevitable whenever a group of developers needs some task accomplished that they view as matching up well with the technical ability of a program manager—like ordering donuts for a meeting. Right after the laughter died down, someone else yelled, "Why, is there a game of golf that needs to be played?"

The other part of the PM's job, once the spec is written, is to make sure it gets implemented. This involves keeping track (without direct management responsibility) of the various phases of the project—development, testing, documentation, marketing. PMs also revise the spec as the project goes along, based on new revelations about what is feasible, or more often, new requests from users (see previous paragraph). In a perfect world, there would not be a great need for PMs once the spec was written, since the spec would be perfect from the get-go and each team would take it and do the right thing. This never happens, so PMs need to hover around the project until it ships. If the development team needs its collective tails kicked, if marketing isn't getting a story ready, if the documentation is not being written, PMs need to identify the problem and work toward getting it resolved, essentially by convincing people that resolving it would be a good thing. PMs like to refer to their task as "herding cats" (generally while blowing nonchalantly on their fingers)—the idea being that you can yell and scream all you want at a cat, but in the end it will wind up doing whatever it wants to do. Since PMs can't fire all the people they depend on, they have to persuade everyone else that what the PM wants is the right thing to want.

Developers are programmers, that is, the people who write the code that ships in the product—a class to which I belonged. Developers are responsible for taking the PM's vision, determining its feasibility, and then producing code that matches the vision. This is known as the implementation, as opposed to the design that the program managers do.

In many fields, the design is considered the locale where real artistry occurs. For example, architects are more revered than the construction workers who transfer their designs into the real world—even though the process of constructing a real building can be quite difficult, since you can draw anything, but you can't build everything. I once heard a friend of mine who worked for an investment bank mention designing some software and then "handing it off to the coders," with the implication that the coders were a lower form of life. But in general, programming is still considered an art in itself, probably because it is such an immature field (one exception is computer games, where the designers are considered the artists).

Developers consider themselves to have the most important job at Microsoft. Of course, so do program managers. Who is right? Having been a developer I'm too biased to answer, but I do know that I always got a kick at meetings where the speaker would ask, "How many of you are developers?" and I would get to stick my hand up.

The third class of technical people at Microsoft are the testers. These are the people responsible for verifying that the product matches the spec, and more importantly, that it does not have any bugs in it—especially bugs that would cause the program to crash and potentially lose work that the user has done. Developers will test code they write to the extent that they care to, but the testers do the real quality assurance on the software.

The technical skills required of testers vary greatly depending on which product they are testing. Testing of some applications involves simply using the applications over and over, according to some script. The tests generally need to be performed on each official build that comes out, because the nature of programming means that you can never be sure when an unexpected error will occur in a feature that previously worked—such errors are known as regressions. This type of testing is quite mechanical (and quite boring). On the other end, testers who test an operating system can wind up writing entire applications that are quite sophisticated.

Testers have a critical function at Microsoft—they are the ones who decide that a product is ready to ship, based on some pre-established criteria of stability, features, and so on (these criteria often magically adjust themselves to accommodate the current state of the product). However, for a variety of reasons they are viewed as lower on the pecking order than program managers and developers.

The three different groups have different functions in various phases of a product. At the start, PMs will be working on a spec. Since everything else depends on a spec, this will generally be done towards the end of the previous product—if this is a new product, the PM team will be formed slightly before the other teams. This is the most intense time for PMs, since the other groups need a spec to continue.

Once the spec is done, the development teams will come up with a plan to develop the product. This involves verifying that the spec is technically feasible (with some back-and-forth with PMs at this stage), dividing up the work, and coming up with an estimate of how long it will take—the first schedule.

Once development starts working on the product, the test team comes up with a test plan. This can be delayed slightly from the development plan, because at the beginning, when the code is starting to be written, there is nothing for the testers to test—there may not even be an official build at this point. This phase is the crunch time for developers—they need to crank out a bunch of code to show that the schedule is meetable, and get the test team started. The PMs, at this point, are tracking everything to make sure progress is being made as needed.

The coding will reach a stage called "feature complete," which means that everything defined in the spec is coded up, although it may not work right. Officially this means everything *would* work right if by some miracle there were no bugs, but the definition of "not work right" can be stretched a bit to include not even being expected to work by the developers (as in, "This feature would work right if only I had written the code to support it"). As this milestone is reached, the burden shifts to the testers, who now have to validate the whole product against the spec, and keep revalidating it as the developers fix bugs, and the inevitable last-minute changes to the spec are made. In the home stretch of a product, the PM team will likely start working on the spec for the next version, and as the product gets close to shipping, the development team will start looking into a plan for the next version.

As you can see, the development team lags behind the program management team to some extent, and the testing team lags behind the development team. There are other groups that also ramp up on a product, when the test team does or slightly later—the marketing team, the user assurance (documentation) team, and the "evangelization" team, who try to get other software developers interested in the product.

During the life of a product, all bugs are tracked in a database that is viewed with an internal Microsoft application called RAID. RAID may have been retronymed (Rapidly Accessible Information Database? Repeatedly Annoy Immature Developers?), but the name really evolved because it is used to exterminate bugs—get it? Anyone can enter a new bug in RAID—anyone inside Microsoft who has permission to access a particular database. External users who find bugs report them to people at Microsoft, who will try to see if a bug for the problem already exists before adding it to RAID.

When a bug is in RAID it will be "assigned" to someone, who will typically be the developer who is going to fix it, but may be someone else—a
tester who needs to get more information about the bug, or a program
manager who needs to design a solution.

When bugs are resolved, they are assigned a resolution. The most
common are "fixed," meaning the bug was actually fixed, and "duplicate," meaning the bug is a duplicate of another bug and it is therefore
unnecessary to keep both bugs open. Other resolutions include "not
repro," the developer could not reproduce the problem; "by design,"
the behavior reported in the bug is what the program is supposed to do;
"won't fix," yes, it is a bug, but we are not going to fix it; and "postponed,"
this will probably get fixed, but not in this version of the product.
Sometimes these resolutions can contain a touch of condescension—
"duplicate" implies the opener didn't scan existing bugs hard enough,
"by design" implies that the user is a moron for not reading the spec,
and "won't fix" implies that the opener should probably find better
ways to spend their time. I have had testers request that I resolve bugs a
certain way to make the testers look better.

RAID is set up so that at each stage—as the bug is assigned around,
resolved, or at any other time—people can append information to the text
description, providing an electronic record of the bug. These running
dialogs, often spread over months or years, can be quite entertaining to
read. Sometimes bugs are written as jokes—people have filed bugs complaining about the quality of food in the cafeteria. One person assigned
his girlfriend a RAID bug containing a marriage proposal (no word on
how she resolved it).

*   *   *

Looking back on the history of Microsoft, you can view the company
as going through three different eras. I'm not referring to the stand-alone

computer, networked computer, and Internet-connected computer eras that everyone else comes up with.

The first era was the era of the developers. This is how almost all software companies start, because without developers you have no code to ship. A small company probably also has some marketing people and some product support people. In this phase, the PMs' functions are divided up between marketing, who help with the spec, and development management, which handles the ongoing supervision of the product. But the developers do the main spec work, which basically consists of putting in features that they want, or consider easy to do. The testing, such as it is, is done by the developers themselves, or by product support, or by anyone that can be enlisted to help.

When I worked at Dendrite back in 1988 it was in this phase. The software was sold to a pharmaceutical company's entire sales force at once; the company had only about five accounts at the time. We would have a development team working on each individual account, so the spec was whatever marketing told us the customer wanted, modulated by what we pushed back as impossible. Testing was very haphazard—we would test our own code, and the product support people would test specific features that had changed or been added, but there was no organized testing for regressions. The end users of the product wound up performing this function (they were unaware of the guinea pig nature of their daily lives), which had the unfortunate effect that most regressions were discovered after panicked phone calls from users, rather than in the relatively calm environment at work.

The typical product of the developer era at Microsoft is DOS, the operating system that preceded Windows. The typical customers of that era were fairly technical users who were probably satisfied with a product whose requirements were defined by programmers—they may have been programmers themselves. They also tended to use the product much as a programmer would, so the Microsoft developers would tend to find and fix most bugs before the end users would. This was a nice feature of this era—developers could rely on their own instincts when determining what features to add and what priority bugs should be fixed in. Speed and reliability tended to be at the top of the requirement list.

The era of developers began when Microsoft was founded in 1975, and continued until the launch of Windows 3.0, in May 1990. At the Windows 3.0 launch, who did Microsoft choose to bring up on stage? The developers of the product, looking slightly bemused at the attention they were getting. They should have been looking slightly worried, because the launch of Windows 3.0 signaled the end of their era, and the beginning of the second era at Microsoft—that of the program manager (given that Dendrite is still in business, I assume that it also moved beyond the developer era at some point).

In the era of the program manager, the typical product was an office productivity application, like Microsoft Word or Excel. The typical users were not technical, but people who worked in an office and wanted to create documents or spreadsheets. Products designed by developers wouldn't cut it, because developers had the wrong instincts for designing products for this market. What was needed were program managers, who could talk to office workers and do surveys and market research and decide what features people really wanted. The result was a product that developers might sneer at—because the features that people liked were not necessarily the most fun to program, or the most challenging. Take a feature like auto-correct, which corrects the word "teh" to "the" automatically. To a developer, a feature like this is hopeless—hard to define exactly, ridiculously simple, and what if the user really wanted to type "teh"? In programming terms, it is a "hack." But program managers will smile and say let's catch the 90% case, and users love features like auto-correct.

In this era, testing became important, because the users didn't think like developers did. For example, a developer who was testing a word processor by typing in a long text might save it every two or three pages, because they assume it might crash at any time. An office worker might not do this, because it doesn't occur to him or her that the computer might crash, so he or she may go for dozens of pages without saving. So a developer may never find a bug that only occurs if the document is rarely saved. Because the users are using the program differently from how developers do, you can't rely on developers to catch most of the bugs by themselves.

The other reason you need testing is so it can prepare itself for the third era, which is (ta-da) the era of the tester.

In the era of the tester, which started around 1995 and is still ongoing, the typical product is a networked application like the SQL Server database software, and the typical users work at large corporations that are running an important part of their business using Microsoft software. It is impossible for developers to do a thorough job of testing software like that in their offices. What you need are testers running suites of automated tests on hundreds of computers networked together. Program management is still around to spec features, but the one "feature" that everyone wants is large-scale reliability, something only the testers can deliver.

With the rise of the Internet, there is another class of software, the Internet service such as the Hotmail email service. Here the users are often novices. They have the same expectation as the corporation; reliability above all, "It just works." They expect their software to be as reliable as their toaster.

Unfortunately, not too many people are aware that Microsoft is currently in the era of the tester—in particular, the testers themselves don't realize how important they are. Many testers seem to feel their job is to find bugs—that their value is defined by the sheer number of bugs they report. They try to find more and more outlandish scenarios in which they can claim misbehavior by the software. This is wrong. The job of testers is to define criteria for allowing the software to ship, and then file bugs for every instance in which the software does not meet that criteria.

In actuality, the preceding division of labor, especially between PM and development, is not always as precise as I make it sound. Many products start development with an incomplete spec; many finish with an incomplete spec, and if the spec is ever finished, it is written after the fact to reflect how the product turned out. Specs for the development and test plans may never exist. In some groups the PMs are the center of the action, while in others the developers are.

Whatever the balance of power in a product team, the overall focus is on shipping software—getting a final product into the hands of end users. The goal is what as known as "release to manufacturing," or RTM, which is when you take a build of the product and declare it the final one, and hand off those compiled bits—the "golden" bits—to manufacturing to start pressing onto floppies or CD-ROMs. It is cheap to keep making new daily builds, but once the CD-ROMs start being pressed, it is expensive to change things. Thus the momentousness of the RTM. (Lately a new acronym has emerged—RTW, "release to Web," for products that are distributed over the Internet. This is somewhat less momentous since it is much easier to update those bits.)

*   *   *

Back in the old cowboy days at Microsoft, when developers ruled the roost, they would add features whenever they wanted. If somebody didn't like a part of a product, chances are they would rewrite it, even if it only resulted in a minor gain for the user. Sometimes developers would rewrite software because they felt the algorithms or data structures lacked elegance. Sometimes it would be the same person who originally wrote it doing this, having had an insight in the meantime. Sometimes people would rewrite software because they did not like the way the code was formatted.

The problem is that all this rewriting and cleaning up and making more elegant take time, and you might wind up with something that is worse than what you started with. Trying to fix a minor bug can inadvertently introduce a major bug.

Certainly in some cases rewriting software can improve it. You spend time planning out software before you write it, but that is all theoretical. Often actually writing a piece of software is the only real way to figure out how it should be done. The problem, to this day, is in being selective in what midnight coding frenzies you are willing to accept. It is very hard to tell someone who has spent countless hours slaving away on what he or she perceives as an improvement to the product that you are going to throw out all that work and keep things the way they are, thank you very much. Much better to try to stop the unneeded crusades early on, and put the developer to work on something more important that helps you ship sooner, not later.

Theoretically, a product is first developed until it is feature complete, then tested and debugged until it has zero bugs, and then shipped. What really happens is that a product is developed until the features that are going to be included are complete—which may not necessarily be what was in the original spec. Then bugs are fixed until there are zero bugs left that are going to be fixed—which is definitely not the same as having zero bugs.

Thinking up new features to add, or changes in features to make them just a little better, can go on forever. It is incredibly tempting, because each individual feature is small enough that it does not seem like it will have much impact on the product—"there's always room for one more." This is such a common pitfall that it has a name, "feature creep." It takes real courage and experience to stand up and say no, that the software is "locked down" and you won't add any more features, that everybody's favorite feature that didn't make it in to the product will have to wait until the next version.

Similarly with bugs. Software doesn't ship with zero bugs—it ships with zero bugs that are deemed important enough to not ship with. As you get closer and closer to shipping, you enter what is called a "ship drive." As each new bug is reported, you need to analyze it carefully to see if it is worth fixing—because implicit in agreeing to fix a bug is the acknowledgment that fixing it may delay the product slightly, which will mean fixing this one bug may prevent the entire rest of the product, with all its nifty non-buggy features, from getting into the hands of users.

Given the nature of software, changing any part of your code, even a minor bug fix, means you need to re-run all your tests, because you never know what effect a change to the code might have. So as you get closer and closer to your RTM date, the criteria for a bug being deemed worthy of fixing get higher and higher. You start to resolve most bugs as "won't fix." You fix only bugs that you classify as "showstoppers"—ones that would pass the mental test of "Would I pull the CDs out of manufacturing to get a fix for this bug in?"

For some reason the term "showstopper" has been defined in the popular press as a bug that is so bad that it makes the whole software stop working, catastrophically failing everywhere, and in such a way that it cannot be fixed and the whole project has to be tossed out. The fact that this doesn't make sense doesn't seem to matter. There is a story about an American chemist in the 19th century who published a paper about preparing an amorphous (non-crystalline) version of glycerine. He received a letter from a European chemist who said that following the same steps he got crystalline glycerine. From then on the American could not reproduce his results either—the letter from Europe had apparently contained a seed crystal that caused the glycerine to crystallize. Software, however, is not amorphous glycerine. Whatever change you make to the source code that puts the software in a broken state can always be undone, since the source control server saves all changes.

Even in showstopper mode, it is incredibly tempting to try to fix that one last bug, because you can always picture the poor user who hits that bug and thinks, "Man, couldn't they have fixed this one also?"

Microsoft is often accused of shipping buggy software, and people are aghast when they learn that products ship with hundreds of known bugs.

There's nothing special about Microsoft; it's the nature of the software business. Unless you stop adding features, you will never have zero bugs. The more hardcore you are about features and bugs, the quicker you can ship this version of the product, and get to work on shipping the next version, which will have all those features and bug fixes you couldn't get around to fixing this time.

*   *   *

In the spring of 1992, Microsoft instituted something called the "Ship-It Award." The idea was to recognize people when a product they worked on shipped. Every employee was given a Ship-It Award, which had room to attach a number of small gold plaques, one for each product he or she had contributed to. In addition, an engraved stone commemorating each product would be embedded in a designated courtyard on campus.

When the Ship-It Award was announced, employees were amused. Part of this was because of the awards themselves, which were big hunks of Lucite inscribed with a message above Bill Gates' signature: "Every time a product ships, it takes us one step closer to the vision: a computer on every desk and in every home. Thanks for the lasting contribution you have made to Microsoft history." The awards have since been redesigned to be smaller and more recyclable, although the quote remains unchanged (in 1999 Microsoft recast its vision to be "empowering people through great software—any time, any place, and on any device." I don't know if anyone plans to update the plaques). A greater source of amusement was the initial email announcing the program; a typo in line one described it as the "Shit-It Award." But mainly, people were amazed that the company would think they would work any harder for a piece of Lucite and some gold plaques.

The Ship-It Award conceals a hidden truth however. Shipping software really is what matters. You can come up with great ideas, and work hard, and do the greatest design, and have the most comprehensive test plan, but the goal of all of it is to get software in the hands of customers. The award was meant to emphasize this, but somehow the way it was presented muted the impact, and today I don't think many people spend time gazing fondly at their Ship-It Awards and thinking about all the customers they have made happy. Which is a shame.

4

Campus Crusade

After I had been doing interviews for Microsoft for a while, I was asked to go to college campuses to do first-round interviews there. I eagerly accepted, first of all because it was a way to get a free trip to some other parts of the country and a few nights in a nice hotel. But what I really wanted to see was the full range of candidates who present themselves to Microsoft. Anyone you interview in Redmond has already been screened in some way—by examination of his or her resume, through a referral from an employee, or through an on-campus interview of the type I was contemplating. I figured if I went on campus, I would be interviewing people whose only qualification, beyond getting into college, was the ability to write their name on a sign-up sheet in the career services office.

Microsoft only goes to certain college campuses, and the list is a pretty selective group, so I wouldn't be talking to just anybody. But college admissions are not perfect, plus there would be self-taught people, or computer science majors who were more toward the bottom of the class, or people looking to test Microsoft's claim that it hired great minds, not specific abilities. Thus the chances of talking to someone completely unqualified looked promising.

Most of the schools Microsoft interviews at are on the East Coast, so you need to fly out the day before you interview. Truly hardcore folks (hardcore about missing as little work as possible) can take a red-eye out, but interviewing on campus is mentally and physically taxing, so it is much better to have a good night's sleep the night before. Since you are flying from Seattle the time change is working against you, so you probably go to work in the morning for a bit, catch a flight around noon, arrive at your hotel around 10 p.m., and try to get some sleep.

Some managers take a dim view of employees going on campus to interview. Once when I asked permission to go to Princeton to interview, the email response was, "If this would be your idea of relaxation (i.e., something you'd rather do instead of spending your off work time at home), I'd say you should go. It's not a good way to spend your work time currently. I'm not trying to be a hardass about this—it's not an issue of not deserving to go. I'd rather send you to Princeton on some other boondoggle after you get [your current project] done."

When Microsoft interviewed at Princeton when I was a senior, the Human Resources department sent out a recruiter to coordinate things, as well as the actual interviewers, but by the time I was being sent on campus they had stopped sending the recruiters. So the boondoggle crew had been reduced to just me and two or three other interviewers.

After a brief orientation from the campus career services people—a bit about the school, where the bathrooms are, that sort of thing—you jump right into a full day of half-hour interviews. In half an hour you have to fetch the candidate from the waiting area, introduce yourself and talk about Microsoft, go over some of the resume high points, ask at least one technical or programming question, wrap up, lead the candidate out, jot down some notes to help you remember the interview, and make at least a tentative assessment of whether he or she should get a "flyback" to Redmond for more interviews.

To add to the time pressure, if you start to fall behind you can't catch up without short-changing someone. You always want to leave each candidate with a good impression, because he or she may have a sibling or a roommate or a friend who is interviewing, and you don't want someone going around campus bad-mouthing Microsoft. In fact dealing with a failed interviewee can be harder than with a good one, since you need to maintain forced enthusiasm without being obvious. So you look approvingly at whatever answers you get, and act tactful when guiding people in the correct direction. You need to leave some time at the end for questions. If there are no questions, you need to make sure to say that is okay. And if there are a lot of questions and the interview runs past its allotted time, you need to steer the candidate out the door without being rude.

All this can be more than a bit stressful. You are supposed to be representing the other geniuses at Microsoft, but you're really just a tired, under-trained geek who is just a few years removed from sitting on the other side of the interview table. One time as I was finishing up with one candidate, the next one walked over, and I apologized for running over by explaining that the previous candidate had a lot of questions. Just small talk, but I then spent the rest of the day stressing over how she might have reacted to me saying that. I pictured her in all her future interviews refusing to ask any questions at all, because someone from Microsoft had implied that she talked too much. Yeesh!

*　　　　*　　　　*

Adding to the general difficulty and time crunch of interviews is the fact that you are also supposed to be on the lookout for program manager, developer, and tester candidates all at the same time.

A distinction used to be made in campus recruiting. At certain schools, candidates were considered only for development and program management positions; at other schools, they were considered only for testing positions. The program manager/developer schools were the Ivy League,

Stanford, and MIT. The test schools were places like UCLA and Brigham Young, excellent schools but a notch below the elite schools where program managers and developers were recruited.

Microsoft eventually realized that this distinction was hurting recruiting. Beyond being a giant slap in the face to the test schools, it made no sense because Microsoft was only seeking the elite, not the average. If you were going to hire an entire class you might be able to justify going to only certain highly regarded schools, where the admissions office has done some of the work for you four years before. But if you are going to be incredibly selective—if even at a school like Harvard you are going to hire only the top two or three people—you need to go to a lot more places, because you never know where an incredible candidate might be. The schools with lower admission standards may have candidates at the bottom of the class who are worse than the bottom of a class at an Ivy League school, but lower admission standards place no limit on how good the top people in the class are.

I don't know whether the change was made because the number of college graduates needed grew so quickly, or because the test schools complained, but the result is that Microsoft now recruits for all three positions at all schools. This means that as you are interviewing candidates, talking about yourself, probing the resume, asking technical questions, and all that, you are also supposed to be figuring out the most appropriate job and adjusting your questions, and your selling if appropriate, towards this.

Still, the foundation had been laid for testers to be seen as a step below the other two. The relative importance of program management and development might oscillate around each other, but they are always above that of testing.

It has always been emphasized by Microsoft management and human resources that program managers, developers, and testers are all just as technically qualified as each other—that they all have the same "skill set" (it goes without saying, almost, that they are all just as smart and motivated and resourceful—that is expected of all Microsoft employ-ees). If you ever say anything even vaguely implying that testers don't require the same technical ability as developers or program managers, you will get shouted down by irate testers (or irate recruiters). Just as there is some slight difference in program managers that causes them to be a little more verbal and into designing, there is supposed to be a slight difference in testers that makes them a little more into testing other peo-ple's code than writing their own.

If that last sounded a little suspicious, it is because it is a crock of 100% pure, unadulterated hooey.

Let me say, before I am drowned out by the shouts of irate testers (or irate recruiters), that I do not mean that testers are not smart, motivated, and resourceful, because they are (as much as the next Microsoftie). And I am not saying that testers are not important to Microsoft, because they are just as important as program managers and developers—and as Microsoft enters its third age, they are increasingly becoming more important.

So the testers are crucial, Microsoft needs them, the stock price would drop through the floor without them. What follows is not meant to be a criticism of testers. Nonetheless it will be likely interpreted as such.

First of all, if you probe a bit to find out what the magic difference is between developers, program managers, and testers, you get some suspi-cious answers. Program managers are described as being "courageous" and "persuasive." Testers are described as being "curious" and "liking to break things." Now, which of those descriptions would accurately describe my one-year-old son? You get the idea.

Consider what testers are supposed to be—people who enjoy testing other people's code instead of writing their own. Does that make any sense? Are there a lot of automobile designers who prefer taking test-drives to doing new designs? Are there a lot of cooks who prefer preparing other people's recipes to concocting their own? Are there a lot of writers who prefer editing? There are a lot of professional critics in this country, but I think the consensus is that most critics are not as qualified as the people they are reviewing, and are mostly whatever-profession-it-is-they-are-criticizing manqués. Keep in mind that testers, unlike editors, are not allowed to fix the bugs they find—merely to report them to the developers.

If you are trained to do X, where X in this case is program computers, then you want to do X as a career. When Microsoft interviewers look for people to do X, they will hire you if they think you are qualified. If they see a development candidate who they think is qualified to be a developer, they won't hire him or her as a tester—they will hire him or her as a developer.

When I first started at Microsoft, I was given an office in a hallway where most of the other offices had testers in them. People in the hall came around to meet me, and one of the things they were curious about was whether I was a developer or a tester. From the outside both look roughly the same—a scruffy-looking individual surrounded by computers—and it would have been gauche to simply come out and ask whether I was a tester (after all, there's nothing wrong with being a tester, right?). So they resorted to questions like, "Who is your manager?" From that they were able to scurry back to their offices, check out the online organizational chart, and figure out that I was, as one person put it, "a commissioned officer."

In all my years at Microsoft I met exactly one person who was offered a development job and instead said, "No, I'd rather be a tester"—and that was universally considered to be a strange decision. Meanwhile many testers I knew wanted to be developers—which makes sense, since that is what they were trained to be. Many people moved from test to development, and this was considered a step up in their career. The only people I saw move from development to test were those who didn't make it as developers but wanted to stick around the company. Meanwhile, moves between program management and development were viewed as completely normal. In fact, it somehow managed to seem like a step up both ways—moving from program management to development was seen as a sign of having serious programming chops, and moving from development to program management was seen as a sign of having a broader, more strategic viewpoint.

But somehow, despite all this evidence around you at Microsoft, you were not allowed to discuss the truth—that testers, on average, were less qualified as programmers than developers were. This is the only group that this rule applied to. You could point out that the user assistance folks (who write the documentation) were not as technically qualified as developers, and everyone nodded their heads and agreed, while at the same time realizing that user assistance is very important and the company would sink without it. But you couldn't say things like that about testers.

Consider the following quote from the book *Microsoft Secrets*, by Michael Cusumano and Richard Selby. A Microsoft test manager is discussing what he looks for when interviewing potential testers: "In the interviewing process, he looks for people who think differently from developers—people who do not take for granted that a feature works and search for non-obvious contexts in which a feature might fail." This is the company line, and it is like, totally bogus. When developers hear this, they know that it is bogus. If a developer doesn't do those things, takes for granted that a feature works, and doesn't think about non-obvious contexts in which it might fail, he or she is a lousy developer. So developers hear this, know it is absurd, and think, "If that is the testers' justification for being my equal, then they aren't really my equal." Which, unfortunately, is the way things stand today.

What this prevented was a real honest dialogue within Microsoft about the role and importance of testers. Testers need to start explaining the real reason why they are as valuable as developers and program managers, not this cooked-up reason. I would like nothing more than for testing to rise up and become an equal partner with program management and development. But whenever people start talking about this, all the program managers and developers start winking at each other. As a result the relationship between PM/development and test is always an unequal one, where the word of PM/development wins out in the vast majority of cases.

You sense that the test manager quoted above understands this at some level. Later he says, "I have to be smarter in a different way than the developer about how the feature should work....You have to be able to understand what a spreadsheet does and how a customer is going to want to use it, and map a million people's use of a spreadsheet onto six months of focused testing by one or two people." Now *that* is what testers should be recognized for, not this mythical, unique-to-them skepticism that is supposedly lacking in everyone else.

Having testers as equal partners is crucial. Testers need to be the ones who decide which bugs are fixed. They should be setting the ship criteria and filing bug reports about areas that don't meet them. They should also be the ones who hold the line and prevent fixing of minor bugs when it is too late in the product to guarantee the stability of the result. Developers and PMs are notorious for wanting to fix everything (developers because they want the code to be perfect, PMs because they are too close to the eventual customers). Testers need to be the dispassionate observers who can say "no" to fixing a bug—not just the upper management of testing, but every individual tester needs to be empowered to say this. Instead, their only power is to file bug reports for everything they see, tossing them on a big pile for the developers and PMs to sift through and do the "higher-order" work of deciding what is fixed and what isn't. Personally I would have loved it if testers had started doing this, but for a lot of other developers and PMs it would be seen as invading their turf, because they think they are on a higher evolutionary plane than the testers.

The result is testers working heads down, trying to file as many bugs as possible. This is crazy. What you wind up with is people testing esoteric variations, on the theory that it is less likely that someone else has already tried them, and they are therefore more likely to find bugs. They wind up finding esoteric bugs that get prioritized down and eventually not fixed. It is like the two people on the assembly line who are asked what they are doing; one says, "I'm riveting" and the other says, "I'm building a car." The testers need to realize that they are a key part of building the software also, and that their job is not to find bugs, but to ensure that the software that is shipped is great.

This all started with recruiting, where if you decided someone should be a PM, you were supposed to start explaining what a great job it was, while if you decided someone should be a tester, you were supposed to start explaining what a great company Microsoft was. Somehow program management is viewed as an acceptable career for someone trained as a developer, even though PMs also wind up not doing the programming they were trained for (more so even than testers). I'm not sure why this is. It is possible that while developers look down on testers, they are merely mystified by PMs—why would someone want to spend time going to all those meetings and writing all those specs? PMs do get a lot of visibility in the company, and will get to meet with Bill Gates much earlier in their careers than developers (testers rarely get to meet with Bill). Perhaps it's because PMs tend to be a bit more outgoing and egotistical than developers or testers, so once they arrived at Microsoft en masse they set about constructing an environment in which they were the most important people.

In fact Microsoft has recently started hiring less technically trained people as PMs, searching for people with "domain expertise"—those whose experience is close to that of the users that a particular piece of software is going to serve. A group working on a graphics editing package, for example, may now hire as PM a graphics editor with an interest in programming, rather than a programmer with an interest in graphics editing. Despite this the PMs keep their status and the testers, who are generally more technically proficient than the PMs, maintain their lack thereof.

*   *   *

In any case, the poor Microsoft interviewer who is on campus now has the additional worry of trying to pick a job for the candidate during the interview.

Say the interviewer is a developer. Looking for a tester is hard because nobody is going to have much training in testing, and nobody is going to jump up and say they want to be a tester, unless they figure it is a good way to get their foot in the door at Microsoft.

Looking for a PM is hard because everything I ever read about what to look for—which was all written by other PMs—amounted to a variation on, "I don't know much about art, but I know what I like." PMs basically want people who remind them of themselves, which was not much help for me, a developer. Just like testing, people generally don't come into interviews wanting to be PMs, although that is usually because they don't know what the job is. At least you can sell someone on being a PM without feeling guilty about it, the way you do when trying to sell someone on being a tester.

The developer doing interviews has not much of a clue how to identify these people, because he knows that what HR has been telling him to look for is either false, or very difficult to spot.

What I wound up doing on campus was resorting to some pretty basic stereotypes. If I saw a great candidate, I talked to him or her about being a developer. If I saw a candidate who I thought was pretty good, who seemed to talk a lot or maybe wrote for the school paper or dressed well, I talked to him or her about being a program manager. And if I saw someone who I thought was pretty good, but not quite good enough to be a developer, I talked to him or her about being a tester.

I'll bet that PMs did a similar thing—people who reminded them of themselves got PM flybacks, and people who seemed real smart but a little quiet got developer flybacks. Testers got evaluated the same as they did by developers.

So there you are doing your on-campus interviews, doing your 12 or 14 half-hour meetings. You quickly start to wonder whether a free flight and hotel are worth it. You have to be "on" for everyone, but after a while you start to bore yourself because you are saying the same thing to every candidate. At the same time you need to vary your technical questions, because the early candidates may talk to the later ones.

On top of that you need to leave everyone with a good impression. I remember one time, the last interview of the day was someone I didn't think was any good, so I was looking towards the clock thinking I could wrap things up a few minutes early and get out of there. Suddenly this guy whipped out a printout of the source code for some assignment he had done at school. A long assignment. You may think that programmers like looking at each other's code, but they don't. At least I don't. Reading and understanding someone else's code is probably the most mentally taxing thing you have to do. Given that my brain was already fried I suggested that perhaps we didn't have time to go over this, but the guy got upset. So I had to paste on my smiley Microsoft face and walk through his code with him, struggling to say something intelligent and stay awake at the same time.

Once you are done with your interviews for the day, you go back to your hotel and vegetate, unless you are busy at work and decide to hop right on a plane back to Seattle. In any case, at some point, while the candidates are reasonably fresh in your mind, you need to rank them and decide what the cutoff is for flybacks.

Theoretically, there is no set number of flybacks per school; you fly back the candidates you think have a reasonable enough chance of being hired that they justify the expense. If this were purely true, then you wouldn't need to rank the candidates from best to worst as you go along. Closer to reality is the truth expressed by one of my fellow interviewers on a trip we took to a school that was not considered to be of the highest caliber. He walked into career services, looked around, sniffed the air, and said judiciously, "We're looking at a maximum of two flybacks each here."

To further compound this unofficial quota system, the campus recruiters at Microsoft used to send out a spreadsheet at the end of the season, listing everybody who went on campus, how many people they flew back, and how many were offered jobs. It was considered a mark of keen interviewing intellect to get a high percentage on this—perhaps not a perfect score, since that might imply you had made the cutoff too early, but something like four flybacks and three offers. One person I recall was shown as 0 for 9; one must assume he was not asked to interview on campus the following year.

Eventually they stopped sending out this spreadsheet, although I am sure they still kept it internally. It did encourage you to be a bit too selective when deciding on flybacks.

Watching the interviews of candidates whom you have flown back from campus can be nerve-wracking. As the on-campus interviewer you will be included on all the feedback email. You are worried about getting a good percentage on the "successful flyback" spreadsheet, and also you get to like the candidates personally and hope they do well. You eagerly await the first, trend-setting feedback, hoping for a "hire." Throughout the day you find your hopes soaring and sinking with each new piece of feedback that arrives in your email inbox. You cheer silently for each "hire"—"I knew you could do it!" Each "no hire" brings disappointment, as you scour the email for clues as to what happened—"I thought you would have answered that! That question wasn't fair!" Sometimes the feedback can be a little harsher. One candidate whom I had ranked as the top flyback from a school had in one feedback, "[He] is a nice guy, but he didn't make the intellectual bar. Then I asked him my array with a repeat question and he gave the very worst answer and he even got that half wrong. I didn't ask him any design questions because I didn't think he was up to the intellectual bar." Ouch! Another flyback said he wanted to be a PM to lead the development process and that he expected to write code. When told he wouldn't, his reply was, "I was misinformed about the job." That would be me, the on-campus interviewer, presumably doing the misinforming. Finally, there was my favorite irrelevant reason for turning down a candidate: "He must have said 'you know' about 1000 times in the course of an hour—I think I counted 10 in one sentence (if you could call it a sentence)."

When the flyback is for a program manager interview, you have to steel yourself to the randomness of the process. I've watched as negative feedback piles up, full of improperly designed VCRs and misestimated ice-rink weights, and thought to myself that this served more as an indictment of Microsoft's interviewing process than any accurate assessment of the candidate. I've seen design questions ranging from "Zero learning curve UI [user interface] for a crane," to spice racks, showers, and remote controls for Venetian blinds. One person wrote of a candidate, "I asked him how he'd redesign my office and he had just about one of the worst responses I've ever heard."

There is interviewer training for on-campus interviews just as there this is for interviews in Redmond, although not much more information is given. At one of these, one guy explained to me that he had a great question that he asked all candidates, and he had found that candidates who could answer this in their half-hour interviews usually did well in flybacks. This seemed a little narrow-minded to me, since a given question might just hit somebody wrong. Also, students who interviewed one year tended to talk to the students the next year about the questions they were asked.

Nonetheless I was willing to go along with this bit of imparted wisdom, until he told me what the question was. It was—hold on to your hat— Kanji backspace! That's right, the same question that one person was using to determine whether to hire somebody as a level 13 was being used by someone else to determine whether college seniors should even be flown back for a full round of interviews. Most college people who were hired back then came in at level 9 or 10 (the levels were completely redone in the summer of 1999; in the new numbering system college hires usually come in at levels in the high 50s, and all the semantics that had built up around the old levels has been destroyed).

I will also point out that Microsoft includes a solution to the Kanji backspace problem on its Microsoft Developer Network website. It is a solution from a book written about writing international software, and the entire text of the book is online. The solution has a minor bug in it, but I doubt that was intentional. It certainly explains the logic needed to solve Kanji backspace, which is the main thing that an interviewee would need to come up with.

Despite these various foibles, I still feel Microsoft does a better job of interviewing than any other place I have experienced. At least it is making an attempt to hire people based on their real qualifications for the job, instead of their personality or the quality of the paper their resume is printed on.

Still, I think there are some improvements that can be made. Interviewers should be better trained—sitting in with experienced interviewers is a great way to do this, and although it is allowed, it is not required and I never heard of anyone actually doing it. People should be given more information on how to identify good candidates, especially for jobs other than their own—for example to help developers identify good tester and program manager candidates. More training should be done on avoiding hiring only people "just like me." Microsoft also needs to pay more attention to previous jobs and experience, instead of believing that it can accurately judge a person solely on one day of interviews. During an interview day, the company needs to encourage more honesty and less follow-the-leader-ing in hire/no-hire decisions, and not treat one "no-hire" as the kiss of death.

I think that Microsoft hires people who are somewhat arrogant, and they therefore assume that they have the knack for interviewing. When they see other people interviewing and confidently stating their hire/no-hire opinion, they are less likely to step up and admit that they have some doubts, and more likely to bluster through. This in turn can come across as arrogant to the candidates, especially when they are having trouble answering a question that the interviewer obviously feels is easy.

In December 1994, a Microsoft program manager named Hadi Partovi, a recent Harvard graduate, sent email to Steve Ballmer, executive vice president of sales, describing the attitude toward Microsoft that he had seen on campus. He quoted one professor as saying, "My guess is that you turn a lot of people off that way too—demanding people to produce code on the spot in a 30–45 minute interview is a ridiculous task and doesn't give you any indication of how well a person will perform as part of a development team. If the technical recruiters aren't savvy enough to talk about technical issues, projects, design processes, and problem solving to learn who the competent people are, they shouldn't be interviewing." As Partovi pointed out, "Although good technical questions really attract the students who like problem-solving, we shouldn't 'haze' interviewees." Partovi later co-founded an Internet startup called Tellme, and was featured in a May 29, 2000 article in *The New Yorker*, written by Malcolm Gladwell. The article discusses an on-campus candidate named Nolan Myers whom Partovi had interviewed and later hired: "[Partovi] remembers that Myers did well on the programming test, and after talking to him for thirty to forty minutes he became convinced that Myers had, as he puts it, 'the right stuff'...Partovi didn't even know why he liked Myers so much. He just did. 'It was very much a gut call,' he says." Proof that the Microsoft-inspired workout warrior method of judging interviews is alive and well elsewhere!

Microsoft has survived and prospered, but problems like this won't become apparent until it is too late. I talked to recruiters and as-appropriates who shared my opinion of the recruiting process, but it never seemed to change. It could be that management reviewed how Microsoft interviewed on a yearly basis, recognized the various flaws, but decided that the tradeoffs were still better than any alternative and continued with the status quo. But if they did this, I, as a low-level employee, was completely unaware of it. From my perspective, interviewing continued on as it had in the past because "it's always worked before," with all assumptions unchallenged. This in turn undermined my confidence that Microsoft would continue to hire the people it needed.

Today Microsoft also has more competition in hiring. It is no longer the cool place where every college senior wants to work. As one former recruiter put it, "Microsoft is not the force in the industry that it once was. Companies are having success recruiting against Microsoft—it is no longer viewed as the threat." Microsoft now has to compete not only with individual companies in Silicon Valley, but with the concept of Silicon Valley as a whole, as a place you move to, work at a series of companies for six months each, and then get the call from a friend or co-worker inviting you to come work at their "pre-IPO" company—what used to be known as a startup.

Microsoft has been successful at hiring good people. But as the company continues to grow and talent becomes scarcer, it may be the good people it doesn't hire who wind up hurting it.

5

Canadian Vacation

On Valentine's Day 1994, Microsoft acquired Softimage, a company headquartered in Montreal. Softimage produced a high-end animation package called Softimage 3D, which had been used to produce the computer-generated dinosaurs in the movie *Jurassic Park*. With my parents still living in Montreal and their first grandchild to show off, I decided in early 1995 to investigate working there.

When the company was acquired, heavy emphasis was placed on those *Jurassic Park* dinosaurs and how cool they were (Softimage did not do the actual animation of the dinosaurs, but wrote software used by professional animators). Less obvious was how this fit into Microsoft's overall business. Microsoft had gotten rich by selling tens of millions of operating systems for less than $100 each; Softimage had gotten where it was by selling a few thousand copies of an animation package that cost over $100,000 each. Moreover, the company had never turned a profit. One article quoted an investment banker as saying, "There's just nothing to compare it to, except, I guess, if General Motors bought a really high quality rollerblade firm....From a financial perspective, that deal was what accountants refer to as a rounding error."

The party-line explanation for the acquisition involved some hand waving, a mention of future synergy with content efforts, and did we mention those neato dinosaurs? When the interactive television group gave presentations designed to prove that Microsoft had a complete solution, it would put "Softimage" as a bullet entry under "content creation," and leave it at that—the synergy was left as an exercise for the audience (such vague synergy-speak was common back then as people tried to figure out how technology and content were going to come together). Craig Mundie, the Microsoft executive to whom the head of Softimage reported, was quoted much later as saying, "We were thinking how tools would evolve and support television in the future and what those tools would have to look like." Brad Silverberg, who was in charge of the Windows 95 team, was heard to comment that he had no idea why Microsoft had bought Softimage.

I later heard of another factor motivating the Softimage acquisition. Nathan Myhrvold, at the time Microsoft's vice president for advanced technology, had decided that Softimage was a cool company and a good entrée into Hollywood, known for throwing great parties at industry conferences. He directed a few of his henchmen to go acquire it. They dutifully flew off to Montreal for a meet-and-greet with Softimage execs, which involved some nice demos of computer-generated dinosaurs but was generally not very fruitful because of the lack of any stated purpose for the meeting. After they returned, a Softimage manager called, and at some point asked, "Are you interested in acquiring us?" To which the reply came, "Are you interested in being acquired?" After which followed a series of more productive meetings, leading to the eventual acquisition.

The big conference for computer graphics people is the annual meeting of the Association for Computing Machinery (ACM) Special Interest Group on Computer Graphics, known as SIGGRAPH. At the first SIGGRAPH after the buyout, held in Orlando in July 1994, Nathan was in his element as he rubbed elbows with the movie folk in attendance.

I was unaware of all this as I started looking into jobs there. A recruiter I knew put me in touch with someone else in Redmond who knew the jobs available in Montreal, and in May 1995 I was given the name Peter Ibrahim to call to discuss openings. We had a nice talk, but he wasn't sure what was available. I then heard from my recruiting contact that all hiring by Softimage had been frozen for a month because of quality control problems. Eventually the gates opened again, and I flew out for an interview on July 17.

Nathan certainly got his money's worth in the cool department. Softimage was headquartered on St. Lawrence Boulevard, universally acknowledged to be the trendiest, hippest, best people-watching street in Montreal. It was located in a reconditioned warehouse, a building that used to have a dance club on the ground floor, on a block stuffed with trendy restaurants, hip clothing boutiques, and alternative record stores.

I stayed at my parents' house and they drove me downtown for my interview. Softimage occupied the second through fifth floors of the building, with the only street access through a glass door, unmarked except for the street number above it. Looking through the door revealed a dingy hallway leading to a stairway and an elevator. Nowadays that look is in style, but back then it was so out of sync with the usual notion of what a software company should look like that my mother got worried. "We'll wait here," she said, "You can run inside and make sure this really is the place."

I took the elevator to the reception area on the fourth floor and was confronted with a vision of glass and metal that would make any modern art gallery proud. Even better, there was an inch-wide gap running through the middle of the floor, walls, and ceiling of the reception area, caused by the building settling unevenly while the foundation was being dug for an addition.

My interview mostly consisted of people telling me stories about their previous jobs, and me slipping in the occasional story about Microsoft headquarters. After being exposed to Microsoft interviews for so long it was strange to have interviews that were all talking, no coding. I suppose if you let someone talk about themselves for most of the interview they will come away with a good feeling and hire you. Halfway through the day I realized that I was not interviewing with the group that made the 3D product, but with a different group working on a product called Digital Studio. This explained why everyone I interviewed with had been hired recently.

Digital Studio was an editing package, known in the trade as a "non-linear editor." It allowed a person known as a video editor to rearrange snippets of recorded video into a coherent final product. It also let editors perform all the other tasks they needed to do, such as touching up images, adding titles (text that appears over the video, such as credits), and editing the soundtrack, all without leaving Digital Studio. It was positioned squarely at the very high end of this market, where complete systems sell for six figures, just like 3D.

I was taken to lunch by Patrick de Grasse, my future boss if I took the job, and Claude Lambert, who worked for Patrick. Patrick and Claude worked on the hardware interfaces team of Digital Studio, which was responsible for integrating the software with some of the specialized video hardware that it used. The restaurant we went to was a place right across the street called the Shed Café. It also had the "crack in the ceiling" look; in fact, it looked like half of the roof was about to collapse on the hapless bartender, but in this case it appeared intentional. During our lunch discussions Patrick explained that 3D was nice, but Digital Studio was the real reason Microsoft had bought Softimage. Meanwhile, as I discovered later, the 3D people had been told that *they* were the real reason for the acquisition.

Right away I noticed how hierarchical the place was. There was a sense that managers were more important than their employees, and managers' managers were more important still. This notion is almost entirely absent at Microsoft. Every manager I interviewed with at Softimage started out by telling me how long he had been a manager, before giving me his technical credentials. At Microsoft first-level managers often had the same "Software Design Engineer" title as the people who reported to them, but at Softimage all the managers had the title of "Project Leader," even if the "project" had only one other person working on it. Softimage used to have retreats where the Project Leaders (PLs) went off with other management types, to ride horses and whatnot, and discuss the product when they had a chance. Out of these meetings emerged voluminous product specifications, which were duly ignored by the developers in the trenches.

After lunch I interviewed with a guy named Darryl Lewis. A team of four people had been transplanted from Redmond nine months before to work on Digital Studio and help teach the "Microsoft way," such as it is, to their new friends in Montreal. Darryl managed the other three (one of whom was actually in the process of moving back to Redmond).

The interview with Darryl was interesting, but not because he grilled me with the tough technical questions I had been expecting given his Redmond background. He dispensed with that immediately, saying that since I was from Redmond he assumed I was good. He then spent the next hour telling me, in great detail, how bad things were at Softimage. The people had no experience, nobody knew what the product was supposed to be, the wrong people were making decisions, management was incompetent, and so on. He advised me in no uncertain terms *not* to take the job.

I was hooked. Darryl had a huge office that looked right out on St. Lawrence Boulevard, and since it was July and bare midriffs were in style, there were belly-buttons a-plenty wiggling by outside. But that wasn't what got me. I figured that I *had* to investigate a place like this, as an anthropological experiment if nothing else. Plus, I was using Softimage as an excuse to work in Montreal while keeping my stock options, so if they'd told me I was going to be shoveling coal I would have seriously considered accepting. So I cheerfully thanked Darryl for his advice, and then ignored it. I'm still not sure if that was the right decision.

When I got back to Redmond I got an offer from Softimage—for a 25% pay cut. Given the higher taxes in Canada, I'd be taking home about two-thirds of what I was in Redmond. Darryl had told me that when he moved out they converted his salary using the current exchange rate and also paid him extra to make up the tax difference—like the Montreal Expos did for baseball players. I complained, but the recruiter in Montreal said that Darryl and the others had been an exception because they had been asked to go, and Softimage had needed people quickly. She explained that my salary had been converted according to the standard rules for relocations to Canada, which appeared to have been invented just for me. She also claimed that someone from Arthur Andersen had done a study showing that even with a lower salary and higher taxes, my money would go further than it did in Redmond. This made no sense, since the cost of living was also higher in Montreal, but she wouldn't budge except to offer me a $10,000 relocation bonus. Since money wasn't the issue, except on principle, I accepted, and on August 18 my family and I flew out to Montreal. I later talked to the person at Arthur Andersen who had done the supposed study. It turns out she had spent some time living in both places, and the "study" was just an impression she reported when someone asked.

*   *   *

At first things in Montreal were great. We were staying in temporary housing near Softimage, and in the evenings my wife and I went out for walks with our son, who was 9 months old, in the stroller. It was fall, a great season in Montreal. I remember looking at the skyline one evening, the same skyline I had seen as a child, and thinking how amazing it was that I was working here with my stock options intact.

Back at work, some big changes were brewing. There was some unhappiness with Martin Walker, Darryl's boss and the head of the

Digital Studio project. Daniel Langlois, the founder of Softimage, was more interested in movies and future projects than the day-to-day running of the company. After I accepted the offer at Softimage, but before I moved to Montreal, I heard that two people from Redmond were going to transfer to Softimage in unspecified upper management positions. One of them was Moshe Lichtman, who had been running the Plug and Play team for Windows 95. The other was Luis Talavera, someone I knew vaguely from my work on networking. Luis had worked on a handwriting-based system called Pen Windows, then went on to manage a lot of the networking components in Windows 95. He had left that team the previous November and was working on a hand-held computer project.

I had interviewed with Martin and liked him personally, but noticed he seemed a bit indecisive during the interview. This turned out to mirror the attitude of the team: although Martin was very smart and people liked him, he went too far in his attempt to make decisions by consensus. A typical meeting with him started with a "Let's go around the room and have everyone talk about what they've been doing," then some issues were brought up leading to a few rounds of "Let's go around the room and see what everyone thinks of that," and the meeting then drifted to a conclusion with no perceptible action items assigned and no permanent evidence that it had ever taken place.

When I arrived at Softimage I learned that Moshe was going to become co-president with Daniel, and Luis was going to take over as head of Digital Studio, with Martin moved to a position under him as head architect. (At Softimage, as at Microsoft, people referred to everyone by their first name, so the Softimage founder and the Microsoft chairman were known respectively as Daniel and Bill.) "Head architect" in a software project often refers to a critical member of the team known for profound insight and respected by all, but it can also mean "former head of the project who is being offered the chance to exit gracefully but who will be fired soon otherwise." Martin was in the latter category, and he soon obliged by resigning, leaving Luis in charge. Months later I bumped into Martin on the street. He was in charge of development at a small software company and seemed very happy.

Luis arrived in Montreal a month after me, and he got the place hopping. Even before he got there he would sit in on meetings by speakerphone and shoot down Martin when he tried to go around the room asking everyone for their opinion. A staple of Digital Studio was the weekly "PM/PL" meeting, where the program managers and project leaders got together to discuss issues too weighty for the ears of the lowly developers. About once a month this meeting would be expanded to include the whole team. Luis decided, correctly, that this class distinction was wrong. Unfortunately instead of killing the PM/PL meeting and having an all-hands meeting once a month, he kept the weekly time slot and invited everyone.

Luis quickly realized that Digital Studio was adrift and was never going to be completed at the current pace. When Softimage was acquired, Microsoft was told that Digital Studio would ship in September 1994; this was eventually amended to September 1995, which as far as I could tell was still the plan of record when I arrived in August 1995. Luis ordered a full review of the project, out of which emerged a real schedule, with a real ship date: October 1996. At least it seemed real at the time.

In the book *Microsoft Secrets* there is a quote about being a successful Microsoft middle manager: "To be a manager or a leader—in essence a manager *is* a leader—you have to have one of two essential things; if you've got both, then you are just set for life. One is you have to be technically as competent if not better than your peers or the people you're going to manage. Two [is] charisma, and generally the managers at Microsoft are not the charisma types."

Luis had both characteristics in spades. He was a master motivator, excelling at getting people fired up about the project. He had many years of experience at Microsoft and he knew what to say when asked questions such as "What is required to ship software?" and "How do you balance employee growth with short-term goals?" When you confronted him with a concern, you would go away feeling like a million bucks. Darryl was planning on moving back to Redmond at the time I interviewed with him, which partially explained the advice he offered during the interview, but after talking to Luis he decided to stick around.

However, Luis was very much an old-school Microsoft manager, and like other old-school Microsoft managers, the thing he valued above all was "commitment."

At Microsoft, commitment is an overused word. Managers state that they want commitment from their employees, who eagerly profess to have it. So what exactly is commitment?

In the 1980s, Microsoft products used to ship long after their planned dates despite long hours by employees. The attitude was, everyone is working hard, so what else could be done? Eventually, Microsoft's customers shifted from single users playing around in their spare time to large corporations trying to run their businesses. Installing an upgrade of software became a coordinated event that had to be planned well in advance. To keep these customers happy, Microsoft had to start meeting its public schedule commitments. Thus the schedule came to be viewed as supreme, and meeting a schedule became the ultimate measure of success.

Meeting a schedule certainly is critically important for customers. Scheduling software, however, has more in common with dart throwing than it does with science. No two pieces of software are identical, so a schedule is little more than a series of guesses. As the joke goes, "The first 90% of the work takes 90% of the time, and the last 10% takes the other 90%."

To alleviate this problem, management hit on the technique of allowing developers to make their own schedules. A developer and his or her manager work jointly to come up with a list of the tasks that need to be accomplished, but then the developer is given sole responsibility for assigning completion dates to each task. As a result, submitting the schedule implies a commitment to meet it—that is, people will work extra hours as necessary to meet their deadlines. Armed with this assurance, management can then present this schedule to their bosses and guarantee that the team will meet it.

In *The Soul of a New Machine* this is referred to as "signing up": "There was, it appeared, a mysterious rite of initiation through which, in one way or another, almost every member of the team passed. The term that the old hands used for this rite...was 'signing up.' By signing up for a project, you agreed to do whatever was necessary for success. You agreed to forsake, if necessary, family, hobbies, and friends—if you had any of these left (and you might not if you had signed up too many times before). From a manager's point of view, the practical virtues of the ritual were manifold. Labor was no longer coerced. Labor was volunteered." At Microsoft you signed up when you submitted a schedule that you yourself had designed.

This idea is seductive, but it contains a major flaw. The flaw is that development schedules are inherently over-optimistic. It is by definition impossible to predict the unforeseen problems. But it is the unforeseen problems, especially those that appear when integrating components from different developers, that inevitably delay things past the scheduled due date. Meanwhile, if you try to pad your schedule with time to allow for this, whoever reviews the schedule will point out that the time allotted is too generous for the amount of work listed.

It is understood that sometimes deadlines can't be met, and certainly the majority of Microsoft products still ship later than initially hoped. But if you are a developer and you are going to slip, you had better have put in a lot of hours. Missing a deadline without working extra hours is professional suicide. As deadlines approach and employees are behind schedule, managers who may be reluctant to explicitly ask an employee to work more hours will instead use phrases like, "I need more of a commitment from you." Even if more hours won't help—if you are blocked by an issue that you can't resolve yourself—you need to put in the face time to show that you care.

Furthermore, it is common to demand schedules without giving employees the information they need to produce a reasonable estimate. A manager will say, "Just give me a number so we can write it down on the schedule." Then those numbers get presented to upper management and wind up set in stone. You are still expected to make good on this "commitment," no matter how shaky the foundation.

Few things are more frustrating than going to ask another developer for help and being told no because he or she is behind schedule. You can be stuck for days waiting for a few minutes of help from someone else. At times you can feel like you are trapped in a *Dilbert* cartoon. Despite this, if the deadline approaches and the developer is behind, the commitment is still expected. And commitment means working more hours.

The real fallacy in all of this is that working all those extra hours doesn't let you ship your software any sooner. Given a piece of software, there will be some resource that defines the critical path. Generally this is a developer, although it might be someone else. If *you* are that resource, and you are working at a constant rate, and how hard you work one week is not affected by how hard you worked the last week, and you are not in danger of burning out, then it is indeed possible that working an extra day will make a large piece of software ship one day earlier. But it is likely that you are not the critical path, so working that extra time won't make the software ship any sooner.

What you do get with people working longer is more features in a product. But since hopefully you have prioritized your features so you work on the most important ones first, the extra features you get are the low-priority ones. And every time you work on some new features, you run the risk that adding them will destabilize the product in some way that takes a long time to detect and fix. You wind up risking the entire product to add the lowest-priority features.

Let's say a team is working on a word processor and has 200 features on its to-do list, with 100 of those being absolute requirements—like being able to print, save files, set margins, and so on. The other 100 are optional and have been arranged in rough priority order. Now let's say the team is getting close to shipping and has 137 features done, and is contemplating working on feature 138. Likely there will be someone running around claiming that feature 138 is absolutely critical and that you can't ship without it, despite previously agreeing that feature 138 was below the "must have" cutoff. As a manager, you will have some developer who has made a schedule that promises feature 138 on time, and is therefore morally "signed up" to do so. You have the option of talking to that developer about commitment and hoping he or she works extra hours to get feature 138 done. But will this ship your software sooner? Of course not! Feature 138, like all features, will involve changes to the code, which can only take longer to do.

Removing feature 138 will mean you only have 137 features in your product, which may make a few users unhappy. But the presence of 137 features that work well and, more importantly, shipped on time, should allay any user angst over missing features 138 through 200.

When you get right down to the last stages of a product, a developer may need to fix a bug, and not fixing it for two days may make the product slip two days. But it is *only* right at the very end that this can be judged accurately enough to make it worthwhile. I never postponed looking at a bug until tomorrow or the next week and later thought, "I should have looked at it sooner." But there were many times when I stuck around late or came in on weekends to look at something, and realized later that it was pointless.

I am not knocking Luis' own work habits. He certainly practiced what he preached; few developers worked more hours than Luis did. But he expected everyone to work like that or be tarred with the "not committed" brush.

As often happens, the technical architecture of Digital Studio was entrusted to the people who worked the most, no matter their experience level, programming skills, or ability to work with others. Often an internal architectural change to a software product becomes necessary, which generally involves making small changes in many areas of the code. Accepted programming practice dictates that this should be done by defining what the change is, preparing directions on how code should be modified, and letting the individual code "owners" make the changes according to a planned timeline. On Digital Studio, the preferred way to accomplish this was to decide on the change on your own, not discuss it with anyone else, come in on the weekend when there were fewer people there, make all the changes yourself, and announce it on Monday as a done deal.

*　　*　　*

Luis' fundamental problem was that he was overworked, to the point that even he could not make it up by working longer. When Luis arrived, his job title was director of Digital Studio. On the organizational chart, he had a director of development, a group program manager, and a test manager reporting to him. The group program manager was of dubious competence, so Luis spent a lot of time dealing with the program management team. The director of development position was open, a "TBH" (to be hired) in Microsoft parlance. Martin had actually been hired for that job, and had been filling in as the overall director. There was some brief hope when Luis arrived that Martin could continue as director of development under Luis, but it soon became apparent that Luis wanted Martin out the door.

The job of director of development stayed open the whole time I was there. There was some interviewing of candidates, and a few offers made, but nobody ever accepted an offer. Softimage was looking for someone just like Luis, and it is hard to find someone as qualified as Luis who wouldn't want Luis' job instead of merely working for him.

Immediately after I arrived, Patrick, who would have been my boss, decided to move over to fill the vacant PM position for the hardware interfaces project. I was moved up to be temporary PL working directly for Luis, a position that was eventually made official. Luis was nominally both my boss and my boss's boss, but he also freely ignored his PLs and planned tasks for the developers. Effectively he was directly managing every developer on the project and liked it that way. This was frustrating for the PLs who were caught in the middle. Counting myself, there were 10 PLs when Luis arrived; six of them left within a year after conflicts with Luis.

Luis unquestionably had many strong positives. He excelled at managing in a crisis. He was the best crisis manager I ever met at Microsoft, a company filled with them. He had an exceptional talent for clearing away unimportant issues to focus on a short-term goal and prioritize what really defined the goal. Since he managed best in a crisis, the unfortunate result was that Digital Studio became one long, multi-year crisis. No huge surprise, since few projects I worked on at Microsoft were not run this way. One consequence of this is that the key developers were always too busy putting out fires to transfer their knowledge to anyone else. At every milestone, they were the only ones who could fix the critical problems, causing a giant bottleneck.

Luis had inherited a lot of people who had been hired before Microsoft bought Softimage, and one thing that became apparent is that if you want to run a group the Microsoft way, you need to have hired the Microsoft way. When Microsoft acquires companies it will sometimes interview all the employees to eliminate the incompetent and the redundant, but I am pretty sure Softimage had escaped that treatment. One thing that had made me nervous about my nearly content-free interview with Softimage was wondering who else's interviews had been that way. The assumptions that you can succeed without much process, that everybody is extremely competent and will do the right thing in a crunch, simply fall apart if you don't have the right people working for you. Heck, most Softimage people didn't really think of themselves as part of Microsoft. One time I got into an argument with an employee who was telling me how Windows sucked and OS/2 was great. Bill Gates came to visit Softimage, and during an employee Q&A someone asked, "Since the Internet is all about free soft-ware, how come Microsoft is still charging for it?"

As part of the employee review process, you submit feedback on your own manager every six months. In December 1995, when I had been there four months and Luis three, the overall feeling was very positive. The first part of the feedback involves grading your manager on a series of questions, such as "My manager understands the range of issues and vari-ables that impact my work," and "My manager sets clear goals for our work group." Number grades are given to each question, with 1 being the worst and 5 being the best. I gave Luis an average grade of 4.4. There were also some essay questions, such as "What does your manager do well that you would like to see him/her continue doing?" and "What would you like to see your manager stop doing, start doing, or do differently?" I praised Luis for setting a real schedule, energizing the team, and getting people focused on finishing the product rather than continuously adding features. At the time, I felt that he had reduced the number of decisions that had to go through him, although people would sometimes still refuse to do something until personally asked to by Luis.

My main complaint was that he was too busy doing 2 1/2 jobs to pro-vide much guidance to the development team. Managers are supposed to provide both informal feedback on an ongoing basis and also sit-down meetings at least every few months, but Luis didn't have time for either. I also pointed out that his personality was starting to wear thin on some people: "One day the build sucks, the next day it's the greatest thing ever. Making joking comments about the quality of someone's code in a large meeting may be a good tension-breaker, but it can also make people wary of really trusting him." Finally I threw in my perennial complaint about managers everywhere, that Luis was chronically late for meetings. I offered some advice: "If he is in a meeting with Daniel that's running long and there's a meeting scheduled with Joe Blow SDE, he should tell Daniel to take a hike."

In June 1996, after almost a year at Softimage, the average number grade on my manager feedback form dropped to 2.8. In my written comments, I took pains to point out that Luis worked very hard and was very committed to shipping Digital Studio, being by far the most important individual contributor to the success of the project. His technical knowledge of the product was impressive. Unfortunately, I wrote, he had basically abandoned managing his people. At that point he had 29 direct reports, including eight managers, five of whom were managing for the first time. By this time the group program manager had been shunted into another job, so Luis was doing the top three jobs by himself. As I pointed out, "Given the complexity of the product and the inexperience of the team, any one of these three would be a more-than-full-time job." As a result, "His only personal interactions with his direct reports consist of the occasional request for status or quick explanation of what a person should do next. His only advice on how to manage people is to encourage them to kick butt, be a force, and other platitudes. Any feel for where things are headed must be deduced from generalities offered up at group meetings."

Luis really did want to help people; he had an open-door policy, but he was so busy that you could never catch him in his office. He had gotten into a vicious circle where he didn't trust most of his team to make the right decisions, but because the team was in a perpetual crisis, there was no time to step back and let people learn by failing. Luis had to micro-manage the team himself, which was driving the other PLs and me crazy. He had held one meeting with his PLs to discuss their jobs. It was a good meeting, with a good discussion, only nothing concrete ever came out of it, and there was no time for further meetings.

I concluded my feedback with the following summary: "We see Luis doing demos for third parties, planning the details of trade shows, reviewing RAID bugs himself, etc. I feel that Luis has so much personal capital tied to the success of Digital Studio that he cannot bear to see these things done by others who may not do them as well as he does. And in one sense he's right: he could do the job of any member of the team better than they are doing it now. But, he's stifling a lot of the opportunity for growth in the team, which in the long run is more important than any one product. Luis has brought DS forward on his own back, but if he left tomorrow I think the team would return to where it was before, and in that sense he has failed them."

6

Demo Crisis

The Microsoft culture is combative, not physically but verbally. It is expected that ideas will be argued about before they are adopted, and that the best ideas will win. Luis brought that culture to Softimage. He was such a great debater that during any discussion he could always come up with some flaws in your logic or some variable that you had not considered. In a sense he was too good, because he could win any argument. But this meant that decisions were being made for reasons other than technical merit. Eventually you could get tired of losing arguments and decide it was easier to agree with him. After almost a year of this I had the sense that despite all the great things Luis said, and despite lots of hard work on everyone's part, we were still not very close to shipping Digital Studio. What we had had instead was a year of demo-inspired crises.

Ah, the mighty demo. For someone who loves a crisis, there is nothing quite like preparing for a demonstration of your product, especially at an industry conference. The market that Digital Studio was aimed at was quite small, so you could put your message out to everyone important with a single good conference demo.

However, there are various levels of realism in computer demonstrations.

The most honest is what I will call a Type 1 demo, which involves a completed or almost-completed product, which you then put through its paces for the audience, in a basically unscripted manner, with perhaps a small checklist to remind you that at some point during the demo you need to show features A, B, and C. A product at this level can also be put out on the show floor for passers-by to play with. If you were giving a Type 1 demo of a car, you would toss the user the keys and tell him or her to take it for a spin.

The next level down is where your product is not complete, but you have some features that work well. The Type 2 demo shows off those features in a way that is calculated to accentuate their perceived value and diminish the perceived value of the features that aren't there, and create the impression that your product is closer to being done than it really is. You may stop at some well-chosen points and say, "Of course, the complete version will be able to do this nifty thing at this point." Or, if you are a little sneakier or perhaps have fewer real features to show, you may say, "I could also do this, but in the interest of time or clarity or [insert excuse/joke here], I won't show it." Allowing show attendees to play with this product can be a little risky, although you can sometimes pull this off if you have someone who knows the product hovering nearby, ready to jump in and redirect users or explain away crashes. A Type 2 demo of a car would involve you driving along with the user, with your own set of pedals, ready to grab the wheel at any time.

The next circle of demo hell is where your product isn't complete and even the things that work aren't that stable. We'll call this Type 3. You guide the product through its paces while avoiding known pitfalls. You may be able to show features A, B, and C in that order, but if you show B first, then A will crash, for reasons that you don't know or care about, or at least would be embarrassed to have to explain. At some point you may discover that A then B then C doesn't work, but A then B then D then C works, so you rework your demo to do that. Or perhaps to prevent C from crashing, you need to use the time between B and C to tell a story that lasts at least 15 seconds. At this point you have a *very* accurate script, which you teach very carefully to the person doing the demo, while also emphasizing that the whole thing must look natural and unscripted. Then during the demo you watch nervously from the audience. Users will almost never be allowed to play with a product in this state. In a Type 3 demo of a car, you would be driving yourself, on a road with no other cars.

People make jokes about computer industry demos and the art of demoing, referring to Type 3 demos. There are various stories in the Microsoft lore about demos of minefield-infested products that successfully fooled the audience.

Rarer, but even more diabolical and counterproductive, is the Type 4 demo. This is where at some point, weeks or months before the demo, you stop working on the actual product and instead start writing a demo. This is a piece of software that looks superficially like the product you are working on, but all it does is the demo. If there are four buttons on the screen and during the demo you are going to press only one, you don't even bother writing any code to handle the other three. It doesn't even need to do what it is claiming to do; it merely has to *look* like it is doing it. So if you are demoing a spreadsheet and want to show how it can sort a column, you start with known data in the column, and when the sort button is pressed, the code can substitute the pre-sorted data that you have calculated in some other way and stored somewhere. This kind of demo can actually be easier to do flawlessly since the code can't do much except its demo—if you press the wrong key nothing happens. But if someone in the audience pipes up and wants you to use a different font or repeat an example, you may be exposed. A Type 4 demo of a car is where the curtain rises on stage and there is the car, but it is custom-built sheet metal sitting on the chassis of a different model, it never leaves the podium, and it is not clear whether there is an engine inside.

Softimage, in its early days, was a master at Type 4 demos. Leaving aside ethical or moral dilemmas, the problem is that you spend some significant development effort on a demo purely to show it at a conference and then throw it away. Although you can show the same demo if there are several conferences in quick succession, in an industry like computer editing everyone attends the same conferences, and after a while they expect to see some change in your demo to reflect the work you have supposedly done in the interim. You may spend a month or two working on a Type 4 demos, and if you have two or three major conferences a year, they consume a significant portion of your time. A development team has enough trouble shipping one piece of software at a time; asking it to simultaneously produce, maintain, and enhance a separate Type 4 demo is suicidal.

Nonetheless, Softimage had in the past attempted just that. Daniel had dreamed up Digital Studio many years before—the concept of integrating all the tools that an editor would use into one package with a consistent user interface (UI) and easy sharing of content. The first demo had been at the National Association of Broadcasters conference, or NAB, in 1994. NAB is *the* yearly conference where folks who produce video go to see new equipment—everything from cables to motor homes outfitted as remote editing suites. Digital Studio at NAB94 was a Type 4 demo all the way—the actual product was not even in development yet. A bevy of Softimage developers had worked crazy hours for months to get it ready, culminating in a final all-nighter in a room they had rented on the show floor itself. But their work paid off; the demo was successful and Softimage even sold some copies of the at-the-time-nonexistent Digital Studio.

The demo was so successful that some competitors saw it, thought to themselves, "Hmm, that's a good idea!" and now were preparing to give demos of their own software at NAB96, two years after the first Digital Studio demo. People were wondering what Softimage had been up to in those two years, so there was a lot of pressure to have a "killer" Digital Studio demo at NAB.

When Martin had been hired, he had gotten Daniel's assurance that there would be no more cooked-up demos; Softimage would show the product with whatever features were working at the time of any given conference—a Type 2 demo.

When Luis arrived he got Softimage on the Type 3 demo bandwagon. He felt it was important to reassure the market that Digital Studio was progressing, and that this was worth any delays that preparing for the demo might cause. A conference demo was a very public display with an unmovable deadline. In short, it was a ready-made crisis.

My very first Softimage demo crisis was an internal one. Moshe worked for Craig Mundie, a vice president who worked back in Redmond (in a curious twist, Craig had in a previous job led part of Team "A" at Data General—the one that lost to the group chronicled in *The Soul of a New Machine*). Craig was coming to visit in late November, and he was bringing his boss, Paul Maritz, who owned half the development teams at Microsoft and reported directly to Bill Gates. Crisis!!

*   *   *

Before explaining the demo, it is necessary to explain a bit more about how Digital Studio worked. Digital Studio ran in one of two different ways, which were referred to (somewhat inaccurately) as the "hardware" and "software" versions.

Personal computers transmit data internally across a hardware component known as a "bus." When you download a file over the modem, the data goes from the modem to your computer's memory, and then from the memory to the disk, in both cases traveling over the bus on the way. The bus has a certain bandwidth it can support, which indicates how fast it can transfer data. For most operations, the bus bandwidth is not an issue; a modem is many times slower than the bus, so the modem is the limiting factor and the bus bandwidth doesn't make any difference. Digital Studio was sending around video streams, which consume a huge amount of bandwidth. The standard digital format for storing the NTSC television signal used in the U.S., known as "D1," consumes approximately 21 megabytes of data every second. This is a higher data rate than a standard PC bus can handle. Hard drives also have a maximum rate at which they can read or write data, which is also generally well below 21 megabytes per second. Thus a standard PC can't handle D1 video on the bus, and even if it could, the hard drive wouldn't be able to keep up. The same bus limitations apply in reverse, when you are trying to play back D1 video that is stored on the hard drive.

There are two ways to deal with this problem. The first is to use an expansion card in your PC that has connectors on the back to send and receive the D1 video at full bandwidth, but that internally compresses each frame before it sends it out on the bus, so the resulting video stream is low enough bandwidth for the bus and the hard drive to handle. In this model, any effects that Digital Studio wanted to do would be done in software. Let's say you had used the video board to capture some compressed video into a file on your hard drive—this file is known in editing terminology as a "clip." The clip might be 10 seconds long and you might want to add a 1-second text overlay (known as a "title") that started two seconds into the clip. You need to add the title to approximately 30 frames (NTSC runs at precisely 29.97 frames per second, but it is often easier to assume it runs at 30 frames per second). Digital Studio would read each of the 30 affected frames from the disk, uncompress it, add the title to each frame by modifying the data, recompress it, and write it back to disk, producing a 1-second clip that had the title in it. This process is known as "rendering." Once this has been done, the result can be played back. Digital Studio would instruct the video card to play two seconds of the original clip, then the new 1-second rendered clip with the title in it, then the last seven seconds of the original clip. The viewer would see the expected result play back seamlessly.

In this "software" version of Digital Studio, the video hardware is only used for capturing clips and playing them back. All manipulation of the clips (the heart and soul of Digital Studio) was done in software.

The "hardware" version of Digital Studio would solve the bus bandwidth problem a second way, by using much more specialized hardware. This hardware would have video inputs and outputs, connected to a special bus and hard drive, separate from those of the main PC, which could handle the required bandwidth. It would also have significant ability to modify the video as it went by. You might be able to tell the hardware to add the title for you. Then you would only have to store the original 10-second clip; when it came time to play back the result with the title, you would tell the hardware "Play back this 10-second clip, and for one second, starting at two seconds, please overlay this title with the following text and font and size and position," and then tell the hardware "go" and it would output the final video. There would be no need to render the special 1-second clip, so storage space would be saved and rendering time eliminated.

*   *   *

So despite the names, both the "software" and "hardware" versions of Digital Studio required specialized hardware, but the hardware version required much more specialized and expensive hardware. Prior to the demo for Craig and Paul, Digital Studio was running a third way, which you might call "true software" mode. It could run on any standard computer. But there was no video capture functionality—it worked on video clips that had been captured by other pieces of software, or gotten from another computer, and stored on the standard hard drive. For playback, it displayed frames as fast as it could, which might be a couple of frames per second.

For the demo, we needed to show better playback, which meant integrating some real video hardware into Digital Studio to let it run in "software" mode. This fell squarely under the purview of the hardware interfaces team, of which I was PL. We used an expansion card called the Targa 2000, from a company called TrueVision. The Targa 2000 could do 30 frames per second capture and playback of compressed video. This was a card that you could buy off the shelf, and you could also buy documentation explaining how to integrate it into your software. So we opened up the Targa 2000 documentation and wrote some code to do playback from within Digital Studio.

Needless to say, the code didn't work at first. Luckily TrueVision had technical support for problems like ours. Since the card was used by various other editing packages on the market, we knew it was possible to make it work; we just had to figure out how. After a few weeks of panic and a lot of email exchanges with TrueVision, we got the thing working, sort of. We could only get it to play back at 15 frames per second, but that looks fine to most people. The rest of the Digital Studio team pulled their pieces together and we gave Craig and Paul a nice solid Type 3 demo. The demo machine was set up so that it had a second monitor that the Targa 2000 output was connected to, so after editing the video in the first monitor, you saw the playback in the second. This looked very cool compared to a typical Microsoft demo and it made you think, "Wow they can show video in a second monitor, they must be working hard." In fact it was easier to do this than to show the Targa 2000 output in the main monitor, but never mind.

After that demo, we focused on preparing for our first real public demo at NAB96. This would be two years after the initial, completely fake Digital Studio demo, and it was judged imperative to show real progress. The plan was to demo a hardware version of Digital Studio, using much more sophisticated hardware than the Targa 2000. We wanted to form a partnership with various high-end hardware companies to jointly integrate their hardware into Digital Studio. The plan was to focus on one or two hardware partners at first, and eventually expand the list.

For the NAB demo, the main hardware partner was a company called Play, headquartered in Rancho Cordova, California, just east of Sacramento.

Play was the offshoot of a company called NewTek, which had produced a piece of hardware called the Video Toaster. The Video Toaster was video-processing hardware, just like what Digital Studio would use for its hardware version. It was tied to a computer called the Amiga, a computer that was in many ways ahead of its time. Commodore, the company that sold the Amiga, had been one of the leaders in home computers back in the late 1970s, in the days before the IBM PC. It bought the company that made the Amiga (at the time the company it bought was called Amiga and the machine was code named the Lorraine) in 1984 and brought the first of several machines out the next year. The Amiga had astonishingly good video and audio processing capabilities. Unfortunately, Commodore never figured out how to market it or get programmers interested in it, and it never caught on as a mainstream computer.

Because of the Amiga's multimedia capabilities, it did attract heavy support in fields such as video editing. The Video Toaster, which came out in 1990, was revolutionary: a hardware add-in that gave you a $5,000 system with real-time video processing just like systems that cost hundreds of thousands of dollars. The quality wasn't quite as good, but the bang for the buck was phenomenal. In 1993 the Video Toaster won an Emmy award for development in television engineering.

NewTek at the time was headquartered in Topeka, Kansas. The big excitement in Topeka was chasing tornadoes, and eventually a group of employees decided that the place was a little too dull. They also felt that the founder, Tim Jenison, had no vision of how to expand the business. In particular, he still wanted to restrict NewTek's product to the Amiga when others felt that the PC was the way of the future. Furthermore they all worked too damn hard, and none of them had any equity in the company, so what was the point? Included in this group were a lot of the engineers, as well as a woman named Kiki Stockhammer, who had been the chief demo artist and consumer evangelist for NewTek. A legend in the video business, Kiki was for most people the visible face of the Video Toaster. As she herself says on her website, "There is nothing more appealing than a technical guru in hot pants showing you how to use the latest and greatest in technological breakthroughs."

The group quit NewTek and relocated to the San Francisco Bay Area. After kicking around some ideas for a new company, they moved to Rancho Cordova and merged with a video hardware company called Progressive Image Technology and a video software company called Digital Creations to found Play in August 1994. Its first product was Snappy, a simple device that would plug into the printer port of a PC and capture still images from a video feed, for example, from your camcorder. Snappy was an immediate success, due perhaps in part to the photos of Kiki looking sultry on the outside of the box.

Snappy was not the real goal of Play. It was designed by a couple of engineers in a few months, so the company could pay the bills while work continued on the real dream—producing the successor to the Video Toaster. Play planned to produce the ultimate video editor, in every way superior to the Toaster. The Toaster had run on an Amiga; the new system would run on a PC. The Toaster had operated at NTSC resolution; the new system would operate at D1, the digital standard for television broadcasts. The Toaster had some cool effects, but the new system would have the ultimate effects, rivaling anything available on a high-end system. The effects engine would be programmable, so there would be no limit to what it could do.

This new system had been dubbed Trinity, and for NAB96 Softimage was going to demo Digital Studio using Trinity. Trinity was a large box that connected to the PC via a single expansion card and some cables. It had its own high-bandwidth bus and plug-in cards, much like the PC but geared towards video processing. The video signal would enter the Trinity through a card that plugged into this bus, be stored on disks attached to the bus, be processed by the effects cards on the bus, and then exit through another card; the video signal would never go near the PC and its poky little bus. Instead, the PC would send instructions through the expansion card instructing the Trinity what to do with the video. This solved the limitations in the PC's internal bus by removing it from the loop.

Play was in a situation with Trinity similar to the one Softimage was in with Digital Studio. Trinity was not a shipping product; it was still under development. The defection from NewTek had been public, and Play had been talking about Trinity at conferences for a long time, so people were starting to ask when they would see real hardware.

At Softimage we were also a bit skeptical. The spec for the software interfaces we would use to control Trinity had been delivered on time in mid-October 1995, but the actual hardware and drivers that implemented those interfaces were another story. NAB was in early April 1996. Play first promised to deliver a basic Trinity system in mid-December 1995, with the video effects engine (dubbed the Warp Engine) arriving at the end of February 1996. The dates kept getting pushed back; at each step we were assured that although the dates for delivery of the initial components were slipping, we would still get the complete package at the proper time. In order to keep pressure on Play's engineers, and on ourselves, we ran with the assumption that what they said was true—every time they missed a deadline we behaved as if they would make the next one. This made it even more disruptive when they kept missing them. For a major demo like this, it is not only the developers who are affected by a slip. You need to allocate some time to test the demo, then more time to redesign the demo based on what works and doesn't work, then time to train the demo artists who will be doing the demo on the show floor.

Finally at the end of January 1996, Play sent up some engineers to Montreal, carrying with them a real live Trinity box. In this early version, the boards were mounted on pieces of plywood inside a plain metal case. It did have real hardware in it, and could play back video under the control of the expansion card in the PC. The input cards were not ready yet, which meant you could not bring live video into the system. The only video it could play was that stored on digital disk recorders hooked up to the system—like VCRs except they store the data internally on hard drives instead of tape. To prepare for the NAB demo, we could detach the digital disk recorders from the Trinity, put the demo video on them, and then hook them back up to the Trinity with nobody the wiser.

On the initial schedule, the Warp Engine had been promised for mid-February. Despite the fact that the initial Trinity box had just slipped a month and a half (and the input modules, which would consume some engineering resources at Play, were also not finished), when Play told us that the Warp Engine would only slip two weeks to the beginning of March, Luis had us all re-do our schedules to depend on its arriving then.

The Warp Engine would allow a variety of effects. What we wanted to use it for in the demo was an effect known as a "transition," used when switching between scenes. The simplest transition, and by far the most common, is the "cut," where the video is showing the end of one scene in one frame and then shows the start of the next scene in the next frame. Doing a cut on Trinity would not require the Warp Engine; you could just instruct the digital disk recorder to switch clips at the appropriate time.

The most basic transition that required an effect was the "wipe." A wipe looks like an imaginary line is moving across the screen, revealing the new scene behind the old one. Wipes are rarely used in movies nowadays, although they used to be popular. The *Star Wars* movies, going for a retro touch, use wipes when the action switches between planets. You can wipe in almost any direction; there are "clock wipes," where the new scene is revealed by a watch hand sweeping around, and "circle wipes," where a circle grows from the middle with the new scene in it or the old scene shrinks into a circle in the middle.

Wipes were considered "two-dimensional" effects, along with some other simple transitions such as a "slide" (which is like a wipe except that the new or old scene moves as it is being revealed or hidden), and effects such as picture-in-picture. The transition used in the old *Batman* television show, where the outline of a bat zoomed out at you and then reversed, revealing the new scene, was also a two-dimensional wipe. This is in contrast to fancier "three-dimensional" effects, such as a page curl, where it appears as if a page is being turned to reveal the new scene, or the opposite, where the new scene arrives on a page being turned down over the old scene. If done properly, the scene that is on the "page" will be mapped onto it as it is turned—that is the three-dimensional effect. Gimmicky effects like this are currently out of fashion except for children's television shows. The show *Barney* uses a 3D effect where the old scene appears to float away, surrounded by sparkles.

The Warp Engine was designed to do even more powerful effects, such as a transition in which the first scene was consumed by flames, revealing the second one. 2D effects are so basic that Play was designing a separate, less expensive card to handle them. That card had long since been postponed until after NAB. Play wanted to concentrate on the Warp Engine, which was the truly unique feature of Trinity. Since a 2D effect is a subset of a 3D effect, the Warp Engine could do the simple transitions we wanted to show in our NAB demo. But as it stood at the end of January, we had no Warp Engine, and only a promise from Play that it would be ready in a month.

There was another problem. The single card that went in the PC to control the Trinity was somewhat non-standard. It was designed for a bus called the VESA (Video Electronics Standards Association) local bus, or VL-BUS. VESA was faster than the original PC bus but slower than PCI (Peripheral Component Interconnect), the current standard. VESA had a brief moment in the sun in 1992 and 1993, when the Intel 486 chip was the state of the art. With the arrival of the Pentium chip and the PCI bus, VESA went out of fashion, and by early 1996 it was very hard to find computers with a VESA bus in them. Worse, some of the other cards we needed to put in the demo machines were designed for the PCI bus.

It was never clear why Play had chosen to make a VESA card instead of a PCI card; there were some vague explanations that the hardware designers had some experience with VESA and PCI was considered more difficult to design for. The VESA card was always supposed to be a temporary measure with the PCI card just around the corner, but when the first Trinity hardware arrived in Montreal, the corner was nowhere in sight.

Play had discovered a motherboard that had PCI slots as well as a single VESA slot. They brought two computers built around this motherboard along with them when they delivered the Trinity system. Unfortunately the fastest processor that this motherboard could accommodate was a 100 MHz Pentium, which was very slow for the time—computers were now running the Pentium Pro, the successor to the Pentium, at 200 MHz. This hodgepodge of slots also seemed to make the computers quite flaky; they kept malfunctioning mysteriously.

During the January visit, Play set up the computers and showed off the Trinity system. The hardware that was there worked well. We got it integrated fairly quickly into Digital Studio, and then went back to waiting for the rest of the hardware we needed for the demo.

The lack of hardware was especially frustrating because Play refused to give us any official status on it. The new pieces of hardware would be ready when they were ready, they were working as hard as they could, nagging them would not help. The most important thing when planning a demo is knowing what you have to work with. If they had told us upfront that none of the extra hardware was going to be available, we could have modified the demo to deal with that, but the uncertainty was killing us. We secretly worried that Play was going to deliver the hardware at the last minute, too late for us to integrate into Digital Studio, and then show it at its own booth at NAB.

In early March, the Warp Engine was still nowhere in sight. With the demo a month away, Luis decided to fly someone out to Rancho Cordova with orders to stay there until the hardware was delivered and integrated into Digital Studio. The obvious choices were either Peter Ibrahim or me, and since Peter was critical to the entire product, while I was only critical to the hardware interfaces team, I was chosen to go.

While I resent having to scramble in response to an imagined or artificial crisis, this was a genuine crisis. Major pieces of hardware were missing five weeks before the conference, and Play's unwillingness to give us any progress reports made planning the demo impossible. The decision to send someone was made late Friday afternoon, and Luis wanted someone to fly out on Monday and stay for an indefinite amount of time.

Luis offered to pay to fly my wife and son somewhere for the duration of my visit to Sacramento. This was a genuinely nice offer on his part, and illustrates some of the paradox of Luis' personality; he did feel bad about the effect this would have on my family and felt guilty for having to ask me to go. It just took something excessive like this for those instincts to kick in. To him, working late nights and weekends in a state of perpetual crisis was not beyond the call of duty. So it was not a question of his not caring about his employees' personal lives, it was more that his threshold was set much higher than mine.

We decided they would stay at our house in Redmond, visiting the friends who had rented it while we were in Montreal. On Monday we all flew out there, and I flew down to Sacramento on Tuesday morning, March 12. NAB was set to start on Monday, April 15, exactly 34 days later.

*   *   *

Play's offices were located in a generic one-story office building in Rancho Cordova, which is itself a generic suburb of Sacramento. When I arrived, Steve Hartford, the main Softimage contact at Play, met me and gave me a tour. The building had four large rooms. One room had offices for the executives, including Kiki (who, sadly, was traveling on business when I arrived). Down the hall was a large room for engineering, containing a maze of cubicles littered with hardware and doors to a few offices, including Steve's. Across the hall was the manufacturing operation, where Snappys were being combined with cables and manuals and stuffed into boxes. Next to that was the room for the designers, who worked on user interfaces and fancy Warp Engine transitions and had a room lit mostly with Lava Lamps.

I was introduced to Paul Montgomery, the president of Play. He sat me down, explained a bit of the history of the company and then had me watch a video. The video was mostly about NewTek, in particular lots of footage of its Christmas parties, narrated by Kiki. This was the first sign of a feeling that pervaded Play. Although it was resolutely *not* NewTek, the founders wanted to be recognized and respected for what they had achieved at NewTek. They wanted to be seen as having the coolness and nimbleness of a startup, while at the same time generating the trust that came with a track record of shipping products.

After the video, Paul came back and talked some more about his vision for the company. I couldn't understand why he was telling me all this. I had a brief, terrifying thought that he was going to offer me a job, but he just wanted me to know "where they were coming from." When I was sufficiently indoctrinated, he released me back to Steve.

I met some of the engineers I would be working with. They were interested in computers and cars, mostly. After leaving NewTek, a bunch of them had got together and fleet ordered Nissan 300ZX sports cars in various colors. Paul took great pride in driving a Ferrari Testarossa as his everyday car. Like a lot of engineers, they collected random amusing knickknacks; Paul had in his office a panel that was used on the bridge of the Enterprise in one of the *Star Trek* movies, alongside the Emmy he had won at NewTek.

They also subscribed to the "work hard, party hard" ethic. The first night I arrived there, someone had decided that they should watch the movie *This is Spinal Tap*. At the appointed hour, nothing would do but that all work stop and everyone troop into the lone conference room to watch the movie. When it was over, everyone went back to work. Another night, someone decided that he was going to blow up a soda pop bottle, so everyone went out to the parking lot, watched the explosion, and then went back to work.

Whatever their foibles, the engineers were to a person extremely smart and extremely dedicated. Paul, *Star Trek* panel and all, was a very impressive entrepreneurial type. And they did have more interesting outside interests than the average programmers. The head of sales was a trained magician. One of the hardware engineers played bass in a rock band. Kiki was, well, Kiki.

What they also had, unfortunately, was a strong desire to do things at their own pace. I think their real goal was to work on cool hardware for a while, go public, make their fortunes, and rub it in the face of Tim Jenison, NewTek's founder. What they did not want to do was be bullied around by Microsoft, or Microsoft masquerading as Softimage.

The building Play was in had a receptionist in the middle and then branched off to the left and right. Play occupied the entire left side, which was entered by a door off the receptionist area that required a cardkey for access. Steve explained that they had recently leased some more office space in the right side of the building, and I would be the first occupant. I sat in the new space all by myself. If I wanted to talk to anybody else, I needed to be buzzed in from the receptionist area. I was also supposed to be met at the door and escorted around.

Officially, that's the way it was. Steve was no more forthcoming on schedules from across the lobby than he had been from across the continent: things would be ready when they were ready, they were working as hard as they could, nagging them would not help. As he said, "We don't have a schedule, just an order of implementation." It took several days to get a phone line in my special office, and Steve got upset because I would ask him about it every day. I guess the phone installer was also working as hard as he could.

Luckily, the engineers were mostly immune to the security fixation that had permeated management from Steve on up. They invited me over to their side of the building for lunch every day. They would let me walk around without an escort (if Steve wasn't watching) and were very open about the status of the hardware (although sometimes they would report my visits back to Steve, who would come complain to me). Unfortunately the news wasn't particularly good; the Warp Engine wasn't going to be ready for at least a week. So I sat around in my new office, waiting for something to happen, on alert in case it did. I had a laptop I had brought with me that I would use to read email (once I got my phone line), play prodigious amounts of Solitaire, and occasionally cook up some pretext to go over to the other side of the building to extract nuggets of information from the engineers. It was especially frustrating to think that my family was living out of a suitcase (admittedly in no great discomfort, since they were staying in their own house), my wife watching my son by herself, while I sat around with my thumb up my rear. At least I finally got to meet Kiki.

After a week there I finally saw a Trinity with a Warp Engine working in the lab. However, that was the one Play was planning on using for its own NAB demo. The set of hardware that Softimage was getting was perennially a few days away from arriving, but something always seemed to be delaying it. And the software drivers that we needed were even further away. Finally on Thursday, nine days after I arrived, Steve admitted that nothing would be ready until the following Monday, March 25. So I flew up to Seattle for the weekend.

When I got back to Rancho Cordova on Monday, much to my amazement the hardware was ready and working as advertised. My time waiting had allowed me to get the code in Digital Studio ready to integrate in, and within a few days, Digital Studio was running on Trinity. There were still oodles of problems with the drivers they had provided—for example, you couldn't do more than one Warp effect in a row, which would make the demo pretty simple. Still I had the hardware in hand, and any software updates could easily be sent over the Internet. On Thursday, March 28, I flew back to Seattle, and the next day we all flew back to Montreal.

The next week was fairly calm. The demo script was cut down significantly to work around issues with the drivers. We would report problems to Play, and then wait for fixes; it was the same story as it had been with the hardware, with us waiting for Play to give us new drivers, and Play telling us to be patient.

One problem in particular involved the keyer. A keyer is a piece of hardware used when you want to overlay a foreground image over a background. The foreground image is filmed in front of a bright blue or green screen, known as a "matte"; the keyer is then used to replace the blue or green areas with the background. This is how weathermen on the news appear to be standing in front of a weather map. In reality they are standing in front of a blue or green matte, and a keyer is used to dynamically overlay them on top of the weather map image (technically, a keyer only analyzes the foreground image and decides what areas of the foreground image should be kept, and which ones should be made transparent; the actual work of overlaying that result on top of the background is done by a separate piece of hardware called the compositor).

Weathermen tend to look like they are floating unnaturally in front of their weather maps, because the division between them and the background is somewhat abrupt. This is known as a "hard-edged key," but the image is seen only briefly, and no one is too concerned about maintaining the illusion that the weatherman is standing in front of a large weather map. In addition, the keying is done live, so you have to set up your keyer to recognize the matte and hope your weatherman doesn't wear a bright green jacket.

When doing keying for a commercial or movie, you have much more time to play with the parameters to the keyer. You can set up a key, play back the composited image, fiddle with the parameters a bit, play it back over and over again until you feel it blends together naturally, creating a nice "soft-edged key." A well-edited commercial should make it virtually impossible to tell what was shot as one scene and what was composited later.

The keyer was one of the selling points of Trinity; it was reputed to do excellent soft-edged keying. A keyer is controlled by a minimum of two parameters: one indicates the basic background color that is to be keyed out, and the other indicates how close to that color a color should be to be keyed out. This is to allow for small variations in the background color due to lighting or different materials. The Trinity keyer was controlled with two parameters, but the documentation gave no indication what each parameter meant. We tried plugging in various parameters at random, but discovered that we either got no keying, or else removed the entire foreground image.

We had provided Play with the exact clip that we were going to key. It showed a man who had been miniaturized being chased by a giant-looking mosquito. The man was the foreground image; he had been filmed in front of a green screen, reacting to an imaginary giant mosquito and running away. The background image was a computer-generated video (generated in Softimage 3D in fact) of the mosquito, plus the actual background for the whole shot—the wall behind them, the ground they were standing on, and so forth. Play looked at the foreground clip and told us the exact values we should provide for the two parameters to key that particular shot well. They still did not explain what the values meant; they were two apparently random numbers, like a magic incantation. We rigged up Digital Studio to pass those two numbers in, and much to our amazement, the keyer worked properly—not a particularly soft-edged key, but reasonable for a demo.

Before we got keying working we had been prepared to remove it from the demo entirely, but now we were able to plan the demo. The demo artist would bring up the dialog box to control the keyer and twiddle a few knobs on the screen, which would change the values of the parameters passed to the keyer. The screen would show the effect of this, which would likely be to transition abruptly from no keying (all you saw was the man in front of his green screen) to keying the entire foreground image (all you saw was the mosquito and background), but enough to indicate that something was happening. He would utter the classic Type 3 demo phrase, "To save time in this demo, we got this set up beforehand..." and explain how rather than continue to fiddle with the parameters until the key looked good, he would load some saved values instead. Then he would press a special button on the screen, added just for the demo, which would instruct Digital Studio to set up the keyer with the two magic parameters that Play had provided to us. And lo and behold, the keying would work, and the man and mosquito would both be seen. Unbeknownst to the audience was the fact that it would only work for that particular image.

A new problem soon emerged, which was that the keyer was very flaky. Sometimes it would key properly, but other times, even though Digital Studio passed the same parameters to the keyer, nothing would happen— the foreground image would be shown in its entirety, with none of the background visible. Play had no idea what was going on. They reported that the keyer always worked for them.

Eventually we discovered that if the very first thing you did after starting Digital Studio was use the keyer, then it would work. However, once you played back a clip, the keyer would stop working until you restarted Digital Studio. In particular, you could not even play back the keyed clip; all you could do was fiddle with the keyer with the video paused. Play had never discovered this because all their tests only did one thing, and then re-initialized the Trinity before doing the next test.

The demo was amended again; the script was reworked so the demo artist would do the keying first. He would keep the video paused and play with the parameters, showing keying swinging wildly between all-mosquito and all-man. Then he would hit the special button and the magic parameters would be provided to the keyer, showing a good key with the video paused. He would then play back the clip. Digital Studio would at that point secretly switch from playing the foreground and background clips with keying enabled, and would instead disable the keyer and play back a pre-recorded clip with the keying already done. This clip was generated using the same two source clips that we were claiming to use—the man in front of the green screen and the computer-generated mosquito and background—composited together on a competitor's non-linear editor whose keyer worked, and then saved back to the digital disk recorder.

So the version of Digital Studio we would bring to the demo would be rigged up so that any time you went into the keyer UI with any two clips, it would always use the parameters that had been predetermined to look good with the giant mosquito chasing the man—no matter if those parameters gave a good key for the footage used. And when you set up a key and played it back, it would always play back the finished footage of the mosquito chasing the man, even if your material was completely different. We would not allow anyone in the audience to come up and play with the keyer after the demo. This was Type 3 demoing at its finest.

Play also didn't fix the problem of being able to do only one Warp effect in time for the demo. We wanted to play multiple clips back-to-back and have nice Warp effects between each of them, but instead we had to pick one particular transition and use a Warp effect. The only other transitions we could use were a cut, which involves butting two clips back-to-back, and a dissolve, which is a transition where the old scene fades out while the new one fades in. It happened that the way Trinity was designed, dissolves were not done by the Warp Engine but by another piece of hardware. To nobody's great surprise, their drivers also had a bug preventing more than one dissolve from being done in a given sequence of clips.

We wound up with a demo where we would do the keying part first, then add some clips, and then have the demo artist say, "To speed things along I'll now put in one transition here and one dissolve here and leave the rest as cuts." The frightening thing is that this would still be a compelling demo and would imply a very well-functioning product. You would have your nice key, then some funky Warp Engine transition, then a dissolve. This "Let's show only one of everything" idea is very common in demos, presented as a time-saver.

There was yet another problem with the demo. We needed to use the clunky machines with the VESA buses to control the Trinity through the expansion card. Thus, any part of the demo using the Trinity would need to be done on one of those machines. But Digital Studio also allowed audio clips to be edited, which used a separate high-end audio expansion card. We discovered that the VESA machines did not have enough expansion slots to fit the audio card. The audio part of the demo was impressive; the audio card had been ready some time before, and that part of the demo was much more authentic than the video part. The decision was made that we would have two machines up on stage during the demo. At a predetermined point during the demo script, the demo artist would switch machines. The person controlling which computer's display was duplicated on the giant screens onstage would need to be alert and switch over at the proper time. It also meant that we would need to have the second machine set up before the demo so that its screen looked more or less like what the first machine display would look like at the end of its part of the demo, to minimize the number of people who noticed the switch.

Such switching is not uncommon during demos for a variety of reasons; a lot of demos have a second machine standing by in case the first one crashes, so this would also provide a backup for us. If the first machine crashed at some point in the demo, then the demo artist could switch to the second one and skip the remainder of the demo involving the first machine (hoping the person controlling the giant screens noticed what was going on and also switched them over). If he did this smoothly enough, people might not even realize the first machine had crashed.

NAB96 started on a Monday, and the previous Thursday we flew out to Las Vegas. Play was supposed to ship PCs and Trinity systems directly to Las Vegas for us to use, but Luis, in what was soon to be revealed as a stroke of management genius, decided that he didn't want to depend on them, so we packed up our entire lab in Montreal—PCs, Trinitys, cables, the works—and brought it with us on the flight. This decision was made the afternoon we were leaving, so the boxes were packed in a hurry. One box consisted of a PC system unit and a video monitor, taped up with no packing material at all to cushion them.

Peter Ibrahim, Chris Lea (the Digital Studio audio expert), and I were flying together. We arrived at the airport each with three carry-on "bags," which were actually boxes of computer equipment each weighing about 100 pounds. The rules on bringing computer equipment into the U.S. for demos are somewhat vague, but generally you can bring equipment in if you are going to bring it out again. We had a printout containing the serial numbers of all the equipment we had. We first went by Canadian customs and showed the boxes and the printout to an agent there. He looked amused and produced some form, which he filled in and stamped. We then went to check in. The check in agents told us we needed a "carnet" describing the equipment. We showed them the printout with the serial numbers. They shrugged and said it was up to the U.S. customs agents to decide whether that was sufficient. In Montreal, immediately after you check in you carry your bags over to U.S. customs agents who are stationed there, meaning you clear customs before you leave. This allows you to land at the domestic terminal when you get to the U.S. We trundled off to customs, each of us pushing a cart loaded with equipment. I was volunteered to talk to the agent since I was the only U.S. citizen. I showed him the boxes, showed him the printout, and explained the situation. He looked at me, looked at the boxes, and made some mental calculation involving how pathetic we looked and what a pain it would be to process all this equipment correctly. Then he waved us through.

When we arrived in Las Vegas, we immediately set up a software development office in a hotel suite. We got in touch with the folks from Play and discovered that the truck they had hired to drive all the equipment from Sacramento had broken down somewhere near Death Valley, and would not be there until the next morning. Luckily we had our whole lab in boxes, which had amazingly all survived the flight intact. After a quick trip to a local computer store to buy some networking cable and hubs, we had all the computers set up and networked, carefully plugged into outlets spread around the suite to avoid blowing any fuses.

The first public demo of Digital Studio was going to be at a meeting for the sales force early Sunday afternoon, the day before NAB officially started. But we still had a lot of work to do, finishing up pieces of code, trying to train the demo artists, and making sure everything worked together—things normally done weeks before you fly out to the conference.

The scene in the development suite was surreal. There were computers scattered everywhere, linked by network wires that were taped down with yellow and black striped tape someone had found, making the place look like a crime scene (luckily, "conspiracy to fool an audience into believing your system can do more than one Warp effect" was not a crime in Nevada). We worked all day Friday, all day Saturday, and then through the night Saturday, right up until they came and carted away the equipment for the demo around noon on Sunday. Luis was right there with us, providing entertainment: videotaping us in our more lucid moments, bringing his kids by (he had flown his family out to Las Vegas for the conference), and occasionally microwaving a CD-ROM. I wound up getting an hour's sleep from 5:00 to 6:00 a.m. Sunday morning. And wouldn't you know it, after all that messing around with the keyer, Peter never had time to put in the final hack of substituting the pre-composited clip for playback—so the entire keyer section was tossed out of the demo.

After the equipment was carried off to the demo, we sat around nervous and sleep-deprived, waiting to hear back. This was a milestone: the first public demo of Digital Studio, even though it was to our own sales force. Finally we got a phone call, telling us that the demo had gone great. Soon after that, Luis showed up at the suite with Daniel, who was supremely pumped up and shook all our hands. As Peter said later, "When Daniel shakes your hand—that's something!"

We professed a willingness to keep cranking away on improving the demo, but Luis said no, we had a demo and that was it. Of course he was right; trying to fix the demo might result in breaking it more, especially in our zoned-out state. Luis marched us out to the pool area, bought us bathing suits, and deposited us in the line waiting for poolside massages.

Sadly, the demo to the sales force was the high point of our relationship with Play. Later Sunday afternoon we had a joint, invitation-only demo with Play at Caesar's Palace, announcing our partnership. The invitations themselves, which had been done by Play, were a little strange; they had a cover image that at first glance looked like the explosion of the space shuttle *Challenger*, but that on closer inspection turned out to be a picture of a blowtorch. The text promised "NAB'S HOTTEST EVENT" (hot—blowtorch—get it?). We showed the same demo we had shown to the sales force, using the same exact hardware setup, which went fine. Steve did the Play demo. At some point he was showing it playing back video, and just at the point where he announced that we would see the video playing, the system froze completely. Evidently he was not as experienced at demos as we were; he was trying to give a Type 2 demo with Type 3 quality equipment. We had experienced similar freezes during our testing and had reworked our demo to avoid them. As I watched the sequence of operations Steve was doing in his demo, I thought to myself, "Uh-oh, this is probably going to freeze the system." The Softimage people, with their own demo already successfully completed, were laughing inside; in deference to the supposed strength of our just-announced partnership, we tried to keep a straight face.

The conference started the next day. The same equipment used in the sales force demo and the joint announcement with Play was moved to a mini-theater in the Softimage booth. As people started to gather for the first scheduled demo, everybody involved in getting the demo ready, from Daniel on down to Peter, Chris, and me, lurked around the booth. A Softimage program manager named Christian Lavoie had done the demos the day before. Christian had been involved for months in modifying the demo to match what the Play hardware could really do. He had been right there alongside us in the hotel suite and knew which parts of the demo had to be done precisely and which could be changed a bit. For this public demo, we had hired two demo artists whose only training had been the previous morning in the hotel suite—at the same time that we were trying to use the machines to finish up writing the demo. Their knowledge of the pitfalls of the product was much more shallow. One small innocent change in the order or timing of the demo could crash the system.

Whenever I watched a demo of any Microsoft product, I always got nervous about it crashing. The demo will have been carefully scripted based on what worked privately, so a crash means that the demo artist made a mistake, or that bad luck caused something to break that hadn't broken before. Even when the product in question was about to be released, and was therefore getting a Type 1 demo, I would still hold my breath whenever something tricky was attempted.

In the case of the demo at NAB96, we were on much shakier ground. We had the second system—the one with the audio card in it—available to switch to at any point, but if we did this too soon it would be obvious that something had gone wrong.

During the first demo, the first computer did crash. But it was late in the Trinity part of the demo; we had already shown the Warp effect and the dissolve and played back the result. The switch to the second machine was done quickly, and the audio part of the demo went well. Thinking back to where we had been a few days before, the whole thing came off amazingly well.

After watching the first demo, Peter, Chris, and I went out to lunch to celebrate, while the Digital Studio demos continued every half an hour. When we came back to the show in the afternoon, we learned that during one demo the Trinity system had crashed very early on, but all the others had gone well. With nothing much else to do at the booth, we wandered around the show floor checking out competitors.

On Tuesday I figured I would have time to explore the show in more detail, but it turned out the NAB96 thrills and chills were not over. With the demos generating some good buzz at the Softimage booth, Play was upset that it was not showing Digital Studio in its own booth, a few aisles over. This was an idea that had been discussed before the conference but eventually abandoned as we struggled to get even one set of hardware working. Now Play wanted us to set up a second complete system in their booth.

This wasn't as simple as it might seem. The hardware for the demo consisted of a PC with the VESA bus, a Trinity, two digital disk recorders with the demo material pre-recorded on them, a monitor for the PC, a video monitor for the Trinity output, and the various cables to connect them all (for the Play booth we were going to skip the audio part of the demo). In Las Vegas there existed, somewhere, two complete systems that Play had trucked to the show for our use, plus the one we had packed up from our lab in Montreal and brought with us when we flew down. Unfortunately, in the hectic days and hours leading up to the conference, we had done some cannibalization of hardware to get one system in which everything worked.

After scrounging around and coming up with a complete set of hardware, I then had to ensure that the PC had the correct version of Digital Studio on it, with all the proper demo hacks included, and that the digital disk recorders had the right material. Finally I had to train the demo artists.

To add to the excitement, all this was taking place right on the show floor. Play had built the booth itself and then taken it apart to ship to Las Vegas. It featured rusted metal walls topped by an eight-foot-high replica of a Trinity system. There was one area where Kiki was doing her presentation (as at every conference, this featured her sitting on an elevated platform, wearing a mini-skirt). A second larger area had a green screen set up to show live keying and compositing using Trinity. Around the back, there was a little demo platform. This was where they wanted the Digital Studio demo, and where I did all the setup for the demo. From the moment I started, people were stopping by and asking if I was going to do a demo. Before I even had the hardware connected one guy started waiting around expectantly for it to start. This is normal; you expect that the demo preparation would have been done beforehand, so when you see someone attaching cables, you assume it would be almost ready to go. Such logic ignored the intricacies of the Play-Softimage relationship. I had to keep directing people who wanted a Digital Studio demo down to the Softimage booth.

Softimage had hired two pairs of demo artists for the conference, but the two assigned to the Play booth demo were the "B" team. Just as the starters get all the repetitions at football practice, these guys had not had a whole lot of hands-on time with a real working Digital Studio system. They insisted on walking through the demo script repeatedly until they had a perfect run-through. If halfway through they clicked the mouse on the wrong place, they started over. At one point the two demo artists started yelling at each other, which resulted in one of them throwing up his hands and stomping off to go walk around the show floor for a while, leaving me and the other guy sitting there with no option except to wait for him to come back. "The Digital Studio demo? It's right down there at the Softimage booth."

This combination of flaky hardware, flaky software, and flaky demo artists meant that it took all day Tuesday to get the demo working. Finally late Tuesday we had a good run-through of the demo, just in time for the show to close and us to get thrown out of the convention center. At least the demo was ready to go on Wednesday, the last full day of the show.

Despite all the behind-the-scenes madness and the incredible hackiness of the demo, NAB96 wound up being a very good show for Digital Studio. Partly this was due to reduced expectations; people had seen both Trinity and Digital Studio demoed before, and were not expecting either of them to be ready, so any progress was welcome. Whatever string and baling wire we had used, it was undeniable that the two *were* working together, that you could use Digital Studio to connect two clips with a fancy Warp Engine effect and then play the result back at D1 resolution. If it were ever finished, the combo would be way cool. The comments we saw posted on the Web after the conference reflect this combination of excitement and cynicism. One person wrote:

> Well, the coolest thing to me was Digital Studio from Softimage. It works in conjunction with Play's Trinity board, and provides NL [non-linear] editing, audio editing, compositing, paint and probably some other stuff. It's very, very powerful and full of cool features. However, it's based on technology that was shown at last year's show and still isn't shipping (Trinity) so who knows when it might actually be available.

Someone else's take:

> I knew it was only a matter of time before Trinity got mentioned here. My boss came back from NAB raving about it and Digital Studio! Looks like we might be getting one...whenever it ships...yum!

How often does someone say "yum" about computer equipment? Then there was this summary:

> The coolest thing at the SI [Softimage] booth, and at the show, was Digital Studio. This package works with Play's Trinity system, and is a NL editor, audio editor, compositing and paint system. The system allows for real-time uncompressed D1 video in and out (as the demo guy reminded us many times) with unlimited layers. Audio is eight channels, but these can be layered for unlimited tracks as well. The editing interface looked pretty easy to use, and allowed for lots of functionality in real time. The best part

had to be the compositor and paint system.
Imagine unlimited layers, imagine painting
on a layer and seeing how it looks with the
composited layers in real time. This thing
is slick. Sadly, it crashed while I was
watching the demo, but it's betaware, and
based on a non-shipping product (Trinity,
which was shown last year), so some problems
can be expected. When the system is shipping,
I expect this hardware/software combination
to become very, very popular.

It is interesting how this review seamlessly merges things that were
actually demoed with things that were only promised by the demo artist.
The comment about "as the demo guy reminded us many times" indicates
that the author knows he is being spun to—but is eager enough to believe
that he buys the whole story.

Technical Digression: APIs

A key concept in programming is the Application Programming Interface, or API. An API is an interface between two pieces of software. The interfaces that Play's software provided for Digital Studio to control the Trinity hardware were an API. An API could be viewed as the software equivalent of a standard connector such as an electrical plug, except vastly more complicated.

Consider the small piece of C from the earlier discussion about code in Technical Digression 1:

```
int i;
printf("Let's count to 10!\n");
for (i = 1; i <= 10; i++) {
    printf("%d\n", i);
}
```

This code can be wrapped in something new, like this:

```
count_to_ten() {
    int i;
    printf("Let's count to 10!\n");
    for (i = 1; i <= 10; i++) {
        printf("%d\n", i);
    }
}
```

What was added was the line that includes "count_to_ten()," as well as another set of squiggly brackets surrounding all of the previous code. This turns the code into a "function," which in this case is called the count_to_ten() function (names are often followed by () to indicate that they are functions). A function is a piece of code that can be "called" by other code. Calling this function means that somewhere in the other code, you can put a line that says "count_to_ten()." This will tell the computer to run the contents of the count_to_ten() function, then continue running the next line of the other code. It is essentially a shorthand for copying the contents of the count_to_ten() function and putting them in the place you want them.

There are two main advantages of this. The first is that it is much simpler and more compact to put "count_to_ten()" in the other code, rather than duplicate all the lines of the function. More importantly, once you are confident that the count_to_ten() function works, you don't need to worry about bugs in it when you call it, as you would if you recreated it each time.

One more change will show the real benefit of functions:

```
count_to_any_number(int x) {
    int i;
    printf("Let's count to %d!\n", x);
    for (i = 1; i <= x; i++) {
        printf("%d\n", i);
    }
}
```

What I did was add "int x" to the first line, and then replaced the number "10" with "x" elsewhere in the code. I also changed the name of the function from count_to_ten() to count_to_any_number(). The "x" is called a "parameter" to the count_to_any_number() function. The name of a function doesn't have to accurately reflect what the code inside the function accomplishes, but it almost always does—for the convenience of any programmers who encounter it.

This allows any other code to include the line count_to_any_number(5) or count_to_any_number(23) and cause the computer to count to whatever number is specified between parentheses. This is known as passing a parameter to a function. Effectively you are duplicating the code in the count_to_any_number() function, *and* going through and replacing the "x" with 5 or 23 or whatever parameter the other code passed. Functions can be defined to have as many parameters as are deemed necessary.

If this doesn't both amaze you and give you an idea of the limitless possibilities of computers, all I can say is that you are missing out. This concept of functions with parameters, containing code that is called by other code that can pass the parameters it requires, is central to all programming. The exact syntax, which I have shown here for the language C, may vary wildly, but the basic concept is universal.

All code can be thought of in terms of what it provides and what it uses. For example, in the little sample above, the code is providing the count_to_any_number() function. Now that this code exists, other code can call count_to_any_number(). Meanwhile the code is using the printf() function, which somebody else has already written. The printf() function does the actual work of printing a number on the screen. It is like a tool used to accomplish the task of writing the count_to_any_number() function.

In computer terminology, providing code to others is known as "exporting" it. A function that is exported is known as an API.

This is the heart of any task that a programmer is assigned. You are told what functions are available for you to use, and what functions you need to provide, and you write the code for those functions. Your code fills the gap between the APIs you call at the bottom layer and the APIs you export at the top layer. There will be similar pieces of code layered on top of you and below you. The exception to this is at the very top of the pile and the very bottom. At the very top, you are not providing functions, but rather interacting with the user. And at the very bottom you need to talk to the actual hardware of the computer.

Code at the top, which interacts with the user, is often known as user interface, or UI, code. Code at the bottom, which interacts with hardware, is often known as a driver. UI code and drivers are not particularly different from other kinds of code. Although UI code has an atypical top layer, at the bottom layer the APIs that it calls are conceptually the same as the ones called by other layers. Drivers have an atypical bottom layer, but at the top layer the APIs that they export are conceptually the same as the ones exported by other layers.

Let's use as a simplified example a program that draws a line on the screen in response to mouse clicks—one click at the start of the line, and one click at the end.

At the very bottom of the code pile you may have a piece of code that can draw a single dot on the video screen and provides a function called draw_dot() that takes as parameters the x and y coordinates on the screen that the dot should be drawn at. This function controls the video hardware directly—it's a driver.

Above this there may be some code that can draw a line, using the draw_dot() function and providing a function called draw_line(), which probably takes two pairs of x and y coordinates, for the start and end point of the line. This function contains the mathematical logic to figure out exactly which dots need to be drawn to make the line look correct.

There is also some code in the system that provides a function to tell where the mouse is, and whether the button is pressed or not. This code may itself be layered on more primitive bits of code, down to the code that talks directly to the mouse hardware.

Above all this you will have the code that uses both the draw_line() function and the mouse functions, which will check for the mouse clicks, get the coordinates on the screen, and then pass those in a call to the draw_line() function. This code is not providing any actual functions for other code to call but is instead responding to what the user does. This is UI code.

API more correctly refers to, and is also used to indicate, a set of functions that are grouped together. So a programmer may use the draw_dot() function to construct a set of functions such as draw_line(), draw_circle(), and draw_square(), and package them together as a graphics API. Then other code could call the functions in this graphics API and not have to worry about the details of drawing lines and circles. In the example shown, it is likely that the various layers were written by different programmers, possibly even in different companies. The fact that programmers know the API being exported by each level is what allows the whole stack to work together.

When Play was designing the Trinity hardware so it could be integrated into software applications such as Digital Studio, it knew that it had to define an API that Digital Studio could call, and also implement a driver that exported that API and operated the Trinity hardware. Those are two separate items. The API definitions are an abstract concept; Play could either invent them from scratch, or borrow parts from other API definitions, or state that its drivers would export an API that was already defined, if an appropriate "video editing hardware API" definition could be found. Play, in fact, defined its API from scratch and sent Softimage a definition of it on schedule, in October 1995. This was useful for planning how we would use that API in Digital Studio, but what was missing was the second part—the actual implementation of that API that interfaced with the Trinity hardware.

Of course, in that situation the hardware itself was also missing. But the hardware without the API implementation would have been useless to Softimage. A similar situation existed when preparing the Digital Studio that ran on the Targa 2000; what we needed from TrueVision, beside the actual Targa 2000 hardware, was the definition of the API that TrueVision's driver exported, and the actual driver itself.

Operating systems today export hundreds of APIs, for drawing on the screen, printing, communicating over a network, and so on. When the operating system is running, the implementation of those APIs—the actual code provided by the operating system vendor—is all present, waiting to be called. What is needed for people who want to write applications that call those APIs is the definitions of the APIs, which is pure information. This is actually a slight simplification because there is a little piece of code, called a "library," that the compiler needs when compiling code that calls an API. But in general the libraries for a particular API are freely available. Typically the documentation containing the definitions of the APIs is packaged together with a CD-ROM containing the libraries in what is known as a Software Development Kit, or SDK. The key point here is that companies have claimed that Microsoft has singled them out by withholding APIs from them, and APIs are generally described in the press along the lines of, "The building blocks that programmers use to write code." This makes an API sound like some sort of mold or adhesive, a physical object that every company needs its own copy of. This is wrong; once an API is documented in an SDK and implemented in an operating system, Microsoft has no control over whose code calls that API.

7

Out the Door

Unfortunately for all those who left NAB dreaming of a Digital Studio/Trinity combo, our relationship with Play disintegrated after the show. Officially we were planning to look at their stuff once they had more hardware or better drivers. Five months later Play sent someone up to Montreal with "improved" drivers. After playing with them for a bit, we discovered that, except for some bug fixes, they didn't do a single thing that hadn't been available at NAB.

Digital Studio still wanted some zippy hardware, both for demos and for eventually shipping with. We settled on a product called DigiSuite from a company called Matrox. DigiSuite could do D1 output with transitions, keying, and other effects, just like Trinity, but using a different hardware approach. Whereas Trinity had one card that went in the PC, which connected to a separate box containing the rest of the hardware, DigiSuite used multiple standard PC expansion cards. The cards sat next to each other on the standard PC bus and were connected together by a separate bus (the "Movie-2" bus) that attached to special connectors on the top of each card. The simplest DigiSuite system had two cards, one that did the basic effects and one that attached to a high-speed hard disk that stored the video; but to do 3D effects you needed another card, and to do D1 input and output you needed yet another card (both these cards were made by separate companies working in partnership with Matrox). So you had to put all four of these cards in a computer, in slots right next to each other, then attach the Movie-2 bus over the top of them. The Movie-2 bus was a rigid circuit board, with connectors located so as to align perfectly with the top of the expansion cards it was connecting to. To attach the Movie-2 bus, you lined up this little circuit board above four cards simultaneously, then gently pushed it down. The actual connector used by Movie-2 was very small but had a large number of tiny pins; if any of the pins on any of the boards bent while you were inserting it, the whole thing wouldn't work.

The next Digital Studio demo was planned for SIGGRAPH in early August 1996, and the decision was made to focus on DigiSuite as the primary hardware platform. Trinity would be shown with the same demo used at NAB. We had been meeting with Matrox since I had arrived in Montreal, viewing it as a backup solution after Play. Suddenly it was in the forefront, and once people were done taking vacations after NAB, we had only three months to get DigiSuite integrated in time for SIGGRAPH.

Matrox was headquartered in Montreal, although it was out in the suburbs, not in a hip downtown location like Softimage. The lead programmer on the DigiSuite drivers was a guy named Tim Cherna, whom I had met when we both participated in a weekend math enrichment program for high school kids run by IBM. Because DigiSuite used standard expansion cards, it could be set up in any current PC system with enough expansion slots. We settled on a system made by a company called NeTpower, which made machines designed to run Windows NT (hence the curious capitalization in the name), and had recently switched over from using MIPS microprocessors to Intel ones. The technical sales engineer that NeTpower assigned to us was a guy named Val Bercovici, a high school classmate of mine. Val was based in Ottawa, which is an hour and a half from Montreal. So with my two main contacts for the SIGGRAPH demo being old friends whose abilities I trusted, and both located nearby, things looked promising for a great demo on Matrox's hardware.

To paraphrase Tolstoy, all happy demos are happy in the same way, but each unhappy demo is unhappy in its own way. With Play there had been problems with the physical distance between the companies, the lack of communication, and the lack of a schedule. Matrox was a short drive away, and it was no sweat for several engineers to come to Softimage, or for several Softimage developers to go out there. Early on in the demo crunch Matrox provided a full-time technical support person to work at Softimage, and as things got down to the wire, they set up a little lab for us at Matrox where a few other Softimage developers and I worked full time.

Matrox was also more than willing to give us a detailed schedule of all their deliverables, hardware, and software. Unfortunately, they were also very consistent at missing the schedule. It was great that I knew Tim personally and could get honest status reports from him, but when the status was that they had slipped again, it wasn't much better than hearing it from a stranger.

Part of the delay was indirectly Microsoft's fault. At the time, the multimedia group at Microsoft (based in Redmond, and completely separate from Softimage) was promoting a new API, code-named Quartz, for controlling video and audio devices. When Microsoft defines a new API, it usually invites some other companies in the industry to comment on it, in exchange for giving them early versions to play with. Matrox was one of the members of the "inner circle" for Quartz and had been one of the most active providers of feedback. The group working on DigiSuite had jumped wholeheartedly into using Quartz as the API to control its hardware, even though at the time Quartz was still in the early beta stage—it was not officially released or even completely finished, but was being given out for other companies to test. This meant the API changed significantly with each new version from Microsoft. In addition, Quartz was not designed, in its initial version, for hardware like DigiSuite, whose users needed rock-solid D1 output. It was designed more for playback of compressed video, either completely in software or using lower-end hardware like the Targa 2000 (the card we had used for the internal demo the previous fall). A lot of what Quartz did involved dealing with situations where the machine could not keep up with 30 frames per second, degrading the frame rate in a nice way so that to a user's eye, it looked reasonable. For a product like Digital Studio, any slip from 30 frames per second (or 29.97 frames per second) was unacceptable, so what Quartz did was a non-issue.

Play, on the other hand, had designed its API completely on its own, to exactly match the hardware capabilities of Trinity. Therefore, on Trinity you had a nice clean API, and our code was talking directly to Play's code. On DigiSuite you had an API that was more general, and therefore more complicated, and was also being asked to do more than it was designed to. Plus, there was an extra layer of software—the Quartz code itself, provided by the Microsoft multimedia group—that could potentially have its own bugs.

Matrox's decision stemmed from a basic difference between it and Play. Trinity was always designed for the perfectionist. Play picked its software partners carefully—Softimage was the only other company preparing a NAB96 demo on Trinity. Play was willing to do the work to define and explain a unique API in order to ensure that it was exactly what was needed. Matrox, whose background in the PC industry was selling large numbers of display adapters, had a more egalitarian approach. It wanted to make its hardware widely available. Choosing Quartz as DigiSuite's API would make it easier on Matrox, because Microsoft was going to do the work of evangelizing Quartz—explaining it and hyping it to the rest of the industry. Programmers who wanted their software to work with Matrox's hardware could get the information they needed from Microsoft, instead of Matrox.

Arguably Matrox made a mistake in going with Quartz at that point, since the API was too immature and not designed for what DigiSuite was trying to do. Evangelizing APIs is one of Microsoft's great strengths. When Microsoft is promoting an initiative like this, it makes it sound like the greatest thing since sliced bread, and it is easy for companies to get swept up in this. Matrox was not naive; its engineers knew a lot more about this kind of hardware than the Microsoft multimedia people they were dealing with, and one of the reasons they got so involved in Quartz was to steer its future direction toward more high-end hardware like DigiSuite. Some companies involved in these early API definitions get star-struck—"Gosh, big giant Microsoft is listening to my advice, I feel so honored, I'm going to use its API." I don't think that was the situation with Matrox, which was an established company selling a wide range of products. If they had not used Quartz at this point they would have had to define and evangelize their own API, and possibly later abandon that for Quartz, which could have been even more disruptive. In the final analysis, the timing of Quartz's appearance in relation to DigiSuite's was bad, and Matrox would have had trouble whether it adopted it then or not.

We had some problems with Quartz, but eventually worked through them in time for the SIGGRAPH demo. Then we hit the real problems.

Digital Studio was trying to stake out the same high ground as Trinity. We wanted the software to be good enough for the perfectionists: the best editing, the best painting, the best titling. Digital Studio was going to sell for over $100,000, but there were other systems selling for over a million dollars. In this industry, it is important to be identified as "high-end." If people's initial impression of Digital Studio was that it was a toy, not suitable for real production work, it would be hard to ever change that perception. Just the fact that Digital Studio was going to be so cheap would cause an image problem—it is the kind of industry where you sometimes have to raise your price to be taken seriously.

The plan was therefore to start out at the very high end, with very high-end hardware, and then possibly later, once a certain cachet had been acquired, sell a cheaper version with cheaper hardware. Going in the opposite direction—starting out mid- or low-range and going up—would be too much of a marketing challenge. For this reason partnering with Play was a good match. Trinity was also aimed at the very high end, and Play had some concerns because the hardware was so radically cheap (in price, not quality) compared with other systems.

The only way to counteract suspicion based on low price is to always show nothing but flawless D1 output whenever you demo publicly. It's OK if the whole thing crashes, because that can be dismissed as a bug that can be fixed. But if you are doing a demo at a show, to an audience of trained video-editing professionals, and your video doesn't look nice—it flashes, or the transitions aren't smooth, or there are mysterious black lines across the screen—your reputation can be sunk for good.

Moving from Trinity to DigiSuite, Digital Studio was already taking a credibility hit because Matrox did not have the hype that Play did. It was viewed as a lower-end company taking a stab at high-end. So the absolutely key requirement for the SIGGRAPH demo was that the video output had to look flawless. Whatever the status of Play's software, whenever Trinity managed to play back video it produced perfect output. In the weeks leading up to SIGGRAPH, we saw problems with playback on Matrox's hardware, where video frames would be solid gray for no apparent reason, or have pink bands across the top, or have the wrong colors. The hardware itself was not to blame; some of the problems turned out to be in Digital Studio, others in Matrox's drivers. The fact that the commands from Digital Studio were being shoehorned through Quartz before they got to Matrox's drivers didn't help. Whatever the case, as problems were fixed others kept appearing. It didn't matter whose code was to blame. We needed to be at least 99% confident that the entire Digital Studio/Quartz/Matrox concoction would work perfectly during a live demo before we could risk showing it at SIGGRAPH.

At this point the fact that I knew Tim and Val personally worked against me. It had been easier to demand harder work from an engineer at Play whom I had only met a few weeks before. Knowing that my actions were going to trickle down to someone yelling at Tim made me a little reluctant to complain. When you need another computer, it is easier to rail at some anonymous support engineer than to complain to NeTpower and know that I would be forcing Val to leave his pregnant wife behind and drive the hour and a half from Ottawa to Montreal to come set it up.

The days leading up to SIGGRAPH were one massive demo crisis. I was mercifully spared all that by my brother Joe, who had decided to get married in Pittsburgh the weekend before SIGGRAPH started. On Wednesday afternoon I gratefully left Montreal, leaving others to handle the last days of the Matrox crisis. Meanwhile, someone else was trying to revive the Play demo we had used at NAB to show at SIGGRAPH. Play had not given us any new hardware or software; it was merely a question of setting up the system again.

The final panic involved getting the hardware to the show, which was in New Orleans. Normally, systems for a show are shipped out at least a week before so you can set them up in time to fix anything that breaks or gets lost during shipping. If you want to continue software development for that last week, you send the show hardware down early, and keep some in your lab to work on, then fly down with the latest software the weekend before the show. Even for NAB, we had been able to take the hardware down to the show the Thursday before the show started. For SIGGRAPH, we had only a few working hardware setups, and they were needed in Montreal so we could get the demo working at all. A more "just-in-time" approach was adopted. The hardware would stay at Matrox all week (along with the frantic Matrox and Softimage developers), then be shipped out from Montreal on Saturday morning and arrive on Sunday morning, the day before the show started.

At 9 o'clock on Friday evening, as the development team was hunkering down for one last all-night session getting the demo ready, the

Softimage shipping department got a call informing them that New Orleans was a small airport and was closed for incoming cargo on Sunday. A plan was quickly cobbled together to ship the stuff to Houston and then truck it to New Orleans. When it reached Houston, no trucking company could be found to drive it to New Orleans on Sunday. Finally, a plane was chartered to fly only our boxes from Houston to New Orleans. The charter cost $10,000, which Luis assigned to the marketing team's budget.

After all that fuss getting Matrox working, and the panic trying to resuscitate the Play demo, it was a little depressing to return from my brother's wedding on Tuesday and see the following email from a Softimage person at SIGGRAPH:

> The team in New Orleans has managed to get
> VERY close to showing DS on Matrox, they've
> decided however that it made more sense to
> demo the most stable version in front of such
> a large audience today, i.e. the s/w [soft-
> ware] only version. Luis told me this ver-
> sion rocks, it will allow us to show off a
> LOT of hot features (without the risk of
> failures), our most important mission at
> SIGGRAPH.

So after all that fuss, and all those shipping expenses, we wound up showing only the "true software" version—no Matrox hardware, no Play hardware—a demo we could have done a year earlier when I arrived in Montreal. The email did not mention conference attendees asking questions like, "Gee, you demoed on Play at NAB four months ago, what happened?!?"

The next conference on the agenda was the International Broadcasting Convention (IBC), a large European show in mid-September (NAB, SIGGRAPH, and IBC are the "big three" of shows for video editing equipment). Although the official story was that we had been only hours from getting the Matrox demo working at SIGGRAPH, and there were five weeks between then and IBC, there was still a crunch to get the IBC demo working. In the end, Softimage did do demos on Matrox at IBC, and despite some crashes they went well overall. By IBC, Play had been completely abandoned.

NAB, SIGGRAPH, and IBC were all clumped within five months. The break in the demo season following IBC gave Softimage a good opportunity to push towards a beta release of Digital Studio. The ship date of record was still October 1996, the month after IBC, but this date was lingering around only because with the product not even in beta and nobody certain about which hardware to ship on, guesses about the final ship date were meaningless. Despite this, right before IBC, one developer was heard to exclaim in surprise, "You mean we're not shipping next month?"

*   *   *

Right after IBC, I moved back to Redmond with my family. There was a small team in Redmond working on Digital Studio—two other people who had transferred back to Redmond from Montreal, and four people working on titling who were originally from a separate company in Atlanta. After Microsoft bought the company, they refused to move to Montreal, and were moved to Redmond as a compromise. Around the time I came back, three of the remaining titling people and one of the former Montreal expats left the team for other positions at Microsoft, so there wound up being just three people in the Redmond Digital Studio team.

In Redmond, I was given as my main task the job of being liaison and integrator of drivers from a company called Intergraph. Intergraph had replaced Matrox as the latest company that Digital Studio was pinning its hopes of shipping on.

Intergraph was an established hardware company, headquartered in Huntsville, Alabama, with a good industry reputation—closer in prestige to Play than to Matrox. It had made a splash at NAB96 with its new "Studio Z" hardware, which allowed playback and capture of a single stream of uncompressed D1 video on a more or less standard PC. The Play and Matrox solutions were two-stream solutions—they could play back two streams of video at the same time. For example, to do a dissolve between two scenes, you have to be playing both the old and new clips for the duration of the dissolve. On Studio Z, Digital Studio was back to the so-called "software" version—not the old "true software" version that had been demoed at SIGGRAPH, but the one that could capture D1 and play it back. You had to render any effect like a dissolve—at each frame in the dissolve, Digital Studio had to read in the corresponding frame from both clips, figure out mathematically what the result would be, then save that back in a separate clip. Changing any parameter of a transition, such as the length of the dissolve, was trivial on Trinity or DigiSuite, but on Studio Z would require re-rendering the whole thing.

Still, Studio Z could do uncompressed D1, which was the main thing. Having to render effects might take some time, but the end result would still be perfect. It is a matter of debate whether it is possible to do any compression at all without producing degradation that is noticeable to the average television viewer; many editors insist on handling only uncompressed video.

Studio Z had other advantages. Primary was the fact that Intergraph had real working hardware and real working drivers ready to go. Two Intergraph engineers visited Redmond in early November 1996 and within a day we had basic Digital Studio functionality working on top of Studio Z hardware. They were also willing to do most of the work involved in integrating it—writing the layer of software that stood between the API their drivers exported and the API that Digital Studio expected to call when talking to video hardware.

The simpler hardware also meant fewer worries about the hardware. Since all Studio Z did, in the end, was capture clips and then play them back—either the original clips, or clips with rendered effects—it was pretty easy to debug problems. If during playback of a rendered effect you saw something odd, like a flash of pink, you could go look at the rendered clip sitting on the hard drive and see if it had the pink in it. If it did, you blamed the Digital Studio rendering code; if it didn't, you blamed the Intergraph playback code. With Trinity and DigiSuite, all those effects had been generated dynamically by the hardware, so you had to figure out what Digital Studio was telling the hardware to do at that particular instant, which was much harder.

The solidity of the Intergraph code exposed the rest of Digital Studio as not quite ready for prime time. The earlier problems with hardware and drivers had been a convenient excuse for explaining the delays. At one point, someone from Matrox came to us and explained that they wanted to add some features to their code for use by other companies that were putting software on top of DigiSuite. They promised that this would not affect the date of what they needed to deliver to us. Luis laughed at this, but at the same time we were busily stuffing new features into Digital Studio, while maintaining that it would not slip. Suddenly having hardware that worked well meant that blame for any delays had to be assigned elsewhere.

Digital Studio did finally manage to get a beta out the door in February 1997. This was not a widespread beta, but rather a very controlled one at a few video-editing houses, each with a Softimage person assigned to hold the editor's hand. The beta was on DigiSuite, but it was the last gasp for Digital Studio running on that hardware; the team was already focused on shipping the final product on Intergraph's Studio Z. This was to be kept a secret from Matrox until after NAB97. Which was fine until Tim called me as a friend and asked, "What's this I hear about Digital Studio and Intergraph?"

Finally, at NAB97, Digital Studio publicly demoed on Intergraph's Studio Z. Although it was also shown on Matrox's DigiSuite, the direction of the product was obvious.

Nonetheless the dalliance with Softimage may not have been bad for Matrox. It certainly forced the team there to improve their drivers in a hurry. They kept working away, and by NAB97 Matrox was shipping DigiSuite hardware to customers, using Quartz as the API. As Tim reflected later, "For all the pain that we had, DigiSuite would have never been as much of a success were it not for the Softimage experience. So I think the next customer that came along ended up with a better company to work with." Microsoft had announced Quartz under the name ActiveMovie, and eventually, after significant input from Matrox, shipped it as DirectShow. By NAB98, Matrox had redesigned the Movie-2 bus and introduced a version of DigiSuite that fit on one expansion card. Several editing packages supported it, and DigiSuite continues to do well in the market.

In the spring of 1997, I left the Digital Studio team in Redmond and moved to the Windows NT team (soon to be renamed the Windows 2000 team). But I kept tabs on Digital Studio, wondering when it would finally ship.

On September 12, 1997, at IBC, Intergraph and Softimage co-sponsored the launch of Digital Studio. "Launch" did not mean that the product was shipping to customers. The mad dash was on to get it out the door by the end of the year. Spurring the team on was the fact that Luis had announced he would retire from Microsoft at the end of 1997.

On December 12, 1997, Play shipped the first completed Trinity systems to dealers. No mention was made of Digital Studio.

Would the Digital Studio team succeed in shipping before Luis left? Unfortunately, the answer was "no." Digital Studio, running on Studio Z, was finally released to manufacturing on January 22, 1998, exactly one month after Luis left.

There was more to come.

*   *   *

On June 15, 1998, Microsoft announced that Softimage was being sold to Avid Technology, one of the leaders in the video-editing field, for $285 million. The Wall Street Journal article about the sale included the following:

> While Microsoft has been a voracious acquirer of technology companies in recent years, yesterday's move surprised many people because it was believed to be the first major instance in which the company sold something.
>
> [. . .]
>
> Craig Mundie, senior vice president of Microsoft's consumer-platform division, said his company had accomplished the goals it had set for itself in buying Softimage, especially in validating its Windows NT operating system for advanced computer graphics. Financial results for Softimage are not disclosed by its parent, but most industry analysts believe it is losing money, like many of its competitors, largely because of the stiff development costs of its products. Mr. Mundie said the unit's financial performance was in line with expectations.
>
> Mr. Mundie said the sale didn't signify a new get-tough attitude by Microsoft that might augur more such sales. "I don't think you can expect this to be a pattern," he said. "We were just being pragmatic in meeting business objectives."

As part of the deal, Softimage employees were prohibited from transferring to Microsoft for one year. Their Microsoft stock options would
be converted to Avid stock options. There would be no exceptions to
this rule, except for Moshe and the Softimage lawyer who had helped
negotiate the sale. They would be allowed to transfer back to Redmond,
options intact (after a few days of panic among Redmond transferees
still in Montreal, it was revealed that they too would be allowed to come
back—but it would be preferable if they pretended they had retired, to
avoid annoying those who were forced to move to Avid). Since there was
no precedent for Microsoft selling off a company like this, nobody could
claim to have been singled out by this deal, but there was mass dis-
gruntlement among the employees.

I ran into Mike Murray, Microsoft's VP of human resources, a few
weeks after the sale was announced. I asked him if he knew how the
employees felt. He said he had been concerned about this, so he had asked
human resources in Montreal about that exact point. The answer came
back not to worry, that all the employees were very excited about the sale.

The stock option conversion for employees was calculated the day the
deal was announced. From the day the sale was announced until it closed
on August 3, Avid's stock dropped from around $39 a share to around $34
a share. Microsoft, meanwhile, rose from around $42 to around $52.
Within a few months, Avid's stock was below $15.

On October 20, 1999, following a loss of six cents per share in the third
quarter of 1999, Avid announced that chairman and CEO Bill Miller, the
man who had bought Softimage from Microsoft, was resigning immediately,
along with Cliff Jenks, the president and COO. After the announcement, the
stock dropped to $11 a share. Microsoft's stock, meanwhile, was above $90.
The announcement discussed the performance of various parts of Avid; no
mention was made of Softimage.

Softimage was still in business, and despite being tossed around by its
American owners, it remained an impressive success story. When Canada
Post announced its Millennium Collection of 68 specially minted stamps,

to be released on September 15, 1999, one of them commemorated Softimage.

*   *   *

Following the August 1998 review cycle, it was announced that Moshe had been promoted to vice president. In the press release, Bill Gates was quoted as saying, "Moshe did an incredible job raising Softimage to new levels in terms of its product strategy and ability to develop large, complex software products. He was central to laying the foundation that Avid, the new owner of Softimage, can build on."

Microsoft's purchase of Softimage had been unusual—a company that was outside of Microsoft's usual area of expertise. The decision to sell it four years later, just after it had finally shipped Digital Studio, was also curious. Perhaps there was no real reason to buy the company in the first place, but having bought it and owned it for four years, why sell it? It's not clear what to make of the whole Softimage experience. Financially the company was just a blip on Microsoft's radar, and although the company was sold for more than twice what was paid for it, the Microsoft stock that was used to buy the company would have more than quadrupled in value during the period that Softimage was owned. Then there is the opportunity cost of the resources that were devoted to Softimage—what Luis and Moshe could have been working on in Redmond if they had not been occupied in Montreal.

It was never clear how Softimage really fit into Microsoft's plans. When the company was bought, it was put under Craig Mundie in the organizational chart, along with all the other whizzy, futuristic (and money-losing) projects like interactive television. In February 1996, Craig's Consumer Systems Division was reorganized to be the Consumer Products Division, and Softimage was handed over to Brad Silverberg, who owned the Internet Platform and Tools Division, on the theory that Softimage was an

Internet tool of some sort. Given Brad's previously noted dubiousness about the whole Softimage adventure, it was no surprise when Craig took Softimage back three months later. As Daniel put it somewhat tactfully in email, "We have looked for a Microsoft 'mentor' that is more familiar with the Softimage business."

Meanwhile, the Softimage marketing team was completely replaced twice. The team was moved to Redmond soon after Microsoft acquired Softimage, causing all the marketing people in Montreal to quit. In November 1996 it was announced that the marketing team would be moved back to Montreal by the following January, which caused almost all of the new people to look for other jobs in Redmond.

Finally there is the late, unlamented relationship with Play. What intangible value would Microsoft have derived from a continuing association with a cutting-edge company, the kind that inspires die-hard supporters? In the December 2, 1998, edition of his nationally syndicated newspaper column, Bill Gates, apparently unaware of his company's brief entanglement with Play, discussed a visit he had made to Play's booth at Comdex/Fall, a huge computer show, the previous month. "Technology kept catching my eye…Play, Inc. put a video-editing suite in a $6,500 box connected to a PC. It could open the video-editing market to lots of new companies."

8

The Show

As the 1980s dawned, there were a variety of personal computers on the market. These computers, also known as microcomputers, were cheap enough that individuals could buy them and put them in their homes. This replaced the previous notion of putting a dumb terminal in the house, which couldn't do anything unless you dialed in over a slow modem to a central computer. Games began to appear that took advantage of the whiz-bang features of personal computers, like graphics, sound, and joysticks.

The three most important personal computer manufacturers at the time had all introduced their first significant machines in 1977—Apple with the Apple II, Tandy/Radio Shack with the TRS-80 Model I, and Commodore with the PET. All had been improved in the interim. Apple introduced the Apple II Plus in 1979, Radio Shack put out the Model III in 1980 (the Model II, a business machine with a different microprocessor, came out the year before), and Commodore came out with the VIC-20 in 1981. The prices of these machines varied, but generally were dropping; the Apple II Plus had cost $1,195 when it came out, while the VIC-20 sold for just $299.

In October 1981 IBM introduced the IBM PC. At the time it looked like just another personal computer in a crowded field, and there was some doubt that IBM, a giant company that earned its money selling computers and services to large businesses and universities, could succeed in the more rough-and-tumble world of home hobbyists and small businesses. At the time, the Apple II, the TRS-80 models, and the Commodore VIC-20 were all viewed as more or less equal, with no single system dominating. The Apple II was arguably the most popular platform, but it was understood by software developers that they would need to write versions of their software for multiple, completely different platforms if they wanted to cover the entire personal computer market. And they did; each of the three systems had hundreds of software titles already on the market.

The IBM PC's chances of success were snorted at in many circles. As a further handicap, IBM also decided to limit where the computer could be sold, to try to control the experience the user had when buying it (and when getting it serviced later). It was sold through Computerland, one of the best-known computer stores at the time; through a network of business machine stores that Sears, Roebuck was setting up; through a network of IBM Product Centers that the company was in the process of creating; and directly from IBM for high-volume sales. IBM intentionally shut out all the small computer stores that had sprung up to sell Apples and Commodores (TRS-80 machines were sold only through Radio Shack stores, but there were thousands of those around the country).

The October 1981 issue of *Byte*, one of the leading computer magazines, had an article titled "The IBM Personal Computer: First Impressions." It described the system as costing from $1,565 to more than $5,000, a price range that stayed remarkably consistent in the ensuing 20 years (although in the last few years the cheapest ones have dropped well below $1,000). For $1,565 you got 16K of memory (that is 16 kilobytes—computers today come with a minimum of 64 megabytes, or four thousand times as much). Storage was accomplished with an audiocassette recorder and a television set was used as the monitor. The article also mentioned that $1,565 got you a speaker, a parallel port for connecting a printer, and a self-test program that ran during power on—things a review today wouldn't even bother mentioning. The fact that all the keys on the keyboard auto-repeated if you held them down was called out as a noteworthy feature.

For $3,005, an increase of $1,440, you got a single floppy disk drive and 48K more memory. For another $1,500 you got color display output (the other systems were monochrome and had no graphics capability), a second floppy drive, and a printer. This system was described as the "expanded business system." Among the things this computer didn't have at any price were a hard drive, a sound card, or a mouse. The processor ran at 4.77 MHz, over two hundred times slower than the one in today's fastest personal computer.

Laughably puny as this machine may seem by today's standards, it was quite advanced for its day. It allowed far more memory to be put in than the existing models, and it had a 16-bit processor, rather than the 8-bit ones in the existing machines, which made it easier for programmers to use all that memory. A 4.77 MHz processor was fast in a day when most others ran at 1 or 2 MHz. A couple of years later, IBM shipped the IBM PC XT, which had a hard drive built in; this was cutting edge for a personal computer.

In addition, the system not only included one operating system, Microsoft's DOS, but there were plans to offer two more when they became available. By supplying various software companies with preview copies of the machine, IBM had assembled a relatively full-featured set of applications ready to work on top of DOS—a spreadsheet, a word processor, a communications package, and a set of business accounting programs. None of these applications was provided by Microsoft; the only IBM PC application that Microsoft was selling at the time was a DOS version of Adventure, a well-known game from the old "terminals and mainframes" days. More important, IBM was interested in actively helping other software developers write software for the system, and helping other hardware developers produce add-in expansion cards for the system—a decision that would have a profound effect on the future of the personal computer.

It is amazing to look at a personal computer today and see how similar it is to the original IBM PC. The basic design of a small keyboard, a main system unit, and a separate monitor is unchanged. This seems obvious now, but back then it was non-standard. Most machines were either one big integrated unit (like the TRS-80 Model III), a keyboard/system unit combo with a separate monitor (like the Apple and Commodore machines), or a separate keyboard that connected to a monitor/system unit combo (like the TRS-80 Model II). The floppy drive was often a separate box connected by a cable. On the original IBM PC the power supply was here, the expansion slots were over there, the floppy disks went in the front, the keyboard plugged in back here, just like today. The only real change is that the power switch has moved all over the place, from its original location near the back right side of the machine (a logical place since that is where the power supply was inside the unit), to a brief fancy for putting it on the back of the machine, to its current more or less standard location on the front. Even the modern tower models, when you take the cover off, look like an original IBM PC standing on its side.

The *Byte* article concluded, "For those of us who dislike giants, the IBM Personal Computer comes as a shock. I expected that the giant would stumble by overestimating or underestimating the capabilities the public wants and stubbornly insisting on incompatibility with the rest of the microcomputer world. But IBM didn't stumble at all; instead, the giant jumped leagues in front of the competition....A superior machine from the start, the IBM Personal Computer should grow in capability as outside vendors begin producing peripheral devices and add-on hardware for special applications." Truer words were never written.

In April 1982, my father bought an IBM PC and brought it home. It came with an extremely powerful version of BASIC, which I immediately

set about writing games in. Writing games is a great way to learn to program. Also, you can impress your friends with your stellar rip-off of the
arcade game Q*Bert, one of my first masterworks. The arcade Q*Bert was
a little dude with a big nose who hopped around on a pyramid of blocks,
trying to jump on each one a certain number of times so they would all
change color and he could advance to the next level. He did this while
avoiding various baddies who chased him around the pyramid, and trying
to avoid jumping off the edge. His only help was some spinning discs off
the edge of some of the blocks, which served as transporters up to the top
if Q*Bert jumped on them. My version of Q*Bert (which I called Q*Bart,
possibly to avoid copyright lawsuits once it earned me millions) was just
like the arcade game except with lame graphics, pitiful sound effects, and
laughable intelligence on the part of the monsters. Also Q*Bart, unlike his
arcade brother, did not have a big schnozz, or utter garbled obscenities
while leaping artistically to his death off the side of the pyramid (tech-y
DOS types may want to know that Q*Bart was represented on-screen by
ASCII character 1, that smiley face that Windows seems to have sup-
pressed). Still Q*Bart ruled in his own little way, and when he hopped on
to a little spinning disc off the side of the pyramid, he was duly trans-
ported to the top with a minimum of fuss.

I eventually wrote other games, all in BASIC, including versions of the
arcade games Robotron and Pac-Man. My crowning glory was a game
called Left, Right, and Fire. You were a little spaceship at the bottom of
the screen, confronting waves of aliens (10 different kinds, each with different patterns of movement!). All you could do was move to the left,
move to the right, and fire (it goes without saying—but let me say it—
that this was where the title of the game came from).

I went so far as to submit copies of Pac-Man and Left, Right, and Fire
to an outfit in California called the Software Guild, which was planning
to make it big by licensing and distributing other people's software. After
an undoubtedly rigorous evaluation, the two games were accepted, but I
never heard from the Software Guild again. I assume the company went

out of business, although I've never found out exactly what happened. A shame, since its promotional material noted its intention of becoming the largest software company in the industry, and it was even planning on going public—very advanced thinking for 1983.

In June 1982, a few months after we bought our IBM PC, my family visited the family of my Uncle Tony, who was a computer consultant in New Jersey. He mentioned that there was a computer show being held in the Atlantic City Convention Hall, something called Comdex. Would my father and I like to go?

In 1982 Comdex/Spring was in its second year, while Comdex/Fall, the original show, was preparing for its fourth year (but had already settled in Las Vegas, where it remains to this day). Comdex stands for "Computer Dealers Exposition," and the main target audience was so-called Independent Sales Organizations (ISOs), companies that resold computer equipment to actual users. At the time, it was virtually unheard of for something as complicated as a computer to be sold directly to an end user—the ISOs were the middlemen who installed the systems, and then for a price supported them once they inevitably broke down. Comdex has since morphed into the pre-eminent North American computer show, having spawned and then merged with a parallel show called Windows World. It is a massive event whose Fall version takes over Las Vegas for a week. It is *the* place to be for anybody involved in computers, and the only remnant of the dealer focus is in the name, which few people understand.

But in 1982 the exhibits were aimed at resellers instead of at end users, so there was a bit of chumminess about it all—"Here's how we can work together to convince people to buy our stuff." Back then ARPANET (Advanced Research Projects Agency Network), the main precursor of the Internet, had only a few hundred machines connected, and putting multiple machines in a single office on a local area computer network was very unusual. Business computers were bought as complete systems, with hardware and software sold as one bundle. The notion of buying updated software or hardware from anywhere other than the company that sold you the original system was foreign and possibly might void your service contract. In this environment, issues like the market share of the computer you were buying were much less important; you were not going to exchange data electronically with other systems, and what mattered was that the software delivered with the computer did what it said it would, and that the company that sold it to you would still be around a year later to service it. Thus a large number of incompatible systems sprang up, each being presented to ISOs as the easiest path to delighted customers. These systems were described as "turnkey," since they were sold as complete packages that the user merely had to turn on. (Some early computers did turn on with a key, and the issue of how a computer should be turned on was the subject of some debate—should it be a momentous act like starting your car, or a ho-hum one like turning on a television set?)

There was a group of companies that were out to overthrow the idea of the turnkey computer. In their model, people would buy computers like they bought other pieces of electronics, from a store that had demonstration models available, possibly offered delivery and setup, and would do warranty service, but otherwise stayed out of the way. The users could buy their own software and hardware upgrades, from a variety of manufacturers, and install them by themselves. This group of rebels were the personal computer manufacturers: Apple, Commodore, and Tandy/Radio Shack. IBM was a partial member; it had released the IBM PC the previous fall, but by limiting the number of chains that sold it was trying to dip its toe into the wild world of personal computers while still maintaining a link to the old service-and-support way of selling computers.

After we got home from vacation in New Jersey, I sat down in front of our IBM PC, and in a burst of age-14 motivation, wrote out a report on the show. Although personal computers were not a major factor at the show, I naturally focused on them, and the report discusses the various manufacturers' booths. I include excerpts here, with my current-day comments interspersed:

Apple Computer was not at Comdex, although there were as many Apples as IBM PCs at the show [meaning, a few dozen of each]. One company, Advanced Logic Systems of Sunnyvale, CA, was showing "the card IBM doesn't want you to buy," which was an 8088 microprocessor on a plug in card. [The idea being you would plug it into an Apple and it would then have the same processor as an IBM PC—without all the supporting hardware, which made it essentially useless for running an actual IBM PC program on, unless you had the source code available and were prepared to modify it extensively.] The Alien Group, from New York, was displaying the "Voicebox" Speech Synthesizer for the Apple. This program even had a face on the screen that moved its lips as it spoke. It also had an easily expandable vocabulary, and could even be taught to speak rudimentary French and German! The same company also made a similar product for the Atari computers.

Although Apple was absent from Comdex, Franklin Computer was not. The New Jersey-based company was showing the Ace 1000, an advanced version of the Ace 100. Both computers are Apple II look-alikes and can read Apple disks. The company, however, denies that it stole Apple's ideas, claiming that its computer is 25% larger and has different internal circuitry.

Even at a non-personal-computer-focused show like Comdex, Apples were on display, with software and hardware add-ons available. Franklin was the major manufacturer of Apple II "clones," a market that Apple actively tried to shut down, to its detriment. The company eventually morphed into making more customized devices and is the same Franklin that manufactures those small translators and electronic Bibles and what-not you see advertised in the Sharper Image catalog.

Apple, of course, was not the only important personal computer man-ufacturer at the time. Commodore had gone for the gusto and bought a 40-by-40-foot booth right near the entrance:

> Another large firm, Commodore, was there, proudly showing off its five new computers. There was the Commodore-64, a VIC-20 look-alike designed for both home and business applications. The MAX Machine is touted as a Computer-Game Machine-Music Synthesizer for under $200. Both it and the 64 use the new 6510 chip, an advance over the 6502. [This refers to the microproces-sor used inside it. The VIC-20 had a 6502, which was also used in the Apple II. The IBM PC had an 8088 processor, the direct ancestor of today's Pentiums.] The three other computers were the P128, a third-generation PET, the B128, a business-oriented micro, and the BX256, an advanced 'B' series computer. All three use the 6509 chip, and the BX256 has an 8088 as well, thus becoming Commodore's first 16-bit computer. They also had a dis-play of VIC-20 games and several demo models.

Commodore had some good machines back then, but could never market them well enough to succeed. There was also Tandy—actually it was the "Contract Marketing Division" of Tandy:

> Tandy, father of the Radio Shack TRS-80 family, had the TRS-80s displayed with Tandy labels. This appeared to be an attempt to sell the computers to businessmen while disassociating them with the Radio Shack name [since Radio Shack was associated with the TRS-80s, which were viewed as toys by businessmen]. Among those displayed was the powerful new Model 16 micro, featuring the MC68000 chip from Motorola.

That MC68000, incidentally, is the microprocessor used in the original Apple Macintosh, which first appeared in 1984.

Besides Apple, Commodore, and Tandy, some big players were also trying to break into the personal computer market. At the time "personal computers" meant a smaller, cheaper computer designed for use by one person as opposed to the larger minicomputers that were used to run businesses. They almost all kept to the old model of requiring support from the company that sold the computer and not encouraging third-party software or hardware:

> Among the other well-known computer vendors present were Hewlett-Packard, advertising the Series-80 family as well as a new color plotter. Digital Equipment Corp. (DEC) had a large booth near the entrance. Among other things there was the new Rainbow 100, a bottom-of-the-line version of its new personal computers, the pet project of founder and president Kenneth Olsen. Intertec Data Systems were showing its new Superbrain II computer, as well as the multi-user Compustar. And a new company, Fortune Systems, was proudly displaying its new 68000-based, Unix-operated 16:32 computer. The computer looked good, but when asked for more information, one official had to resort to asking around for pocket-knives to open the cabinet containing it.

I remember the Fortune 16:32 because it was very slick, with great graphics support built in. It was an example of a personal computer that was technically far superior to the IBM PC, yet met with no success in the marketplace. There certainly was a lot more diversity in computers back then. All those manufacturers were offering their own unique hardware and operating systems and software—in some cases on several different incompatible models. If you go to a computer show now and look at different hardware vendors, they are all selling machines that are basically the same, to the extent that when you say "personal computer" now, you know it is going to run Windows and have PCI slots and use a VGA display. The differentiation is in price, or in features, such as which has a better sound card. Back then everything about each of these personal computers was completely different! The only completely different line of computers now is Apple's Macintosh—for a current total of two, compared to the dozens back in 1982.

At the same time, few of those computers had anything available for them, in terms of expansion, beyond what the manufacturers had lined up (the exception was the existing 8-bit machines, the Apple II and TRS-80 and Commodore machines, but they were a hardware generation behind the IBM PC). In my report I mentioned third-party hardware and software for the machines I knew—Apple, Commodore, TRS-80, and of course the IBM PC. But don't think that I ignored software and hardware for other systems. There just wasn't any. Nobody was showing software for the Fortune 16:32 or hardware for the Digital Rainbow 100, except in the Fortune and Digital booths. Digital did not even allow other companies to sell floppy disks that worked with the Rainbow; they had to be bought from Digital.

There were other personal computers at the time that were selling quite well, including the Atari 400 and 800, the Texas Instruments 99/4A, and the Timex/Sinclair ZX80 and ZX81, which I mentioned in my report:

> Timex, the company which manufactures the Sinclair ZX-81 microcomputer, is now selling the tiny machine under the name Timex/Sinclair 1000. The new version has twice as much memory (2K to 1K) [that is not a typo] and a lower price than the ZX-81.

The ZX-81 was sold in Britain for £69.95 assembled, or £49.95 in kit form. The Timex/Sinclair 1000 sold for $99 in the US. It was a very small machine with a tiny keyboard, designed to be connected to a television set for output. Because it was so cheap, it was popular among people who wanted to buy a computer for their home to tinker with, with no particular intention of using it for anything useful. According to the Jones

Telecommunications & Multimedia Encyclopedia, in 1982 over 600,000 units of the Timex/Sinclair 1000, Commodore VIC-20, and Atari 400 and 800 were sold, while the Texas Instruments 99/4A sold 530,000, the TRS-80 Model III sold 300,000, the Apple II Plus 270,000, and the IBM PC only 200,000. Despite their high sales numbers, most of those systems were viewed as ways to play games or just play around with a computer; Apple, Radio Shack, and Commodore, because of their relative longevity in the market, were the companies that had the most support among third-party software developers. They were the systems that some adventurous businesses were using for the important tasks that had previously been the domain of the ISO-sold systems—a shift that eventually reached maturity when the IBM PC arrived.

Booth size and location is a pretty good measure of status of a company. Attendees entering the main exhibit hall at Comdex/Spring in 1982 were confronted with Digital Equipment Corp. on their right and Victor on their left. Behind Digital were the aforementioned Commodore and then Onyx Systems. Behind Victor were M/A-Com OSI and then CompuCorp. To the left of Victor was IBM. Those were the seven largest booths at the show. Onyx and Victor had the very largest ones, 60 feet by 40 feet.

If you have never heard of Onyx and Victor, you are not alone (Victor has actually been making calculators for over 80 years; it made a brief foray into computers in the early 1980s). IBM is still around today, approaching its 90th birthday, and Digital, the largest player in the mini-computer market and probably the most watched company at the 1982 show, stuck around as an independent entity until June 1998, when it was bought by Compaq, a company that was founded in February 1982 to sell PC clones. For the record, Onyx, Victor, M/A-Com OSI, and CompuCorp all sold various types of business computers, some quite impressive for their time. The Victor 9000 had 128K of memory standard, three serial ports, a voice digitizer (!), two floppy drives, and an 800 x 400 pixel display. It even ran Microsoft's MS-DOS, essentially the same operating system included with the IBM PC. In short, the system easily outperformed an IBM PC, but like every other personal computer exhibited at Comdex that year (except the IBM PC), it has been consigned to the scrap heap of history.

In fact almost no company that is anybody in the world of personal computers today existed back then, much less exhibited at that show. Intel and Motorola were in business, but not present. The PC clone market did not exist (Compaq and others were in the process of inventing it), so Dell and Gateway had not yet been formed. Novell, now a major force in personal computer networking, was a small company that had shipped its first networking product the year before, and was not at the show either.

One group of companies that *was* there were the IBM PC add-on hardware manufacturers. The computer itself had been introduced barely nine months before, but already a "Big 3" of add-on vendors had been established: A.S.T., Quadram, and Tecmar. Tecmar was the most aggressive: the story went that the founder had camped out in front of a Sears Business Center (which was selling IBM PCs) on the day they became available, and bought the first two sold. This eagerness had enabled Tecmar to get into the official Comdex program (A.S.T. and Quadram only made it into the last-minute Addendum) and even buy a full-page advertisement in it ("First, the IBM Personal Computer, The Next Step...Tecmar"). Naturally in my report I had my eyes open for anything IBM PC-related:

> IBM was at Comdex, although, as at last year's Comdex/Fall in Las Vegas, it did not display its new Personal Computer. Interestingly enough, although IBM did not officially display the IBM PC, there was one hidden away, driving its new Experimental Plasma Display. [Plasma was a cool technology for flat-panel displays.] The IBM PC had a Tecmar expansion chassis and was referred to as the "Token PC" by one official. This was more than made up for by the dozens of IBM PCs at other booths [I meant dozens of IBM PCs in the whole show put

together, not the dozens you will find in any single booth at a modern Comdex], as new vendors jumped on the IBM PC bandwagon, offering everything from memory expansion (a popular idea) to speech synthesizers. The Cleveland company Tecmar was there, offering its line of more than 25 expansion devices for the IBM PC. Among these was an expansion cabinet which is an almost exact duplicate of the IBM PC's System Unit. The cabinet gives the user seven more expansion slots, coming to the aid of the many who find themselves with only one or two slots open after adding a display, printer, disks, etc. [The original IBM PC included none of those connectors on the motherboard; it had five slots available, but the cards for the floppy drive, printer, display, modem, memory, and so on each occupied a slot of their own, so they got used up quickly.] The cabinet also has space for a 5 or 10 megabyte Winchester hard disk, also supplied by Tecmar. [The term "Winchester" refers to a type of hard drive, originally developed by IBM in Winchester, England, in which the read/write heads float on air just above the surface of the disk. Today this type of hard drive is so ubiquitous that the term is no longer needed.]

Many other companies offered hard disks for the IBM PC, some of which fit snugly in the second disk drive slot. One of these, Corona Data Systems of Chatsworth, CA, was offering a 5 megabyte (or MB) disk for $1195 (although it would only sell one per person, and that only to dealers). [By way of comparison, you can currently buy a 5 *gigabyte* drive, with one thousand times as much storage as a 5 megabyte drive, for about $100. The head of the McGill Computing Center, where my father had bought his computer, was also at the show, and he pulled out his checkbook to try to buy a 5 MB Corona Data Systems drive right there on the floor. But he was refused because he didn't fit their definition of "dealer."] Other hard disk manufacturers were Davong, Atasi, and VR Data.

Both A.S.T. and Quadram were displaying combination cards for the IBM PC with 64K–256K parity memory, a serial port, a printer port, and a real-time clock. [The original IBM PC did not have a clock that kept time when it was off; you had to reenter the date and time each time you turned the computer on.] Not to be outdone, Xedex Corp., a new company from New York, was showing the Baby Blue CPU Plus, a card that gives the user a Z80B chip as well as 64K of memory. The card allows the use of thousands of existing CP/M programs on the IBM PC.

The Z80 was another popular 8-bit microprocessor of the time, roughly on par with the 6502. There was a lot of this "Let's put a second chip of a different type in a computer" going on back then. You may recall "the card IBM doesn't want you to buy" from Advanced Logic Systems, which was an 8088 microprocessor on a plug in card. The Baby Blue CPU Plus had the same problem, which was that since you weren't duplicating the whole computer, just the chip, you couldn't actually run existing software from another Z80 computer with this (despite what I wrote above, which must have been based on starry-eyed listening to a Xedex salesperson). It was useful only if you for some reason were obsessed with writing Z80 assembly language on your IBM PC, or you wanted to take the time to port a Z80 program to work with this hardware (which might conceivably be easier than writing a new program from scratch). And you couldn't make assumptions that anyone else had one of these godforsaken cards, so it would be useful only for software you were writing for yourself. These cards have mostly died out, mainly because with one main PC standard, there is no need for them.

The nascent IBM PC market also had room for some early competition among applications software:

Comshare Target Software, from Atlanta, was professing to end the calc wars [meaning the spreadsheet wars—at the time almost all spreadsheets had names that ended in "calc"] with its new PlannerCalc spreadsheet, priced at only $50. Other combatants such as Visicorp (Visicalc) and Sorcim (SuperCalc) were absent from the show. [Visicalc was the heavyweight, the first spreadsheet, whose Apple II version had been the first personal computer "killer app"—people bought Apple IIs just to run Visicalc.] MicroPro, home of the WordStar word processor, was displaying its new IBM PC version of its #1 product. [We had an illegally duplicated copy of WordStar for our computer. It was astonishingly slow, even allowing for how slow the original IBM PC was. Using it was like surfing the Web over a really slow modem. Imagine hitting the "Page Up" key and it taking multiple seconds to redraw the screen. Each time. While editing a program stored on your own computer!] They were also giving away a free visor to everyone seen wearing a MicroPro button and carrying a MicroPro bag (I wore the button and carried the bag for the entire show, and didn't win anything).

The very first instances of the major application categories (word processing and spreadsheets) to be sold for the IBM PC were hastily-ported versions of applications that ran on the Apple II or similar machines—WordStar, Visicalc, and a database known as dBase II by a company called Ashton-Tate. These versions tended not to take advantage of the hardware in the IBM PC, so they were quickly supplanted by applications that were written natively for the IBM PC—the spreadsheet 1-2-3, which was Lotus' first product, or the word processor WordPerfect, which established WordPerfect (known back then as Satellite Software) as a force in the IBM

PC world. This pattern of ported versions being replaced by upstarts who used a paradigm shift to establish themselves was repeated when Windows came out, with Microsoft Word and Excel being the beneficiaries. It may be in the middle of happening again with the shift to the Internet.

The other company of note that was at Comdex was good old Microsoft. It's not clear exactly what Microsoft was hoping to accomplish at Comdex (anymore than what A.S.T, Quadram, and Tecmar were hoping to accomplish). I guess it was trying to sell MS-DOS and its programming languages to whatever minicomputer manufacturers happened to be around, but doing this at Comdex was like hawking Asteroid-B-Gone at a dinosaur convention. The IBM PC was fast becoming a phenomenon and maybe Microsoft was going to every show it could find. Someone had the foresight to book a good-sized booth (20 feet by 20 feet), although it was in the less visible West Exhibit Hall.

Microsoft was far from being the behemoth it is now. Its listing in the Exhibits Guide reads as follows: "MICROSOFT will exhibit a full line of system software for microcomputers including operating systems, languages and application software. Featured products include: MS-DOS, a single-user operating system for 8086/8088 microcomputers; Multiplan, an electronic worksheet for numeric planning applications; and Time Manager, a personal information and organization system for individualized schedule and record keeping. Microsoft's regional sales reps will be on hand to meet with dealers and distributors." Micro-SCI Standun Controls Inc. and Micro Warehouse—the companies before and after Microsoft in the alphabetical list—each had a longer blurb.

What did Microsoft see as it gazed from its booth off in the boondocks? As it happened, a competitor of sorts was right next door: SofTech Microsystems, publishers of the p-System, one of the other operating systems that IBM intended to offer with the IBM PC. On another side was Intech Systems, an OEM (Original Equipment Manufacturer, meaning it manufactured finished computers) and distributor of various computers and printers. Digital Research, publisher of the third IBM PC operating system, CP/M-86, was buried against a wall off in the distance (Digital Research was not related to Digital Equipment Corp.—when people talked about "Digital," they meant Digital Equipment). Of course I took note of these folks, although briefly:

> Digital Research was displaying its new Concurrent CP/M [an advanced, multi-tasking version of CP/M] while across the west hall rival MicroSoft [note my old-fashioned spelling of it] was showing its MS-DOS operating system, the one used by IBM for the IBM PC. SofTech Microsystems was also there, with a new version of the UCSC p-System, designed for the 68000 chip. [It also was showing an IBM PC version of the p-System.]

Also on display at Comdex was the Osborne 1, which was the first portable computer and also the first to come with a full suite of software bundled with it:

> At the Osborne Computer exhibit, one could see the Osborne 1 portable computer. This machine comes equipped with a free software package whose value is only $200 less than the cost of the entire computer. When asked about the Osborne 2, one official replied "Adam hasn't decided when to release it," his reference to the president by his first name showing how small the company was.

Adam Osborne was an early computer visionary/crackpot. The Osborne 1 was an all-in-one system that weighed 24 pounds and had a 5-inch display. It did not run on batteries and was not designed to sit on your lap, but rather to be carried around and then placed on a desk and plugged in for use. The software bundling concept was also novel for the time. The computer sold for $1,795 and the bundled software (the CP/M operating system, BASIC, a word processor, and a spreadsheet) nominally was worth over $1,500. This mostly shows how overpriced software was and how few copies companies expected to sell (the two being related).

Osborne was able to convince software manufacturers to sell him copies of their software for bundling with his system, at a price far reduced from their normal retail, in exchange for the potential of higher sales if the Osborne 1 took off (the machine sold reasonably well—55,000 copies in 1982 according to the Jones Encyclopedia—but the company went bankrupt two years later). This didn't hurt the software companies much since it is doubtful they would have sold full-price copies to the people who bought Osborne 1s. It is an interesting aspect of software development that when a hardware manufacturer is bundling your software with his computer, your cost for each extra copy sold is exactly zero.

Also out there were something known at the time as HHCs:

> The hand-held computers, or HHCs, were at Comdex. Both Sharp and Panasonic exhibited such products. The Sharp was connected to a neat four-color printer which outputted a diagram of the system. Panasonic's HHC, The Link, had a complete line of accessories, including three printers, two modems, and even a suitcase to hold everything.

These are way-ahead-of-their-time precursors of the current hand-held devices, such as the Palm Pilot. Along the way this type of device went through several acronym shifts and they are now known as PDAs, for personal digital assistants.

Comdex/Spring in 1982 featured the personal computer at one of its most diverse moments, with a mix of the old guard of Apple, Commodore, and Tandy; various new, incompatible personal computers; and the IBM PC—which within five years swept all the competition aside and became the undisputed standard. And implicit in all of this, of course, was the rise of Microsoft.

9

Roots of Evangelism

While much has been written about how Microsoft designs, writes, and markets software, almost nothing has been written about one of the key factors in Microsoft's success—how the company evangelizes software. Nothing, except for the quality of the people it hires, has done so much to set Microsoft apart from its competitors. Microsoft has succeeded by producing a very limited number of operating system platforms, and then tirelessly evangelizing them.

The term "evangelism" has religious connotations, and in some ways they are not misplaced. In the software industry, evangelism means getting software writers at other companies to write code that works with your software. In particular, when you are writing an operating system, you want to present it to other software developers as a platform on which users can run their applications. The other developers have to have faith in you—faith that enough people will buy your operating system that it becomes a reasonable platform for their software. It can be an advantage to be one of the first to write software for an operating system that catches on, because you will be ahead of other companies in your understanding of it. This makes other developers very receptive to evangelism. But if they learn how to write software for an operating system that captures no market share, they have wasted their time.

When it works, evangelism becomes a virtuous circle in which people buy the operating system because it has so many applications available for it, and people buy applications because they run on a popular operating system. Currently, Windows is the most popular operating system by far, benefiting from just such an effect. But it didn't happen by accident. Microsoft's evangelism efforts are what put it there.

Evangelism takes many forms. Evangelists plan conferences for developers from other companies. They make sure that the software development kits (SDKs) that those developers need exist. They bring the developers to the Microsoft campus to meet with Microsoft developers. They run the Microsoft Developer Network (MSDN), which provides subscribers with a monthly CD-ROM containing programming information and developer tools. They work on logo programs, such as those little "Designed for Microsoft Windows" stickers you see on hardware and software. But when you get right down to it, at a technical level what they are trying to accomplish with all this is to get software developers to write software that uses Microsoft's APIs.

A modern operating system, such as Windows 98, has many layers that together export hundreds of APIs, for use by other layers and by other programs. Those programs may in turn use those APIs and export APIs for yet other programs, layers on layers on layers.

When a programmer chooses which operating system to design code for, he or she is also implicitly choosing which API he or she will use. Operating systems such as Windows 98, OS/2, Unix, and the Macintosh OS all generally have different APIs for doing the same thing.

Consider drawing a dot on the screen. The API call that operating system A exports to do this might be called draw_dot(). The API call on operating system B might be called dot_draw(). Operating system C might call it draw_pixel(). If you had written code to run on operating system A and you then wanted to compile it for operating system B, you would need to go through your source code and change all references to draw_dot() to be dot_draw()—a simple change that your editing program can probably do for you, but one that could be tedious if you have a large program.

It gets worse. A function to draw a dot will generally take two parameters, the x and y coordinates on the screen. But perhaps the draw_dot() function of operating system A has the first parameter defined to be the x coordinate and the second defined to be the y coordinate, while the dot_draw() function of operating system B might have y first and x second. Now it becomes more difficult to do this replacement automatically.

Finally, the origin used by the two operating systems might be different. That is, the coordinate (0, 0) might be the top left corner of the screen on operating system A, but at the bottom left on operating system B. Or it could be that before drawing anything on the screen in operating system A, you need to call a special function initialize_screen(), but this is unnecessary on operating system B. Sometimes the whole model that an operating system exports for accessing something like the screen is different, which affects the way you design your program.

The result is that the process of moving your code from one operating system to another—which is known as "porting"—can be extremely time-consuming. Writing your program to run on two operating systems— "cross-platform development"—often means writing two separate versions that export the same user interface, but are internally very different, because they call the APIs of the two different operating systems.

What this creates is a concept that I will call "weight." A real-world example is home videotape formats. The current standard format is VHS, which won out over Betamax in the late 1970s. You probably have some VHS tapes in your house; they create weight. Your local video store has VHS tapes; that creates more weight. What this weight does is prevent new video formats from appearing. (It was the gradual accumulation of this weight that killed Betamax. VHS acquired a lead over Betamax in sales, primarily because it allowed longer recording times, and the weight of more VHS players and more VHS tapes fed on itself, until Betamax died out.) It is possible to copy tapes from one format to another if you have a VCR of each kind and some cables, but it is time-consuming—just as it is possible, but time-consuming, to modify your source code to run on a different operating system. This "law of increasing returns" applies to other standards also, from electrical voltage to plumbing fixtures. In some cases there can be several standards, but each will have an area in which it dominates. For example, some areas of the world use 110 volts for electrical power, while others use 220. What is unlikely is that you will have multiple equivalent standards in one market. And in the world of software, which can be transmitted anywhere virtually instantaneously, the whole world becomes one market.

So, if you have written your code to run on operating system A— your source code contains calls to the API that operating system A exports—then we can say that operating system A has generated weight. The work you need to do to port your program to run on operating system B is figuratively equivalent to lifting the weight.

APIs originally were not *intentionally* designed to be different from each other. It was simply that cross-platform development was not a priority for API designers. Windows and OS/2 do in fact differ in where the origin is located in their respective graphics APIs (upper left for Windows, lower left for OS/2). Windows evolved that way because PC hardware in the early 1980s had the origin in the upper left, and since there was no reason to change it, that stuck. OS/2 was designed with the origin in the lower left to match software that ran on IBM mainframes, which probably had the origin placed there to match some even older hardware. In a situation like that it is easy to come up with arguments for why each of the two ways is "right," but neither group wants to change to match the other because they would be hurting people who have weight invested in their operating system. So the difference—and hundreds of similar ones—persists, to the annoyance of programmers trying to do cross-platform development.

The big benefit of weight is that it tends to produce future revenues for the company that is generating the weight. If a user owns applications that run on operating system A, and has a choice of upgrading to a new version of operating system A or to a new version of operating system B, he or she will tend to pick operating system A because of the application weight it has generated. Recognizing this, in recent times operating systems vendors such as Microsoft have been eager to define new APIs that increase the weight their operating systems generate.

This can be a tricky business. First of all, defining an API is no guarantee that it will be used. If you make an API set that does the same thing as an existing API set, but it is perceived as being different just for the sake of being different, programmers may revolt and refuse to call your API—essentially boycotting it, saying, "We would rather not supply this functionality at all, just to avoid calling your API that we don't like."

More importantly, defining APIs is work, and documenting them and supporting programmers who call the APIs is a lot of work. It is almost always the developers who define APIs and do the basic documentation. The time spent doing this could instead be spent writing or improving code.

When I was working at Softimage, we came up with a standard API that Digital Studio would expect to call when talking to video hardware drivers. Initially this was just a convenience, since we ourselves wrote the first instance of code that exported this API. That code sat on top of the API that Play's drivers exported. We didn't have to worry too much about everything being defined clearly since the interface was only called or exported internally—walking down the hall to talk to someone could clear up any questions. Later, having that interface made it much easier to move to Matrox's hardware, since we only had to write a new version of the layer that exported it, keeping the core of Digital Studio unchanged. Doing a second version also allowed us to be more confident that the API we had defined was sufficiently generic to cover any other hardware that needed to be supported. When it came time to integrate in the Studio Z hardware, we were able to give Intergraph's engineers a spec for the API and let them do the work. That was the evangelism part. But this required a lot of work by me, Peter Ibrahim, and others to clean up our initial work and make sure that the interface was well defined and well documented. As we went to support each new type of hardware, we would discover more changes that we had to make in the API, meaning that the existing code had to be changed also. We also had to take time out from our other work to help Intergraph's engineers with any questions or problems they had. This is the hidden cost of evangelism.

*   *   *

The computers from Apple, Radio Shack, and Commodore that dominated the pre-IBM PC era all came with interpreters for a dialect of the programming language BASIC. From a user's perspective, there was no separation between the operating system and the BASIC interpreter. When you turned the computer on, it would start up in the BASIC interpreter, allowing you to type in programs in BASIC and then run them (the BASIC command "RUN" told the computer to execute the current BASIC program that was loaded). You could also load programs from a floppy disk and run them; this is how some third-party software was distributed—as a BASIC program on a floppy.

Each of these machines had versions of BASIC that differed slightly both in the core dialect they supported, and in extensions that were specific to the hardware and operating system they ran on. Luckily, there wasn't much hardware to be specific about. A lot of programs were simple enough that they didn't need to worry about this (they had to worry about differences in the core dialect, but not in the hardware). If programmers wanted to get fancier, for example by displaying graphics on the screen, the BASIC probably had some simple extension that supported setting a pixel on the screen to a certain color, and reading the current color of a pixel. Reading and writing files on the floppy drive (these machines rarely had hard drives) was also generally done differently in each machine's dialect, but again the level of support provided by the BASIC was very simple: just opening files, reading and writing bytes, and closing the file. The various BASICs would provide some way to communicate over the parallel port (the port to which printers were connected) and the serial port (the port to which modems were connected). Anything more complex than that would be handled by the BASIC program itself; for example, programs would need to deal with the differences between the various printers and modems that were connected to the parallel and serial ports and send out the proper command sequences for each one.

Those BASIC extensions were an API, although at the time nobody thought of them that way. They created weight for the particular systems they ran on. Manufacturer-provided resources to help programmers use those APIs were very limited, however. A computer would ship with a BASIC manual that documented all of the commands, but if you had any questions you would ask a friend who had the same model computer, or read the various magazines that sprang up to support each of the hardware platforms. Active evangelism on the part of the manufacturers, in the form of maintaining lists of programmers for their platforms, providing them with special methods of support, and keeping them apprised of future updates, was unheard of.

Hardware evangelism was similarly nonexistent. Each computer came with a keyboard and an output to connect to a television set, plus a random assortment of customized connectors for attaching tape drives, floppy drives, joysticks, and whatever other hardware was supported. The machines tended not to have generic expansion slots as modern PCs do, so the opportunity for third parties to design hardware for these platforms was limited (one exception to this was the Apple II, which did have expansion slots and some third-party hardware industry around it). Some of the machines were expandable (for example, more memory could be added), but the new hardware was generally sold by the same manufacturer that sold the original computer. Some third-party hardware, such as faster floppy drives, did exist but that hardware was designed without input from the original manufacturer, by reverse engineering the hardware it was replacing, not by reading a manufacturer-provided specification on how to integrate new components into the computer. None of the manufacturers wanted clones to exist the way they do today with the PC.

There was another restriction on adding hardware, which was that the BASIC language included with each computer was not expandable. If your BASIC supported only one floppy drive, there was not much point in a third-party company designing hardware that allowed a second floppy drive to be added. Actually, that is a slight oversimplification. Although the BASIC instruction set nominally imposed a limit on what hardware could be accessed, the various versions of BASIC all had instructions that let you read and write any port or memory address in the system. This throwing up of the hands by the BASICs' designers provided a way for a program to access any new hardware that the original BASIC did not support. Essentially it allowed you to include a driver for a device as part of a BASIC program—but every program would need to include its own "driver" for every special piece of hardware it wanted to access. This direct access to memory and ports also provided a method for wayward programs to crash the system in amusing ways. Since programs could write over any area of memory, they could write over their own code, or over parts of memory that the operating system was using.

There was a second way to create software, which was to write it directly in assembly language. Each of these machines had a specific microprocessor, although it wasn't particularly emphasized (this is hard to believe in these days when the first thing any computer ad announces is the model and speed of the microprocessor). For example, the Apple II had a processor called the 6502, developed by a company called MOS Technology. MOS Technology produced a manual on the 6502 that explained its instruction set, and others wrote books that explained it in greater detail. These explained only the 6502 itself, though; they did not include details on the particular floppy drive controller that Apple had included in the Apple II, or the display adapter, or the keyboard chip, or the joystick port, or the tape port, and so on. All that stuff which was hidden from a programmer by the BASIC interpreter was suddenly exposed to anyone writing in assembly language, and had to be dealt with. Assembly language is also more complicated to write and more confusing to debug.

Given that, you might wonder why anyone would write in assembly language. In fact, at the time most software was written in assembly language. The BASIC interpreters were somewhat wasteful of memory, and very wasteful of processor speed (the 6502 in the Apple II was an 8-bit processor running at 1 MHz—roughly 10,000 times less powerful than a state-of-the-art microprocessor in the year 2000). Writing in assembly language let you manage the memory (which on some machines was as small as 4 *kilobytes*—just 4,096 bytes) as you wished, and attempt to squeeze as much speed out of the processor as possible.

*   *   *

People's interest in writing in assembly language was also connected to another preoccupation of the era, which was copy protection. If you shipped your software as a BASIC program, it was easy for someone to load the software on their system, then put a new floppy in the drive, save the program to that floppy, and give it to a friend, saving the friend the trouble of buying the software. If someone had a machine with two floppy drives (such a machine was considered advanced in 1980—and hard drives were essentially nonexistent, so the alternative was a machine with only one floppy drive), he or she could copy the floppy directly. Distributing your program in BASIC also meant that others could view the source code, since BASIC code was interpreted and thus delivered in source code form (some BASICs allowed you to get around this, by marking a program such that the system could load and run it, but casual users would not be able to view the source or save it).

Now, you might be saying to yourself, I can take my floppies with Microsoft Word on them (or almost any other software sold today) and make copies of them and give them to my friend. So what has changed in 19 years? In fact it has gotten much *easier* to illegally copy software this way (it is illegal now, just as it was back then). The current thinking in the software industry is not to worry about the ability to physically copy software, but instead to focus on increasing the benefit of having a valid copy—printed manuals, cheap updates, and other incentives—or to allow physical copying of the software, but have some other restriction that prevents the copy from working.

Back then, however, the focus was on preventing physical copying, and the simplest way was to have your floppy not be readable by the standard operating system on the machine. The operating systems on those PCs did not multi-task; the computer did one thing at a time. Also, nobody had hard drives. So if a user wanted to run a program, he or she would put the floppy in the drive, turn the computer on, run the program, then turn the computer off. Thus, it was possible to put your program on a floppy that essentially contained its own miniature operating system, which only loaded and ran your program, and which was stored on the disk in a format that only it could read. This disk was "copy protected" because if you tried to copy it with the standard operating system, the operating system would not understand the way the data on the floppy was arranged and therefore could not read it.

In parallel with this art of making floppies that were unreadable by the operating system, there evolved an art of converting copy-protected disks into non-copy-protected disks. With special hardware it was not that hard to copy a floppy that was protected, but that was considered too easy, and in any case that meant copies could only be made by people who had the special hardware. The real goal was to take the files as stored on the copy-protected disk and convert them into files stored on a disk in the standard operating system format. Then the files on the disk would be readable by any computer and could be copied by anyone. The people who achieved this feat were known as "crackers."

The war between the coders and the crackers went on for a while. To get the data from a copy-protected disk, you had to figure out how the data was stored on the disk. The weak link in any copy-protection scheme was that the disk format had to be similar enough to the standard one for the computer to be able to perform its initial boot up off it. People wrote very convoluted boot code that used very convoluted file systems, but fundamentally the code, and therefore the layout of the file system on disk, was all traceable with enough time and energy. Once the disk format had been figured out, the files stored in it could be read off the disk and stored back on a floppy that used the standard file system.

At that point the cracker wasn't necessarily finished, because the code in the cracked program might itself want to read the disk—say to access a high-score file for a game (games were among the most elaborately copy-protected programs, since the people who cared a lot about playing games were the same ones who tended to be crackers). The cracker would have to find all the code in the program that was supposed to access a floppy in its own proprietary format, and replace it with code that accessed the floppy in the standard format. Some programmers would scatter random checks in their code to verify that the floppy the program was running from was still in the original format. These had to be unearthed one by one, a job made more difficult by the fact that the software authors, in an attempt to foil crackers, generally tried to disguise the checks as much as possible. Usually a cracker had to play the entire game to find all these hidden checks.

There was one last task that any cracker had to do after cracking a game, which was to modify the game so as to announce to the world who had cracked it. Crackers didn't put in their real names, but used "handles" like Crackowitz and The Smuggler, as they still do today. The crackers did not do this for money; they did it for enjoyment, for notoriety, and to get more software. A network developed for trading cracked Apple II games, but the only currency anyone in this network cared about was more cracked Apple II games. Thus if you knew someone who had some cool new games, he probably already had every game you had, so you would have nothing to trade with him (not that people were worried about legality—they just didn't want to be bothered with making a copy of a disk unless they got something in return). If you were the first to crack a game, you would have the ultimate trade bait with which to get games from other people.

The coder/cracker wars got progressively nastier, with programs coming out that would react violently (to the extent possible) when they determined that they were running as a cracked copy. The program might delete all the data on the floppy—morphing into a virus on the spot. For a game this might not be so bad, but with a word-processing program this could mean the loss of any data you had saved. Thus, using a cracked program for any real business entailed a slight risk. A clean crack of a program would have all the checks, as well as the code meant to delete the data, removed—but you could never be sure, except by built-up word-of-mouth, that a crack really was clean. Later, companies developed floppies with "weak bits," which, rather than always reading 1 or 0, instead randomly read one or the other. The program would read the bit a large number of times, and if it never changed, it would assume it was not running off the original floppy. So the cracker would have to find the code that read the weak bit and remove it. And so it went. An entire industry developed that provided tools for other companies to use to copy-protect their software. Eventually, the crackers "won" and the copy-protection industry died out (except for extremely high-end software—Softimage's software is still copy protected, although with a different method than is described here, and naturally there are cracked versions available that have the copy-protection checks removed).

*　　　　*　　　　*

The upshot of all this was that back in the early 1980s a lot of people were writing code in assembly language, which meant they didn't even have BASIC extensions to help them deal with the hardware. To read from the keyboard, or display text on the screen, or print anything required a lot of code; knowledge about what particular code was needed evolved through experimentation, and was traded through a network similar to the one for cracked games, where the way to get information was to provide some of your own. Eventually books appeared with titles like *Inside Apple II*, which collected in one place the details of how to access the hardware, but still, writing assembly language code for the Apple II, or for Radio Shack or Commodore machines, was a daunting task. Some manufacturers made it even harder: Texas Instruments had a plan to charge royalties to anyone selling software for the TI 99/4A.

The IBM PC changed all this, primarily due to a couple of decisions that IBM made in the interest of getting the system finished more quickly. The first was to design the hardware using parts from third parties, rather than designing its own. The second was to license operating systems from third parties, rather than writing its own. Famously, two beneficiaries of this decision were Intel, which made the 8088 microprocessor that was included in the first IBM PC, and Microsoft, which produced DOS, the first operating system sold for the IBM PC.

In the article titled "The IBM Personal Computer: First Impressions" in the October 1981 issue of *Byte*, the second paragraph reads: "The hardware is impressive, but even more striking are two decisions made by IBM: to use outside software suppliers already established in the microcomputer industry, and to provide information and assistance to independent, small-scale software writers and manufacturers of peripheral devices." Microsoft was one of those "outside software suppliers."

Choosing off-the-shelf components meant that third parties could buy those same components and make their own PCs. Intel was an established microprocessor maker (Intel scientists had designed what is considered to be the first microprocessor back in 1971), and the 8088 was an existing part, so there was no question of Intel's not selling it to other manufacturers. DOS, on the other hand, was designed expressly for the IBM PC, and IBM could have tried to prevent Microsoft from licensing it to other companies. Through a combination of IBM not caring enough to do that and Microsoft having the foresight to keep its options open, the agreement between IBM and Microsoft allowed licensing to others (IBM called their version DOS, and it was commonly known as PC-DOS, while Microsoft called it MS-DOS, but it was the same operating system).

IBM did produce one essential piece of the original IBM PC, the BIOS (Basic Input/Output System) which tied the operating system and the hardware together. This was proprietary and owned by IBM, which had no intention of licensing it to anyone else. The BIOS is a crucial piece of the computer that hides many of the details of the hardware and exports the API that the operating system uses when running. Without IBM's BIOS, other manufacturers would not be able to produce their own versions of the IBM PC—or so IBM thought.

IBM did one other thing, which more than anything else may have been the key to establishing the PC as the dominant standard for the next 20 years (so far). The October 1981 *Byte* article alludes to this: "The published documentation of the IBM Personal Computer DOS will include the source-code listing of the BIOS...and of the diagnostic programs executed automatically when the computer is turned on...the company plans to publish a hardware manual with drawings and industry-standard specifications." What IBM did was publish a purple-bound book called the *Technical Reference*. This book is an amazing collection of pinouts, schematic diagrams, register descriptions, and various other details that make sense only to a hardware engineer. But it included all the details of the hardware workings of the IBM PC; in particular, how cards that plugged into the expansion slots were designed. As a final gesture of brilliance, it included a full source-code listing, with comments, of the original IBM PC BIOS.

This source listing was not to be confused with today's "open source" concept. It could have been, but IBM did not want that. IBM had copyrighted the BIOS, and it was very careful to specify that no rights were being granted to copy the code in the BIOS listing. But the BIOS listing was effectively complete documentation on what APIs the BIOS provided (these were known as "BIOS interrupts," but were functionally like any other API, albeit the absolute bottom level of software API). With the BIOS listing in hand, software developers knew exactly how to write software that bypassed the BASIC interpreter that was included with the IBM PC. There was no need to wait for the "Inside the IBM PC" books to come out (although they did soon enough)—the answers were all there, in the tiny type of the *Technical Reference*, if you only took the time to understand it.

Publishing this book was extremely progressive on the part of IBM. Normally hardware details had to be reverse engineered by buying cards that the manufacturer had made and figuring out how they worked—a tedious, inexact process. To figure out how a BIOS worked, programmers would trace through it using software called a debugger, which gave them only uncommented and possibly incomplete code. A review of the *Technical Reference* in *PC Magazine* captures (somewhat breathlessly) how cool this seemed: "As I removed the manual from its binder, I could feel the excitement building, as if I were about to go on an exciting journey, a journey in which the 'treasure' would be the valuable secrets of how the IBM Personal Computer operates. Glancing at the clock, I noticed it was early in the evening; the next time I looked at the clock, it was early in the morning!" The review ends by suggesting that the manual be used as a college textbook.

As an added bonus, IBM soon after came out with the *DOS Technical Reference*, which expanded on the already extensive technical information provided in the standard DOS manual from IBM. Today's computers come with slim operating system manuals that discuss only user issues, such as how to copy a file, with the programming details available in a separate SDK. Back then it was assumed that a significant numbers of users would also be writing programs. (This may have inadvertently frightened some non-technical users, who while leafing through the appendices of their new DOS manual would have discovered, as an example, that DOS interrupt 24 was the critical error handler vector, with the helpful note that "For disk errors, this exit is taken only for errors occurring during an INT X'21' function call. It is not used for INT X'25' or X'26'.") As a result, the DOS manual that IBM provided was quite technical, and the *DOS Technical Reference* went even further, documenting the extra functionality that DOS provided to applications that it launched.

Among other things it documented how to write "terminate and stay resident" programs, or TSRs. Normally DOS programs ran one at a time, exiting completely before the next one ran. A TSR, on the other hand, could inform DOS that it was going to stick around and lurk while other programs ran. This allowed a programmer to do things like put a ticking clock up on the screen, or have an electronic notepad appear when a certain keystroke was hit. A company called Borland International, which later became one of Microsoft's main competitors in software development tools, had one of its first successful products with a TSR called Sidekick, a very early personal information manager that would pop up on screen when the user hit a certain key. Sidekick had a variety of simple tools, including a calendar, an appointment book, a phone book, various calculators, and a note editor. This all worked thanks to the TSR support documented in the *DOS Technical Reference*.

The parts of the regular *Technical Reference* that discussed how to make expansion cards opened up similar doors for those seeking to produce their own expansion hardware. IBM had some hardware cards ready to go when the IBM PC shipped; one let you add up to 64K of memory, one had a serial port for connecting a modem, one had a parallel port for connecting a printer. Immediately companies such as Tecmar, Quadram, and A.S.T. sprang up making their own expansion cards. The most popular early design was the multifunction adapter, which featured a whopping 256K of memory, a serial port, a parallel port, and whatever else companies cared to throw on there.

What IBM had done with the *Technical Reference* was jump-start both hardware and software evangelism for the PC. At the time, nobody really knew what evangelism was or how it contributed to the process. All they saw was a flood of new hardware and software. The flood was large enough to help the PC overcome the one true competitor it has had since it was released, the Apple Macintosh. The Macintosh was released in 1984, less than three years after the IBM PC. The Macintosh had a more elegant design, including a graphical design and user interface that was light years ahead of DOS, and was shipped by a company, Apple, that had come to understand the benefits of software evangelism: while the "Inside Apple II" books were published by others, the "Inside Macintosh" books were published by Apple. But Apple vigorously opposed hardware evangelism and kept the Macintosh hardware proprietary for a decade. Then, after a brief fling with allowing clones in the mid-1990s, Apple pulled the design back in, and it remains proprietary to this day. Despite all its advantages, the Macintosh never challenged the PC for superiority. The reason was that the PC, clunky as it was, had so much more software, and so much more and cheaper hardware, that a large majority of computer users continued to favor it over the Macintosh. And the reason for all that software and hardware was the seed that was planted by the *Technical Reference*, which created so much weight behind the PC.

It has become accepted doctrine in recent years that IBM did all this unintentionally, that it blew it when it made its computer architecture open. In fact IBM intended this all along. In the second issue of *PC Magazine*, dated April/May 1982, there was an interview with various IBM employees in Boca Raton, Florida, where the IBM PC had been designed. Don Estridge, who was in charge of the whole project, was quoted as saying: "We believed that a very wide array of software would be one of the key factors in the widespread use of the Personal Computer. There is no way that a single company could produce that much software; even if it were possible, it would take too long. So we needed to have the participation of other software authors and companies." Bill Sydnes, the engineering manager, when asked about third-party hardware, stated that the IBM PC was "designed to be open." He expressed admiration for the exploits of Tecmar, one of the first manufacturers of plug-in hardware, which already had more than 20 products available—most of which competed with (and improved upon) hardware that IBM was selling. He summarized things by saying, "The definition of a personal computer *is* third-party hardware and software."

While IBM was actively encouraging the development of all this hardware and software that worked with the IBM PC, what it didn't want duplicated was the machine itself. Unfortunately for IBM, including the BIOS listing in the *Technical Reference*, which was so useful for the hardware and software vendors it was encouraging, had another unintended consequence. Because it was a complete source listing, it allowed someone reading the source to come up with complete documentation on what the BIOS APIs did. The person who had written this documentation was "tainted"; he had seen the BIOS listing. However, he could hand the documentation to someone else and tell them to write a BIOS that matched the spec exactly. This was a long, arduous task, but when a company called Phoenix accomplished it, the result was a BIOS that performed like the original, but could legally be licensed to anyone else. IBM protested, but Phoenix had solid documentation backing up the fact that its BIOS had been developed via a "clean room" process—nobody working on the BIOS had seen the original IBM PC BIOS source code. Since Microsoft was freely licensing MS-DOS to anyone who wanted it, a computer manufacturer could now buy a BIOS from Phoenix, MS-DOS from Microsoft, a microprocessor from Intel, and various hardware components from their manufacturers, and produce a clone of the IBM PC that accepted all the same plug-in hardware and ran all the same third-party software.

Despite this, companies continued to come out with their own new designs. Early issues of *PC Magazine* in 1982 had ads for a new personal computer by NEC called the Advanced Personal Computer (APC). The ad copy stated that this machine had "better price/performance than any personal computer on the market." In case there was any doubt about which personal computer it was referring to, the ad headline claimed, "NEC's new Advanced Personal Computer gives Charlie the blues"—IBM was using Charlie Chaplin to advertise the IBM PC (the NEC ad also featured some film stills of Chaplin looking unhappy). The ad stated that the machine had more storage and better graphics than any-thing out there. I don't doubt that this was true, but I can't say for sure because the ad is vague and I have no personal memory of this machine. This is probably because it sank like a stone. Why? The ad copy made it clear: "Our software includes a full set of general accounting packages, word processing, mailing list management, business planning, database management, and communications. And we're readying more." The two key words were "our" and "we." NEC was following the old model of doing it all themselves, and it was doomed.

Even some of the early makers of PC clones did not get it. They came out with machines that had 8088 microprocessors and ran MS-DOS. But they didn't have exactly the same BIOS or hardware. In most cases the machines were *better* than the IBM PC—the changes they made were improvements. But once a machine was different in any way from the IBM PC, people could not depend on being able to use any IBM PC hardware or software with it. In those days it was common for different machines to require a slightly different version of each third-party application. If a company was selling a word processor that ran on a standard IBM PC, a hardware manufacturer might go to it and say, "Your program is written in 8088 assembly language and uses MS-DOS function calls, both of which our machine has. However, we made some small changes in the BIOS API to get better graphics performance, so could you please produce a version of your application that uses those new API calls and start selling it to our users?" Companies used to agree to this and maintain various slightly different versions of their software for slightly different systems. This sort of situation still exists today with Unix. But with the advent of the IBM PC, software writers instead started telling the hardware manufacturers, "I'm not going to bother stocking all those different versions. I'm going to produce one version that runs on a standard IBM PC under DOS, and it's up to you to ensure that your hardware can run it."

The gold standard for compatibility was a game called Flight Simulator. Flight Simulator showed the user a first-person view from the cockpit of an airplane, and in order to do this as smoothly as possible it was written to take advantage of a lot of specific features of the IBM PC hardware. As a result the program would fail to run correctly on some early PC clones. Microsoft and Intel eventually evolved official compatibility tests that manufacturers had to pass if they wanted to claim to be a proper clone, which nowadays grants them the right to slap a "Designed for Microsoft Windows" sticker on the machines. Nothing like that existed back in the early 1980s, so Flight Simulator emerged as the unofficial litmus test: If a computer could not run the standard version of Flight Simulator, it was not considered PC compatible. The slightly-better-but-different PC designs died out pretty quickly. (Many versions later, Flight Simulator is still around today, and is now sold by Microsoft.)

A similar attitude about supporting multiple operating systems was in the process of dying out. CP/M-86 and DOS both ran on the IBM PC, and according to the old model, software application writers would have produced separate versions for the two operating systems. After all, both were going to run on the same processor and on a machine with the same BIOS, so there would only be some small differences. But DOS jumped out to an early lead, and from then on software writers saw no need to support CP/M-86 (or the third operating system offered, the p-System).

Why did DOS get the early lead? In some ways it was according to plan: in the interview in the second issue of *PC Magazine*, the manager of programming and publications for the IBM division that produced the IBM PC states that he expects that the "great majority of users will use DOS," although the reason given is that it includes a BASIC interpreter. Mel Hallerman, a senior programmer on the project, adds that although he expects there to be "a nice market for all of [the three operating systems]," the "overwhelming majority will be DOS-based." In fact, DOS obliterated the other two right out of the gate. First of all, it cost $40, while CP/M-86 was $240 and the p-System was $675. (CP/M-86 was made by a company called Digital Research. I have heard that Gary Kildall, the company's president, was horrified by how much IBM was planning to charge for CP/M-86.) Second, DOS was available when the IBM PC shipped, whereas CP/M-86 and the p-System did not appear until the next year. So software writers eager to produce something for the IBM PC had to use DOS, and at that point the battle was over. In late 1982 Digital Research came out with an improved version called Concurrent CP/M-86, which allowed multitasking and had four different consoles that you could toggle between at any point. This was a huge advance over DOS, but it was universally ignored in the marketplace.

However, Microsoft was not content to just sit back and let the pricing and availability advantages ensure the success of DOS against CP/M-86 and the p-System. The strategies it used were an interesting foreshadowing of future battles.

First of all, from a product standpoint, Microsoft made DOS "fun" by including some sample programs written in BASIC. One of these was a game called DONKEY, which featured a badly drawn donkey standing on a two-lane road. A black strip going from the top to bottom of the screen, with a dotted line down the middle, was the "road." The donkey never moved from the center of the screen; instead, the dotted lines on the road moved to give the appearance that the donkey was cruising down the road (or rather, because the donkey always looked exactly the same, it gave the appearance that the donkey was shuffling sideways down the road while staring blankly into space). Occasionally a car would appear in one of the lanes at the top of the screen and start chugging desultorily down towards the donkey. The only control the user had over this was the ability to press a key to move the donkey to the other lane, to avoid the cars. I remember playing this game on our new IBM PC and finding it incredibly compelling. In their book *Gates*, Stephen Manes and Paul Andrews make the claim that Bill Gates himself wrote DONKEY. The book also describes the reaction when a team at Apple got a new IBM PC to play with and discovered DONKEY: "The sheer bozosity of it had the Macintosh gang in stitches." Despite its lexicon-bending awfulness, DONKEY and an assortment of similarly goofy programs included with DOS provided something easy to demo when showing off the machine, and since they were written in BASIC, the source code served as a useful sample of how to use the various graphics and sound extensions that Microsoft had included in MS-BASIC.

Microsoft also needed to combat a perception problem with DOS. Digital Research sold a product called CP/M, which was by far the most popular operating system for 8-bit microcomputers—the kind of machines that were being hawked at Comdex in 1982. Programmers who had written software for the old CP/M needed to make a decision about what to do to get their software working on the new IBM PC. Should they port it to DOS, or to CP/M-86?

There was more to worry about, because the whole 16-bit microcomputer market—which at the time looked like it might include a lot more than just the IBM PC—was up for grabs. CP/M-86 already existed for other 16-bit machines, and Microsoft was making MS-DOS available for them. So Microsoft wanted to ensure that it won not only the IBM PC battle, but also the whole 16-bit battle.

The very first issue of *PC Magazine* had an article comparing the three operating system choices, for which the author interviewed representatives from each company. Digital Research had hired a company called Johnson-Laird, Inc. to port CP/M-86 to the IBM PC. The president of that company, Andy Johnson-Laird, was quoted as saying, "The operating system is to a computer what gasoline is to an automobile. It's only a means to an end. The novice user should not give a damn about what kind of chip is inside the computer. Rather, he's asking, What can I do with it? I say, forget about the chip *and* the operating system. The only time you have to worry about the operating system is when things go wrong."

From Microsoft, the author of the article interviewed Chris Larson, the product marketing manager for DOS. Larson avoided any comparison between an operating system and a fungible product like gasoline, or any mention of how it should be hidden away unseen. Instead he jumped right in swinging: "CP/M was designed around 8-bit hardware, when technology was less advanced. DOS was designed around concepts of a 16-bit operating system called Unix." It would be charitable to merely laugh at this statement. To produce DOS for IBM, Microsoft had bought an existing operating system that was written by another company. The author of that operating system, Tim Paterson, had written it in a hurry, and although it is unclear whether, in his haste, he actually stole code from a version of CP/M, the internals of the two operating systems were very similar. The only 16-bit concept that version 1.0 of DOS took from Unix was the term "16-bit." In any case the "bitness" of an operating system is mostly a red herring, an advantage for users only in that it makes it slightly easier to for programmers to write programs, so presumably better programs will result.

Larson continued, "Microsoft's languages, such as BASIC, FORTRAN, and COBOL, will only run on the IBM Personal Computer if DOS is the operating system. There's no way a user can get a Microsoft product onto his machine if he's running CP/M-86." Microsoft was stating that it would never port its applications to CP/M-86, and especially, that it would never port its languages, which are tools that third-party developers use to write other applications. This ties in with the evangelism effort; languages that only ran on DOS would produce applications that only ran on DOS, thus keeping the third-party developers in the DOS camp. Microsoft was just another small company at the time, so this was not going to generate cries of abuse of monopoly power as it would today, but it was already using what leverage it could against CP/M-86.

Larson then discussed a "myth" concerning CP/M-86. "There is a confusion in people's minds about the possibility of translating 8-bit CP/M software into 16-bit CP/M-86 software…a hobbyist *might* be able to do it, but a typical end-user wouldn't. We believe vendors and programmers will translate their best programs into 16-bit source code, and it's just as easy to translate a program written for CP/M into DOS as it is to translate it into CP/M-86. So you will be able to get CP/M software without having to get CP/M-86." At this point Johnson-Laird popped back into the article to shoot another arrow into his foot, admitting that CP/M-86 has a "legacy" of 8-bit software to live up to. "Why does CP/M-86 do that? To provide continuity. Certainly, Microsoft's DOS runs programs more rapidly than CP/M-86 can, because it's freed from that constraint."

Notice the striking differences between the statements by Larson and by Johnson-Laird. Larson attacked the competition on dubious technical grounds that might frighten off non-technical users, pointed out that Microsoft software wouldn't run on the competitor's operating system, and finally addressed software developers who were considering which

new operating system to support. Johnson-Laird downplayed the significance of the operating system and freely admitted that CP/M-86 was
slower than DOS. Interestingly, the article doesn't mention the one fact
that was indisputably in Microsoft's favor, which was that at the time,
DOS was out and shipping, and CP/M-86 for the IBM PC had not yet
been released. Nowadays this would be hyped to the ceiling, but back then
people assumed that it was reasonable to compare a shipping operating
system to one that had not been released, because people would be willing
to wait a bit to get the system they wanted, and because the representative
of the future operating system would be forthright about how it compared
(keep in mind that in this case Microsoft, future target of much vilifica-
tion for its habit of pre-announcing software, was the company with the
operating system that was actually shipping).

The article was actually about a seminar that Microsoft had sponsored
Microsoft came up with another initiative to help DOS. The company
signed up Lifeboat Associates, the largest vendor of 8-bit CP/M software,
to publicly support MS-DOS as the standard operating system for all 16-
bit microcomputers. Most folks back then weren't paying attention to this
kind of maneuvering, but an article in the third issue of *PC Magazine*
summarized things nicely: "What this amounts to if you are a CP/M-86
fan is an outright declaration of war." The article continued, "Microsoft
and Lifeboat seem to be saying that just because CP/M became the de
facto standard operating system for 8-bit microcomputers doesn't mean
CP/M-86 should be the standard on 16-bit micros. Instead, they say, PC-
DOS, developed by Microsoft on the IBM Personal Computer, should be
the standard operating system not only for the PC but for all 16-bit
micros."

The article was actually about a seminar that Microsoft had sponsored
in Silicon Valley, with Lifeboat's support, entitled "16-bit Operating
Systems." So Microsoft had taken a company that could have been one of
the major backers of CP/M-86 and instead signed it up as an ardent MS-
DOS supporter. Larson gave a presentation at the seminar, debunking
more myths about CP/M-86 (CP/M-80, which he refers to, was old 8-bit

CP/M). The myths included the following: a CP/M-86 machine could run CP/M-80 software; there were a vast number of CP/M-86 programs; CP/M-80 was the only viable 8-bit operating system; any good 8-bit software existed under CP/M; and there were more CP/M-86 systems in the field than MS-DOS systems. He was correct in all of these assertions—the Apple, TRS-80, and Commodore machines had lots of software that was not written for CP/M, and MS-DOS was already dominating the 16-bit field. But what Microsoft was really trying to do was prevent any of those from becoming true, especially the one about there being vast numbers of CP/M-86 programs. In the end Larson stated, "It is *not necessarily* [italics added] more convenient to translate CP/M-80 software to CP/M-86 than to MS-DOS," casting doubt in software developers' minds without saying anything concrete.

At the seminar, Paul Allen, one of the founders of Microsoft, gave a presentation about XENIX, a Microsoft implementation of Unix. The idea he was pushing was that MS-DOS and XENIX were part of a family, and that users could migrate to XENIX (as opposed to some other, non-Microsoft operating system) if they needed more power. This specific idea, MS-DOS to XENIX migration, never went anywhere, mostly because XENIX never particularly went anywhere. But the idea that Microsoft would take care of you as your operating system needs grew certainly turned out to have legs.

Microsoft was also trying to emphasize the fact that it was hardware-agnostic, that MS-DOS was not tied to the IBM PC. Although the author of the *PC Magazine* article called it PC-DOS, and in fact complained about the multiple names, by this point Larson and Allen were careful always to refer to it as MS-DOS (unlike the interview two issues earlier in which Larson called it simply DOS). The message to developers was, Microsoft will take care of you. If you port your applications to MS-DOS, we will handle porting MS-DOS itself to any 16-bit hardware that turns out to matter, and your applications will come along for the ride.

So way back in 1982, Microsoft was already out evangelizing its operating system against the competition. Selling it cheaply, having the hardware manufacturer present it as the standard, making it "fun," attacking the competition on technical issues, not porting applications to competitors' systems, making sure that its developer tools ran only on its operating systems, signing up potential competitors as partners, talking about a "family" of operating systems—these are all the techniques it would use later with Windows. And above all, the most important one, evangelism: getting out there and selling other software developers on its operating system, explaining why everyone else was going to be developing for it and they should too. The battle between MS-DOS and CP/M-86 could have been decided by a gradual swaying of opinion based on magazine articles and word of mouth, but Microsoft jumped in and ensured it ended before it began.

Once the IBM PC flattened all the other new 16-bit machines, the 16-bit microcomputer market was reduced to just the IBM PC market. At that point, merely because it cost one sixth what its competition did and had a six-month head start running on the IBM PC, DOS would certainly have won the battle no matter what Microsoft did. DOS established itself as the standard and continued on for the entire decade of the 1980s. Digital Research eventually abandoned CP/M-86 and instead came out with a clone of MS-DOS called DR-DOS, affirming the DOS API as the only one that mattered.

10

Rising

While Microsoft was busy guiding the software development environment for the IBM PC, things were a little complicated on the hardware side. There was no equivalent to DOS, no single standard that everyone could follow. Instead there was an adversarial relationship between IBM and the companies making PC clones. Although IBM had initially planted a strong stake in the ground with the *Technical Reference*, after that time hardware evangelism for the PC drifted a bit, with no company able to set a clear agenda. Since all the manufacturers needed to adhere to a common standard but there was no formal procedure for changing the standard, there was relatively little room for innovation. The basic PC design did not change much through about 1987, although the microprocessors got faster and the number of peripherals available grew tremendously. In 1983 IBM came out with an update to the IBM PC called the XT, which had a built-in hard drive, and in 1984 the company came out with the AT, which had an 80286 microprocessor, an improvement on the 8088. Clone makers quickly matched these advances.

IBM eventually decided that the clones were bad because although the IBM PC market had exploded, far outpacing that of Apple's Macintosh,

IBM itself had only a small share of it. On the theory that it was better to rule in hell than serve in heaven, in the mid-1980s the company came up with a plan for a computer with a proprietary hardware design and a new BIOS, running a brand-new operating system. The goal was to exercise control over third-party hardware and software companies, replacing the open evangelism that existed with the IBM PC and DOS.

This new design was dubbed the PS/2, for Personal System/2, and the operating system that it would run was called OS/2. IBM teamed up with Microsoft to develop OS/2, under an agreement known as the JDA, for Joint Development Agreement. Microsoft had JDAs with several companies it was working with, but the one with IBM was referred to internally as *the* JDA. OS/2 was not restricted to PS/2 machines, but the name intentionally implied it was, much to Microsoft's annoyance. IBM also planned to develop, without Microsoft's help, an expanded version of OS/2 called Extended Edition, which featured database and communications support to allow better connections to existing IBM mainframes. Extended Edition would run only on IBM hardware. IBM's expectation was that the industry would get hooked on OS/2 running on their existing hardware, then start looking longingly at Extended Edition, buy PS/2 machines from IBM, and be nicely enveloped in the IBM cocoon.

OS/2 was meant to replace DOS and offer a graphical user interface (GUI). One big problem with DOS was that the operating system, and therefore any applications running on it, was limited to using 640 kilobytes, or 640K, of memory. OS/2 would not have this limitation. Microsoft did not particularly care for IBM's plans for world domination, but it did want to help users get around the 640K barrier. Microsoft was in a bit of a dilemma over OS/2 because for a couple of years it had been developing Windows, its own GUI that ran on top of DOS and extended beyond 640K, and attempting to evangelize it to other software developers as the platform of the future. However, Microsoft still felt at the time that it needed IBM's blessing to succeed, so it stepped in line behind OS/2, devoting the lion's share of its own resources to writing OS/2. In the meantime, Windows development continued as a skunk works project within Microsoft.

One difference between OS/2 and Windows was that IBM was controlling the evangelization of OS/2, of which there was rather little. Meanwhile, the Windows team, desperate to get anybody to pay attention, was aggressively trying to distribute SDKs that contained details on how to write applications for Windows. (The BIOS listing for the IBM PC was the first PC SDK, but later ones dispensed with the source listing and replaced it with more complete documentation of the APIs.)

OS/2 was also designed to fit into the entire IBM line of products. IBM had come up with an architecture called Systems Application Architecture (SAA), aimed at unifying the API and user interface across its entire product line, from mainframes down to PS/2 machines. So a number of decisions were made in designing OS/2 that had to do with fitting it into SAA, rather than what was appropriate for the personal computer industry.

Parallel to this software battle was a hardware battle evolving between IBM, with the PS/2, and the so-called "Gang of Nine": nine clone makers who were being shut out from the hardware details of the PS/2. The PS/2 was not, functionally, very different from the PC—it had the same basic internal layout, had an Intel microprocessor, and used similar components such as hard disks—but in the most significant respect it was very different. The main area in which third-party hardware vendors could add value was in plug-in expansion cards. The bus that the original IBM PC used had come to be called Industry Standard Architecture (ISA), and hardware manufacturers were well versed in how to make hardware to plug into it. The ISA bus was getting a little creaky, particularly in terms of how fast it could transfer data. For the PS/2, IBM had designed a new, faster bus called the MicroChannel Architecture (MCA), but it wasn't planning on licensing this to the Gang of Nine. In the meantime the Gang had developed its own improvement on ISA, called Extended ISA (EISA). EISA had one big advantage over MCA, which was that you could plug an old ISA card into an EISA bus, while MCA required all new hardware. In both cases this was intentional, because the Gang of Nine wanted as much support as possible for their new bus, whereas IBM wanted as little support as possible for its new bus until it had time to make sure it had control over it. Since the Gang of Nine was anxious to get other hardware vendors signed onto their new standard, they were sending out detailed specs on EISA to anyone who asked.

IBM also made another significant decision in designing the PS/2 that was related to the breadth of its product line. It did not want PS/2 sales to cut into sales of its minicomputers. As a result, it designed the initial PS/2 machines around the 80286 processor that had been used in the IBM PC AT back in 1984. The clone makers, meanwhile, jumped aggressively on the more powerful 80386 processor. This was especially significant because the difference between the 80286 and the 80386 was even more fundamental than the difference between the 80386 and its successors— the 486, the Pentium, and so on. In particular, the 80386 had extensions that allowed multiple DOS applications to be run at the same time.

IBM's decision to design the PS/2 for the 80286 also affected OS/2. Requiring that OS/2 run on 80286s engendered a series of compromises, particularly in support for existing DOS applications, that could have been avoided if it had run only on 80386s or better. Since there were no existing PS/2 machines to support, this would have been a perfect time to jump to the 80386, but IBM didn't want to produce a machine that was too powerful.

So there were parallel situations in software and hardware, with new, backwards-incompatible systems (OS/2 and MCA/PS/2) that were backed by the industry heavyweights and were getting a lot of PR about how they would dominate the market, competing against the scrappy underdogs (Windows and EISA) that promised a smoother migration from the old way. The new systems were hampered by IBM's desire to integrate them into its entire product line. Most important, tight control was being maintained over their evangelism, while Windows and EISA were aggressively evangelized.

It should come as no surprise to anyone (particularly anyone who was paying attention to the PC industry in the early 1990s) that Windows and EISA won out over OS/2 and MCA.

Microsoft eventually had to make a decision about OS/2 versus Windows, since it made no sense to continue to support both systems. In particular, supporting both did not send a clear message to software developers about which operating system they should be developing for. OS/2 was the official favorite, but Windows kept improving with each release, while OS/2 was being revised much more slowly. And it was heck of a lot easier to get an SDK for Windows than it was for OS/2. Not sending a clear message to software developers is bad evangelism—just about the worst mistake you can make for a company in Microsoft's position.

In May 1990 Microsoft released Windows 3.0, which was designed and optimized for the 80386 processor (although it would also run, in a more limited way, on an 80286). Windows 3.0 was a slick product with good support for multiple DOS applications. Suddenly the eye of the hype hurricane began to shift from OS/2 to Windows. Microsoft had also been developing a newer operating system, code-named NT, which was supposed to be the next version of OS/2, but IBM was beginning to get nervous about NT because it had no control over its development. The upshot of this was the famous IBM-Microsoft "don't call it a divorce" divorce, in September 1990 (about six months after I started working at Microsoft). The JDA was torn up; Microsoft got the right to continue to improve Windows, while OS/2 development was handed over to IBM. NT, which had been known as NT OS/2, now became Windows NT.

Interestingly, in the period leading up to the divorce, while the official evangelism drum was being beaten to other software companies to encourage them to develop for OS/2 and not Windows, there was one notable group of skeptics who put Windows ahead of OS/2. That group was Microsoft's own Applications division. It had continued to work on Windows applications, with the upshot that when the divorce was announced and it became obvious to everyone that Windows was going to win out over OS/2, presto! The Applications division was ready with Windows applications, ahead of everyone else.

In the minds of Microsoft conspiracy theorists, that whole incident is the foremost example of Microsoft dirty tricks. Microsoft, this line of thinking goes, intentionally trumpeted OS/2 to mislead other application vendors, pushed ahead with Windows while sabotaging IBM's valiant attempts to make OS/2 great, while at the same time Microsoft's Applications division paid lip service to OS/2 and concentrated on Windows applications for release when the trap was sprung.

This argument is logical in a way. There is nothing in the events as seen externally that particularly contradicts it, and the emergence of Windows in 1990 gave Microsoft a lead in operating system sales that has only grown in the ensuing decade, just as the emergence of Microsoft's Windows applications in 1990 gave the company a lead in applications that has grown likewise. The events of 1990 set the tone for the decade, setting Microsoft on a path to see its sales grow from less than $1 billion to almost $20 billion.

I can honestly say that this is not what happened, although of course this won't convince anyone who believes I may also be a member of the secret Microsoft conspiracy. The sequence of events would have required too much manipulation of IBM—IBM would have to have been supremely competent at developing operating systems, while simultaneously being completely incompetent at managing its relationship with Microsoft. The opposite is closer to the truth—IBM at the time was of dubious competence in developing OS/2, and if anyone was holding the operating system back, it was IBM. On the relationship side, Microsoft was still the tail to the IBM dog. IBM had threatened to boot Microsoft out of the JDA because of its continuing development of Windows. Microsoft initially tried to downplay rumors of trouble, leading to a famous quote from Steve Ballmer, at the time the head of the Systems division: "Our relationship is like two bears making love in the woods. We're going to move the world together. If the press is hearing rumbling, it's only because we're changing positions." It took a lot of guts on Microsoft's part to allow the relationship to be severed. It was still very unclear within Microsoft if it was a brilliant idea or a fatal mistake (or, as someone put it, if Microsoft would now be the bear on top or the bear on the bottom).

Not long after OS/2 development was handed over to IBM in late 1990, IBM suddenly adopted the plan that Microsoft had been pushing since the start of OS/2 development—restrict it to 80386 or better machines, give it good multiple DOS application support, and have it support the Windows API. The result was OS/2 2.0, which was a good product—but one that reflected Microsoft's desires for OS/2, not IBM's. More disturbing to Microsoft, it seemed that IBM was signing up some computer manufacturers to bundle OS/2 and getting a start on evangelizing it to software developers. Was it possible that it had figured out the secret of Microsoft's success? Microsoft's plan was to "squeeze" OS/2 between Windows on the low end and NT on the high end, but NT didn't endear itself to software developers when Microsoft failed to ship its first version until mid-1993. In the end, IBM botched the evangelism of OS/2, it never made much headway, and the "squeeze" worked to perfection. OS/2 remained a fringe product used by a small flock of believers.

Why did the Microsoft Applications division stay focused on Windows? The division was simply a more informed consumer of Microsoft evangelism than the rest of the industry. It heard all the fuss about OS/2, but could also see what was going on with Windows. Bill Gates had given the Applications division considerable freedom in choosing which platforms to develop for. In addition, the applications already ran on an Apple Macintosh, which had a GUI-based operating system. This had been accomplished by isolating the platform-specific parts of the applications into a separate layer, allowing most of the team to work on "shared code" that would run on any platform that had a platform-specific layer written for it. The Applications division had written this layer for the Macintosh and for Windows; once it was written for OS/2, the team could support all three platforms without too much extra work. This made it easy to hedge their bets in the Windows vs. OS/2 battle, and simply drop the OS/2 layer once the dominance of Windows became apparent.

Keep in mind that back then, the only important market for applications was in DOS applications. In the DOS world, the word processor market was dominated by WordPerfect, which was published by a company called Satellite Software International, which renamed itself WordPerfect Corporation in 1986. 1-2-3, published by Lotus Development, was the king of the spreadsheets. Microsoft had been struggling for a few years in the DOS market but had not had much success against the entrenched competitors. Thus, Microsoft saw the arrival of the GUI operating systems as an opportunity, whereas WordPerfect and Lotus saw it as a risk to their market dominance. WordPerfect and Lotus were still concentrating on DOS while doing some work on GUI versions of their products; they focused that work on OS/2 because, based on the official story that IBM and Microsoft were hyping, that appeared to be the safest approach. Microsoft's Applications division, meanwhile, knew it wanted to move away from DOS toward GUI applications, and therefore focused aggressively on the Macintosh and Windows. In a way this was easier than for the other applications vendors, since it wasn't betting the whole company on this strategy. In another sense it was harder, because the Applications division was directly exposed to the wrath of the Systems division of its own company when it refused to concentrate only on OS/2 applications.

There is no disputing the fact that the OS/2 debacle was a major mistake on Microsoft's part. But the mistake was not made in 1990 when Microsoft abandoned OS/2. The mistake was made back in 1987 or so, when Microsoft agreed to artificial limitations in OS/2. And the core of the mistake was that it sent a confusing message. When the confusion was resolved with Microsoft dropping OS/2 to focus on Windows, it created a lot of ill will among software developers, the same software developers whose help Microsoft needed to ensure the success of Windows. For an API provider like Microsoft, other developers are by far the most important market. Bad evangelism can be worse than no evangelism at all.

Luckily, the OS/2 team did not understand evangelism. IBM's strategy for selling operating systems was to get its sales people and management out to tell people who were thinking of buying the operating system that it was great. But if you don't evangelize an operating system to the people actually writing software for it, and back that up with development tools and technical assistance, you won't get the third-party support, and you will inevitably lose the long-term battle for the market.

*   *   *

Starting in 1990, Windows was on the path to becoming the standard it is today. Microsoft continued to invest significant resources in evangelism to ensure that it stayed that way. When Microsoft was developing Windows 95, the successor to Windows, it cranked up the evangelism machine to new heights. The PR blitz was perceived by the media as a campaign to convince end-users to buy the operating system, but that wasn't the main goal at all; people were going to buy the operating system anyway because Microsoft had already locked up deals with almost all the major computer vendors to pre-install Windows 95 on every new computer they shipped. The real target for the PR blitz was other software developers.

Those developers had built up a lot of weight around the existing Windows API, which was known as "Win16" because it was a 16-bit definition. While the 80386 processor itself was a 32-bit processor, information passed between an application and Windows via the Win16 API was in some places limited to 16 bits, meaning that the largest number allowed was 65,535. This was usually not an issue—a 16-bit API does *not*, as is often reported, run half as fast as a 32-bit API, and Win16 used 32-bit numbers in most places they were needed—but programmers would occasionally bump into one of these limits. Microsoft knew that Win16 was growing obsolete and wanted to move developers to a new 32-bit API called Win32, which Windows 95 supported. Win32 "widened" the Win32 API from 16 to 32 bits and also added some new capabilities. But although Win32 was certainly the easiest API to port a Win16 application to, the fact that developers were going to have to change APIs at all was an opening for other operating system APIs. It meant that developers could move instead to OS/2's API, Presentation Manager, which was also 32-bit. (Presentation Manager was abbreviated as PM, thus colliding with the abbreviation for Microsoft program managers.) So Microsoft had to convince software developers that Win32 was without a doubt the future API they should use. Microsoft needed to create a huge buzz around Windows 95 that the company could point to and say, "See, everyone is going to be running Windows 95, whose native API is Win32, so you had better move your applications to Win32 or you will be left behind." This would convince third parties to invest their development dollars in Win32 rather than Presentation Manager. The press missed this point completely, and talked about how Microsoft would never recoup its marketing costs with individual sales of Windows 95—a complete non-issue.

Microsoft's Applications division also needed to be convinced that Win32 was going to succeed. Nobody at Microsoft was considering writing Presentation Manager applications, but the teams were happy with their Win16 applications. The Win32 API had been supported on Windows NT since 1993, but Windows NT also ran Win16 applications. Despite various entreaties from the NT group, the Applications division had been reluctant to invest resources in porting their applications from

Win16 to Win32 when the only result would be that they would run slightly better on Windows NT, which was viewed as a non-mainstream operating system. Once Windows 95 supported Win32, the Applications division quickly ported all their applications over. This was another example of the independence of the Applications division, the same freedom that had allowed them to keep developing Windows applications in the late 1980s despite the supposedly imminent coronation of OS/2.

Windows 95 and the shift to Win32 were absolutely critical, so it would have been impossible to over-hype it. Microsoft sure tried, however. On the day that Windows 95 shipped, a barge with a 40-foot-high Windows 95 box on it sailed into Sydney Harbor. The Empire State Building was lit with the Windows 95 logo colors: orange, green, blue, and yellow. A 500-foot-high Windows 95 banner was hung off the CN Tower in Toronto, while someone holding a notebook computer running Windows 95 rappelled off the top. Microsoft bought the entire run of *The Times* of London, so it could give it away free with a Windows advertising supplement stuck inside. Artists painted the product logo on fields in Britain. Microsoft produced a 30-minute infomercial called "Microsoft Presents: The Start of Something New," starring Anthony Edwards from the television show *E.R.*, that touted the benefits of Windows 95. Microsoft spent $12 million to acquire the rights to the song "Start Me Up" by the Rolling Stones, for use in the television advertising campaign associated with the launch. Comedian Jay Leno was hired to emcee the launch event, held in a giant tent erected on a soccer field on the Microsoft campus.

The whole planet, it seemed at the time, got sucked into the Windows 95 launch. My favorite was the Royal Ontario Museum in Toronto promoting its "Spiders!" exhibit in the fall of 1995 as "Widows 95"—something Microsoft had nothing to do with! When Microsoft announced it was delaying the release of the French-Canadian version for a few months, to prevent people from buying it and reselling it in France, Quebec Premier Jacques Parizeau proposed a meeting with

Microsoft to discuss it. (I was in Montreal during the launch, having moved there four days before to work for Softimage.) The press was completely sucked into this. Partly this was due to amazement that something computer-related could generate such hype, but it was also fueled by the hype itself. On the day of the launch, computer stores everywhere opened at midnight to sell copies to folks lined up around the block. People were fighting each other once the doors opened to grab as many copies as they could. I heard one person interviewed who admitted he wasn't going to install it right away, and therefore had no need to come down to the store at midnight; he just wanted to be part of the event.

At roughly this point I decided that the world had gone crazy. People were lining up at midnight to fight over software they didn't need, just so they could tell their grandkids they were there? As a Microsoft employee I found this both fascinating and unnerving. What had become of the company I had joined five years before? It seemed Microsoft had crossed some threshold into the mainstream consciousness. When I called mail order catalogs to order clothing and gave my Microsoft shipping address, I got asked about Windows 95.

The story went that Microsoft decided that "Start Me Up" was the perfect song to launch Windows 95 because the new user interface featured the new "Start" button so prominently. The Rolling Stones were reluctant to license any of their songs. Microsoft marketers approached Mick Jagger, who quoted the ludicrous amount of $12 million, expecting them to say no. Instead they accepted immediately. I loved that story, even though I didn't know if it was true. The mere fact that it might have been true was enough. Microsoft's money was as good as anyone else's, and Microsoft had a lot of money. The press loved this story too, and I'm sure the company got more than $12 million in free publicity from it.

The event still resounds in the collective consciousness; I recently heard the fuss over *Harry Potter and the Goblet of Fire*, in which people also lined up at midnight on the first day it was available, described as "Windows 95-type marketing."

Setting aside $200 million worth of hype, there are many parallels between Microsoft's evangelization of MS-DOS as the new 16-bit standard in 1982, and its evangelization of Windows 95 as the new 32-bit standard in 1994. The company used all the same tactics. One key difference is that in 1994 it was trying to convince people that there was a more natural migration path from Win16 to Win32 than there was from Win16 to Presentation Manager. This was the opposite of what it was doing back in 1982, when it was claiming that migration from CP/M-80 to CP/M-86 had no particular advantage over CP/M-80 to MS-DOS. (Microsoft was wrong in 1982 back when nobody cared, and right in 1994 when the whole world was watching, so it didn't get ridiculed over this flip-flop.) Microsoft hyped the fact that the new operating system had twice as much "bitness" as a user feature, implying that somehow this would make software run twice as fast, when this is not true at all. In fact, since the main advantage of more "bitness" is that it allows a programmer to more easily use large amounts of computer memory, it arguably leads to bigger, slower programs.

*   *   *

While Microsoft was establishing the Win16 and Win32 standards for PC software, over on the hardware side extensions to the BIOS continued to be standardized by ad hoc coalitions of BIOS and systems vendors, with other vendors adapting standards once they were well received by others. Gradually Intel began to take control of more and more of the remaining hardware standards. A prime example was the contest between PCI and VESA. Both were replacements for the EISA bus, which was starting to show its age. VESA was designed by a group of video-card manufacturers, video displays being the main expansion part that needed more bus bandwidth. VESA arrived around 1992 and quickly became something of a standard appearing on motherboards from a variety of manufacturers. VESA expansion cards for a variety of non-video hardware, such as hard drives, began to appear. At the same time, Intel was readying a new standard, called PCI that it was planning to evangelize to hardware vendors. Despite VESA's head start, PCI won out in an astonishingly quick demonstration of the power of Intel's evangelism efforts.

That is how the situation sits to this day, with Microsoft setting and evangelizing software standards, and Intel setting and evangelizing hardware standards. Both companies remind me of how covert operations like the CIA "run" their agents, letting them live their day-to-day lives as they please, but intervening at key points to set their overall direction. Just as Microsoft handles its software developers, trading inside peeks at future APIs in exchange for feedback and promises to use those APIs, Intel sets the agenda for hardware manufacturers to follow. If Intel starts talking about a hardware extension that it wants manufacturers to implement, the chances are very good that almost every PC sold a few years later will include it. The sudden, coordinated appearance on virtually every PC at once of features like ACPI (Advanced Configuration and Power Interface), USB (Universal Serial Bus), and AGP (Accelerated Graphics Port) is a testimony to Intel's skill in this regard. (ACPI is a standard for power management; USB is a new external plug-in connector; and AGP is a way to speed up the process of sending data to the video card.)

*   *   *

In some cases an operating system will support multiple APIs that do the same thing, with the aim of being able to run programs that call either API. This seems a noble goal, but it has a paradoxical negative effect. The problem is that the system is generally supporting two similar APIs because one of them is owned by somebody else and is to some degree a standard, and the other is a new API that the company writing the operating system is trying to evangelize. OS/2 is a well-known example. Originally OS/2 had its own basic API, Presentation Manager, for the basic functions of an operating system such as windowing, printing, interacting with hardware devices, and so on. Meanwhile, Microsoft Windows also had its own API, Win16 (and later Win32).

As time went on there were far more programs written for the Windows API than for Presentation Manager. After the Microsoft divorce, IBM started supporting both the Windows and Presentation Manager APIs in OS/2, and therefore was able to run applications written for both systems. This was no small task; the Windows API has hundreds of functions defined in it, each of which had to be supported perfectly. You might think that this dual support would make OS/2 the choice, since it could run both kinds of applications, and Windows could run only one kind—even though that kind held a vast majority. Certainly OS/2 supporters, and IBM management, felt this way. In fact, it had the reverse effect. Because both systems supported the Windows API, software developers felt no real need to write applications for Presentation Manager. At that point, OS/2's advantage—that it could run Presentation Manager applications—shrank to almost nothing, since there were so few Presentation Manager applications. And the fact that OS/2 could never quite get the Windows API support done perfectly, and that the Windows API was constantly being added to by Microsoft and OS/2 had to play catch-up, meant that people with Windows applications tended to choose Windows as the preferred operating system to run. So OS/2's support for Windows effectively killed Presentation Manager, which doomed OS/2.

For the same reason, it is very hard to get a new API going when there is already an industry standard in place. You need to do twice the work, since you have to support both the industry standard and your new one, and even then it is hard to offer a compelling reason why the new API is worth switching to.

There is an important lesson here, which is that it is good to create some weight with a good basic API such as Windows that covers all the basic areas of programming. Nobody will be able to write a program for Windows without making it specific to the Windows API in some way—even if all the application does is put up a window and print some text in it. But when it comes to some of the more peripheral parts of your API—aspects that only some applications will use, such as control of a certain piece of hardware, or a particular type of communication over the network—it can be a burden to have your own API definition. If your API for some small part of the system is in second place, so that you need to support the first-place API also, you have signed the death warrant for your API, so you might as well drop it and throw in with the first-place one.

The extra work of defining your own API for this specific function doesn't buy you a larger number of applications weighted towards your operating system (each application may be a bit *more* weighted towards the operating system, but that is less important). So at that point all the evangelism needed to support your API is not worth the trouble. This is a lesson that Microsoft does not seem to have learned. Microsoft continues to define new APIs that duplicate existing standards, and then crank up the evangelism machine behind the new API. In many cases the new API is slightly better, but if you add up the cost of having to deal with the two APIs, you see that such situations are bad both for the industry and for Microsoft.

Microsoft seems to have bought into the notion, which the media trumpets, that owning API definitions is a huge strategic advantage, and the more APIs the better. I disagree with this completely. Microsoft has a bad case of API-itis, with no cure in sight. First of all, defining an API is work, and getting industry feedback is work, and evangelizing it is work. Microsoft has an evangelism team to help with all this, but the process still has a significant impact on the development team. Moreover, once you have defined an API, you need to keep supporting it for a while, and can't make too many changes to it, to avoid annoying software developers who bought into your evangelism work. Sometimes you will keep a bad API just for this reason.

In addition, the advantages of owning APIs (beyond a basic weight-creating API such as the Win32 API) are usually overstated. The most typical example given is the "hidden API"—where Microsoft allegedly puts an API in the operating system, but tells only Microsoft's application writers about it. This would allow the Microsoft applications to appear better than those from competing companies. The system could support a standard API for drawing lines on the screen, but then also have a hidden API that draws them much faster. So applications from other companies would call the slower API, giving Microsoft's applications a speed advantage.

I was never privy to any knowledge about hidden APIs, although there was at least one case reported in the early 1990s (an API called DirectedYield, which allowed multiple applications to run together more smoothly. Microsoft was eventually forced to document it). I am sure the myth far exceeds the reality, and in any case Microsoft has long since realized that hidden APIs are a bad idea, and not just because they cause complaints from competitors and make the government come snooping around. Keeping third-party application writers happy, which helps the operating system sell, is more important than giving Microsoft's own applications an unfair advantage.

What happens now is somewhat subtler. When Microsoft defines a new API that the operating system exports, it tends to release information about it gradually to a progressively increasing circle of software developers, including those at Microsoft. This is so that the API can be looked over by application writers, to see if it meets their needs, and offer suggestions for changes and improvement—essentially a beta test for the API. This is what happened with Matrox and the Quartz API. Once a small circle of developers approves of it, then the circle is widened a few times. Once the API is deemed acceptable, it is released to everybody. I recall one case where someone in the NT group was discussing a new NT API that was going to help Microsoft's Internet Information Server product run faster. The guy then explained, "And now we're going to tell Netscape all about it also" (Netscape being Microsoft's main competitor in the Web server market).

So the real haves-vs.-have-nots division is not between Microsoft's application developers and the rest of the world, but between the developers at the companies deemed worthy of these early peeks and the rest of the world. The big advantage is that once the API is finalized, the early adopters have been working with it for a while, and have code that calls a version of the API that is at least very close to the final version, if not identical. Thus the extra work they need to do to support the final version of the API is much smaller than for a company that gets its first look at the API definitions when they are released to the world. In addition, the more privileged few will have had a chance to offer suggestions before the API was set in stone. Naturally Microsoft's applications groups are among those deemed worthy of this insider status.

There is also a notion that because Microsoft owns, say, an API for communicating over the Internet, it can exercise some control over the applications that call that API. In this misguided vision, code in the Microsoft operating system will detect, for example, that the user is buying a book over the Internet, and decide to redirect a few pennies into a Microsoft bank account. Or it will see someone buying a book from a competitor and instead pop up a suggestion that the user buy a Microsoft Press book. First of all things like this, while theoretically possible technically, would be extremely tricky to get right. Second, you need to convince software developers to use your APIs, which means you are asking them to trust you that the API is useful, is not buggy, and will continue to be supported. The reason that Microsoft puts a lot of effort into documenting its APIs is because there are several operating systems on the market, and Microsoft is trying to lure developers to use the API that Microsoft defines. If you start messing around doing sneaky things in your API, developers will stop trusting you.

Using a particular API in an application creates weight for the operating system, but it also creates a reverse weight because as the operating system is upgraded, it needs to keep supporting the applications that are out there. There were rumors in the old days that the Microsoft Systems division would give the Applications people a hand by ensuring that the Applications guys' main competitor didn't run on the new operating system, forcing the competitor to rush out a new version of its application. If this ever occurred, it was stopped when it was realized that this was hurting the operating system more than it was helping the application. Then there followed a period where Microsoft would ship operating systems that didn't intentionally break other applications, but the test team wouldn't do much checking of other applications; if they broke that was considered the other company's problem. Now, Microsoft aggressively tests existing applications against new releases of its operating systems. Sometimes an application will unintentionally depend on an API in the operating system working incorrectly, and when the API is "fixed," the application stops working. Microsoft used to consider this to be an application problem, but now realizes that it is a combined operating system-application problem. It will often consult with the application vendor in cases like this, and occasionally the solution to the problem is to leave the "bug" in and change the documentation for the API so it matches what the API actually does—thereby taking care of the bug and keeping the vendor happy at the same time.

*   *   *

Because software is so easily layered, many people have come up with the idea of writing a layer that hides the differences in the APIs exported by each operating system. This code goes in the "middle," between the application and the operating system, and is known as middleware. It allows the application to call the same API on all operating systems—the

API that the middleware layer exports. It might define that the origin is in the top-left corner, and that you draw a dot with a function called show_dot() whose parameters are x first, then y. And so on and so forth for every other function.

Once a middleware writer has defined all this, he or she writes the appropriate layer for each operating system. These layers will always export the same functions, but internally they will call the appropriate API for each operating system. So you will need one bit of middleware for each operating system. But once the middleware is written, applications that call the API exported by the middleware can be moved much more easily from operating system to operating system. Since there are far more applications than operating systems, this is viewed as an overall benefit. The ability to write an application once and then move it around thanks to middleware is referred to as "write once, run anywhere."

The latest incarnation of middleware to make news is Java, designed by Sun. Java is two things combined—a programming language, like C, and a set of middleware functions that abstract the operating system. The two are separate; it is possible to write a program in Java that does not call the Java middleware, but instead calls the operating system directly. Such a program, however, would be considered heretical by some. This is because Java also has a third component, as a religion that is worshipped by believers who see it as the solution to the problems of cross-platform development.

As a language, Java is conceptually similar to a language called C++, which is an extension of C. Java is quite elegant; in many small ways it is an improvement over C++—but the followers of the Java religion are interested in its middleware aspect, not the programming-language aspect. Unfortunately for the believers, Java suffers from the same two disadvantages that other middleware suffers from—slow performance and lack of flexibility. The performance is impacted by the overhead required to pass each API call through the middleware layer. The lack of flexibility arises from the requirement that the middleware layer run on many different operating systems, which may have different capabilities.

Java has been packaged all together as both a language and an API, but I see no reason this must be so. I would rather see Java viewed as a language that can be written in either a portable way or a platform-specific way—just like C++. The middleware aspect would be an option, but not a requirement.

Unfortunately, defining middleware is seductive to programmers. You get to study all the APIs you are going to abstract, and then use your quick-firing brain cells to synthesize them all into one perfect abstraction—or so the theory goes. Then when people have questions, they have to grovel in front of you for answers. Hero time! Since programmers benefit the most from middleware—both defining it and using it—they will continue to produce middleware layers, and the middleware dream will continue to rear its ugly head.

Technical Digression: Middleware

Why does middleware have performance and flexibility disadvantages?

Middleware confers a slight performance disadvantage because every API call that an application makes has to run through code in the middleware that converts it into the corresponding API of the underlying operating system. This code runs quickly in general but over time it can add up—this is known as the "overhead" of using the middleware. Luckily, these days processors are fast enough that the extra processing time is not usually noticed. For most applications, factors such as design, ease of use, and features are more important than raw speed. A word processor only has to be fast enough to keep up with the user's typing—any faster than that and it just sits there waiting for the next keystroke.

A far bigger deficiency of middleware is its lack of flexibility. Because middleware has to run on multiple operating systems, it tends to simplify the API that it exports, a sort of least-common-denominator effect. Operating system A might allow you to display 16 million different colors on the screen, but operating system B might only allow 256, or perhaps the designers of the middleware API are worried that some future operating system will only allow 256, so they define their API to only allow 256 colors. Thus your application running on operating system A might be artificially limited in how many colors it can display, compared to an application written "natively" to operating system A—that is, one that calls operating system A's API directly. Remember that middleware is primarily a benefit to programmers—making it easier for them to move their applications to different operating systems. The user benefits indirectly, on the theory that the programmers will use the time saved in other ways, such as adding features to the application, or making it more robust. But to a user running operating system A and wondering why the application he is running can only display 256 colors, that is cold comfort.

The other aspect of this lack of flexibility occurs when a new feature is added to the API of operating system A. A typical case is a new type of hardware, like a scanner. The programmer has a choice of either waiting for the middleware to be updated to export a corresponding API, which may take awhile (if it ever happens), or else calling the new operating system A API directly, which ruins the cross-platform aspect of the software.

People claim that middleware can allow an application to run on any operating system and that this is a benefit to users. They are getting things backwards. Their thinking is based on the notion that people first pick an operating system, and then scout around for some applications to run on it. Some techies and purists do pick the operating system first, but most people have specific tasks they want to do on their computer and don't spend a lot of time worrying about the operating system. They first choose applications that can help with those tasks, and their criteria in choosing an operating system is simply that it runs those applications. The fact that the applications can also run on a different operating system doesn't matter to them, because they only have one operating system. Right now there is one main operating system, Windows, and if you buy that you can be assured that virtually any application you want will run on it. If you buy some other system, you need to do so with your eyes open to the fact that you may be shutting yourself off from some future application that you may want.

There are other problems with middleware. It may cost money. The middleware layer is more code, which means more opportunity for bugs. Middleware definitely has a place in programming, for cases where performance is not critical, the tasks the program is trying to accomplish are fairly standard, and cross-platform compatibility is important. However, Java is being touted as a replacement for Windows, which has a lot of performance-intensive applications, and runs on a hardware platform that is constantly changing with the addition of new hardware such as the USB bus. The history of personal computing is littered with the remains of failed middleware products; the "killer apps" for the PC have always been the ones that were written natively for the operating system.

The p-System, the third operating system that IBM sold for the original IBM PC, was middleware very similar to Java. You wrote code to run on an abstract "p-machine," and p-machine emulators were written for each different type of computer. The sixth issue of *PC Magazine* reviewed the p-System, and a sidebar in the article probably sums it up best: "The benefits to the system's developers, program developers, and users is the ability to transport the entire computing environment without loss…on the other hand, the hypothetical machine design of the p-System can be regarded as an annoying, time-consuming overhead by the end-user of a finished program." P-System emulators existed for many different machines before the IBM PC came out, including Apple, Commodore, and TRS-80 machines. In an environment like that, with so much variety of machines and no dominant standard, something like the p-System made some sense. But once the PC arrived and swept away almost everything else, the need for the p-System disappeared (and so, rapidly, did the p-System itself). Despite what Java adherents will tell you, the computing environment on the Internet is still very homogeneous because the vast majority of computers are PC clones.

In an earlier technical digression I showed a function count_to_any_number() that called a function called printf(). Printf() is part of a standard layer of middleware (called the "standard I/O [input/output] library") that is generally available with any C compiler. It is fairly limited in what it can do—for example, it does not include any standard graphics functions. If we look at the current situation with Java, Microsoft is being tarred in the press for trying to "corrupt" Java by adding in its own Windows-specific Java extensions. Yet nobody objects in the world of C if you write your own alternatives to the standard I/O library. Microsoft did this in Win32, Apple did it with the MacOS APIs, and so on. The standard I/O library functions are there for those who want to write portable code, and the platform-specific APIs are there for those who want to take better advantage of what each platform offers. Nobody complains that the platform-specific APIs are "corrupting" C or the standard I/O library.

Middleware is similar to Esperanto, the "universal language" created over a hundred years ago. Esperanto might be marketed today as, "speak once, be understood anywhere." Yet Esperanto, although it has a few million speakers, is not used in any place where you might think it would be useful—the United Nations, for example. Instead, a lot of effort is put into simultaneous translation, the equivalent of porting a computer application to a different platform. A native speaker of a particular language who switches to Esperanto will lose some richness of expression, just as someone writing an application natively for a platform will lose some richness and flexibility when the application is ported to run over middleware. I see no reason why any current or future middleware will ever be able to overcome these inherent flaws and gain significant application weight.

11

The New New Thing

If Microsoft made a mistake in the early 1990s, it was its continued, decade-long ignorance of Unix as a competitive threat. In April 1994, Dave Cutler, the head of NT, invited Gordon Bell, his mentor at Digital Equipment Corp., to give a talk to the NT team. At the time, the team was mainly focused on beating OS/2, and the networking team within NT was intent on taking down Novell. Bell said to ignore all that, that the real competition was Unix (or actually the various Unix versions, which he referred to collectively as "Unices"). He compared it to driving on a highway at night, where you focus on the taillights of the furthest car you can see, and if you pass it, you will have passed all the others without even noticing. Bell told the team to forget Novell and OS/2. If NT beat Unix, it would blow by Novell and OS/2 and all its other competitors.

Bell was right, but the NT group—and Microsoft in general—ignored his advice, until the Internet arrived to open Microsoft's eyes to the threat. Not surprisingly, Microsoft's main operating system competitor as of mid-2000 is a Unix variant, the Linux operating system. At the time Bell gave his talk, the many different flavors of Unix made things difficult for application writers since each Unix required slightly different versions of their applications—a hopeless situation for someone trying to evangelize the platform. In addition, Unix tended to run on proprietary, closed hardware systems, which were expensive. But Linux runs on a PC and uses all the same peripherals, so the hardware is cheap and there is a reference platform that third-party software developers know will be available on any Linux system. It is not surprising that Linux has quickly become the most talked-about flavor of Unix.

Linux is also different because it was not developed by a single company, but instead used what has come to be called the open source development model. This meant it was developed in parallel by thousands of software developers around the world, collaborating using the Internet and working in their spare time and for no tangible financial reward.

Most importantly, the source code they work on is freely available to all.

An early example of this advantage of open source is from the book *Basic Computer Games*, first published in 1978 by *Creative Computing* magazine (which had been founded in 1974 as the first home computing magazine). The book had no CD or floppy included; the games were listed in source code form, as a series of instructions in the computer programming language BASIC. People who wished to play the games would need to type in the code, letter-perfect, to be able to enjoy such games as Change (which computed the correct change for any amount up to $100), Dice (which repeatedly rolled a pair of dice and reported the number of times each total came up), and Letter (in which you tried to guess which letter of the alphabet the computer had chosen).

A more sophisticated game was Football, which simulated a game of football between the player and the computer. This was a longer game, almost 300 lines of BASIC. If you read the source, you could see exactly how the computer modeled the game. As an example, at a certain point in the game, there was a one-third chance that the program would print out "GAME DELAYED. DOG ON FIELD" before continuing. (There was a comment before this little bit of code that said "Jean's special." The book noted that John Kemeny, a Dartmouth professor and later president who co-invented the BASIC language in 1964, wrote the game. His wife was named Jean, and I assume she came up with the dog on the field idea, which was then immortalized in the source code.)

The first advantage of providing source code was that it allowed people to adapt the games as needed to get them running on their own systems. The BASIC language was not completely standardized, so there were small variations in the version available on each computer system. The listings in the book were for Microsoft 8080 BASIC running on a MITS Altair 8800, which happened to be a later version of the very first piece of software that Microsoft ever sold. There was a brief section at the front of the book with explanations on how to convert the games into Radio Shack BASIC, Apple II BASIC, DEC BASIC PLUS, HP BASIC, SWTPC 6800 BASIC, MSI Disk BASIC, TDL ZAPPLE 8K and 12K BASIC, Sol BASIC (Extended and 5K), PET BASIC, Cromemco 16K Extended BASIC, Ohio Scientific BASIC, IMSAI 8K BASIC, North Star Disk BASIC, PolyMorphic 11K BASIC, and BASIC-E. Rather than provide the games in all these formats, the authors could count on the individual users of these systems to convert them. If a new system arrived with a new, slightly different version of BASIC, users of that system could figure out how to convert them. I could take these programs today and get them working on any version of BASIC available, running on hardware that did not even exist when the book was published.

The second advantage of having the source code available was that it served as an example for others who wanted to write their own software. Someone wishing to write his or her own computer bowling game might be intimidated by the task of starting from scratch. But he or she could take the bowling game in the book and start to improve it bit by bit. At each stage there would still be a working game. At the end there might not be a single line of code left from the original game, and yet the original game would have been indispensable in the creation of the new one. If a novice programmer wanted to tackle a smaller program, he or she could start out with Name (described as "a silly little ice-breaker to get a relationship going between a computer and a shy human"), which was 25 lines long and merely prompted the user for his or her name, then proceeded to print it out backwards, then with the letters alphabetized.

The final advantage of having the source available was that people could change the game as they saw fit. For example, the source code for the football game specified that when the player attempted a short pass, it would be intercepted 5% of the time, cause a sack 10% of the time, be incomplete 40% of the time, and be complete 45% of the time. The following lines of BASIC code controlled this:

```
1280  IF  R<.05  THEN  1330
1290  IF  R<.15  THEN  1390
1300  IF  R<.55  THEN  1420
```

It was quite easy to modify them to change the chance of each result occurring.

David Ahl, the publisher of *Creative Computing* and the person who assembled the games for "*Basic Computer Games*," discussed this phenomenon in the book's introduction, after talking about how fanatical some people had become about playing computer games:

> What happens to a fanatical cult when you open the temple doors and let everyone take its source into their own homes? Obviously, we don't know since the temple hasn't been open that long, but it seems obvious that this same generation of kids that can't do manual math or use a slide rule because of the pocket calculator may learn that a TV set [which virtually all home computers used as a display back then] can throw some actively challenging things their way instead of just passive images.

This software was distributed as source code for reasons of necessity, but also with an eye to the advantages of that model. It wasn't called "open source" back then. Few people worried about who owned the copyright on any modifications made—games like this were not viewed as worth protecting. But the same principles and advantages that guide the open source movement today were alive and well back in 1978.

The programs in *Basic Computer Games* were simple enough that they simply worked, as long as the code had been typed in correctly (and modified appropriately for the user's version of BASIC). With a large, complex program like Linux, there are sure to be bugs. Having the source code available is a huge help to programmers who are trying to diagnose and fix them. When debugging you are looking at the assembly language code, which is obscure, but if you have the source code handy you can generally figure out which bits of assembly code were generated by the compiler for each bit of source code, and so figure out where in the source code the bug is. Better yet, if someone has the source code handy they can actually modify it to fix the bug. If a single programmer (or a single company) is the only person with the source, he or she is the only person (or company) who can fix the bugs.

This is why I always get nervous when somebody I know reports a problem they are having with some piece of software and asks me to look at it. Sometimes the problem is a mistake in using the program or not understanding how a particular feature works. But sometimes it is a real bug in the program, and there is nothing I can do to fix it. There is no equivalent of climbing under the sink with a big wrench; without the source code and some time to understand it. I am helpless. I feel especially helpless when the user is my son who thinks that I personally have written all the Disney software he uses, and is firmly convinced that his Daddy can fix anything.

If you have given out source code to others, there is the possibility that *they* may fix a problem themselves, and report the fix back to you—and as a programmer, I can say it is very nice to receive a bug report that includes the necessary source code fixes. As a programmer who also uses other people's software, it can be very nice to be able to debug and fix a problem yourself rather than have to report the symptoms and hope that they can diagnose the problem and get you a fix in a timely manner.

*   *   *

Most people at Microsoft hold the open source model in contempt, because the difficulty in a lot of software development is not so much adding features on an individual basis but rather integrating the changes. Picture two men working on a blue car; one decides to go off and make a new door, and the other decides to paint the car green. Each individual piece of work is accomplished with no trouble, but when the first man returns, he will find that his nice new door is the wrong color. Neither one is solely at fault, but there is nonetheless a problem with the car. How to fix this? You can try to restrict the times when you allow "global" changes to the car, such as painting it; you can try to have some central person aware of all changes in progress, so he can discover such conflicts before it is too late; you can ask the painter to yell out, "I'm painting the car green!" before he starts, and hope the door worker hears him. Microsoft has tried variants of all of these, but still has problems integrating changes even within a single development team, where everyone works in the same building. The feeling is that solving such a problem with an open source project the size of Linux, where changes are arriving from all over the world on no particular schedule, would be impossible.

Nonetheless, Linux keeps improving, and that is why Microsoft needs to be very wary of it. I once read an article about Ken Griffey Jr., the baseball player. The article pointed out that as of when it was written in the mid-1990s, Griffey had improved his hitting totals each year he had been in the major leagues. Thus, it was impossible to know what level he was eventually going to reach. It was possible to guess—it was unlikely, for example, that Griffey would hit 100 home runs in a season, but until he had a year in which his numbers stayed the same, or went down, you just didn't know. The same is true of Linux. It has continued to get better with each release, and therefore there is no telling how far the open source model can take it. Linux may someday come out with a version that is 10 times better than anything that a Microsoft development team can produce. This may not be likely, but the possibility hasn't been *disproved* yet. A few years ago, the debate in operating systems was mighty NT against much smaller Solaris and BeOS and OS/2 and FreeBSD. Now there are only two that matter, NT and Linux, and they are being talked about as equals.

Why do people write code for Linux? This mystifies Microsoft people, who are used to being rewarded for their work with good reviews, bonuses, stock options, and promotions. Linux gives you none of that. Yet imagine you were an amateur guitarist, and you heard that the Rolling Stones were accepting worldwide submissions for inclusion on their new album. Not much at first—perhaps a five-second guitar solo. But if they liked it, they would use it, uncredited, on the album. And you might get to write a little more next time. Would you dedicate some part of your free time to this? Most programmers enjoy programming, and do it as a hobby at home. Devoting those hobby hours to Linux garners you recognition and respect from your peers at the same time—another way to earn your wings as a programmer. When I was a kid I used to play the board game "Careers," in which you could earn three kinds of points—Love, Money, and Fame. Working on Linux in your spare time won't give you any Money points, and it is doubtful you will pick up much Love either, but within the open source community, you can score big-time in the Fame department.

Detractors say that Linux will have a hard time finding programmers to do the "unsexy" work, that everyone will want to work on games and nobody will want to write drivers for SCSI adapters. In fact, a lot of driver work on Linux is done by someone who has a new piece of hardware for which no driver exists, so they write one. The work may not be sexy, but it is necessary for the person with that hardware. The desire to "scratch an itch" provides more than enough motivation. In any case, different programmers tend to be interested in different kinds of code, for whatever reason. Microsoft, being a company with salaries and a supervisory hierarchy, has the ability to order someone to work on something he or she doesn't want to work on, but I never recall this happening. People worked on things that interested them and projects still got complete coverage. There is no reason that the same should not be true of Linux, especially given the size of the Linux community. Linux empowers any user worldwide who has the desire and ability to write that SCSI driver. It may be hard to find someone who wants to write SCSI drivers, but opening it up to the entire Internet community is a good way to start.

Just to be safe, the main Linux distributors, such as Red Hat and VA Linux, are starting to hire people to work on Linux full-time, which will give them some ability to direct what they work on. These companies are taking a calculated gamble that it is worth paying people to do work that is then made available to all their competitors (as the Linux source code licensing agreement dictates), because it will advance Linux as a whole. They might wind up with a smaller part of the pie, but it will be a much bigger pie.

Linux also addresses the two biggest concerns for Microsoft—recruiting and evangelism.

Linux solves the recruiting problem quite neatly. Microsoft, in its interviews, tries to simulate in one hour the work that the employee will be doing. Linux does not "recruit" per se; to contribute to the project, you have to provide some code, which is reviewed by other people. Thus, a Linux "interview" is a perfect simulation of working on Linux, since it *is* working on Linux.

Related to recruiting is the issue of retaining people. Once people are hired at Microsoft they become used to the benefits, the free soda, and the stock options. Since Linux does not "capture" people the same way, there is not much that can be done to force them to keep working on the project. At the same time, there is no particular reason for people to leave; people don't need to stop working on Linux because they are moving to a different city, or because they have other interests that prevent them from devoting 40 hours a week to it.

This loose affiliation also has an advantage in getting rid of people. Although technically Microsoft employs everyone "at will," and can fire people at any time for no reason, in practice loss of unvested stock options may lead someone to file a wrongful dismissal lawsuit. As a result it is first necessary for a manager to carefully document underperformance over a period of time before firing anyone. In the Linux world, you can simply stop accepting code from someone. A Finnish programmer named Linus Torvalds wrote the initial core of Linux, and he still remains the final judge of what changes are accepted. People may complain about Linus' decisions, but they won't (at least not yet) sue over it—and whom exactly would they sue, and on what basis? In some other Unix versions, such as the one known as BSD, people have sometimes responded to such slights by "forking" the code—producing their own version in which they became the final arbiter of what changes were accepted. This is confusing to users and messes up the evangelism. Thus far the Linux community has successfully avoided this trap, through a combination of enlightened self-interest and respect for Linus.

Will the sudden arrival of IPO money in the Linux world mess things up as envy rears its ugly green head? In this view, it was considered okay for Red Hat to make a few bucks selling copies of something that had been developed for free by others, but it wasn't okay for the founders to become billionaires after the company went public, selling copies of something that had been developed for free by others. When Bob Young, CEO of Red Hat, goes on television and talks about "the open source model that we developed at Red Hat," as he is prone to do, that may annoy some people in the open source community. Still, I don't see what negative effects would actually result. If a single programmer gets upset and stops working on Linux, it will not have any effect on the product. People, even core software architects, leave Microsoft all the time and it continues to ship software (and as I discussed above, there are fewer reasons for someone to "leave" Linux). Even if an entire company such as Red Hat went under, all the work it had done on Linux would still be available to others, so Linux itself could continue.

The main point about a select few making all the money is that this is the way things used to be. When I worked in my first job at Dendrite International in the late 1980s, there was *no* equity given to anybody except top executives. I worked long hours for straight salary—no stock options, not even a bonus—while the founder of the company made millions and alternated driving to work in his BMW and his sport utility vehicle, which he parked right by the front door so everybody got a nice look at them. When the company went public, employees were given the chance to purchase a whopping 200 shares each. In today's climate Dendrite might be forced to give out a little more equity to attract people. But the notion that if you work hard on something for two years you should expect to get millions of dollars when IPOs start happening is a recent, and possibly short-lived, phenomenon.

What about evangelism on Linux? In one sense Linux does perfect evangelism because ultimately the source code precisely defines every API that the system exports. For a certain type of programmer who wants to write applications and drivers for Linux, this is enough, since these programmers will be happy to read the source code when determining how the APIs work. And if they want to help define a new API for, say, interfacing with a new class of hardware, they will jump right into any technical discussion going on. On the other hand there is another, larger, group that would rather have good documentation and invitations to events where new APIs are presented and discussed at a higher level—evangelism Microsoft-style. At the moment this does not exist for Linux. Certainly books have been written on how to program for Linux: since the source code is available, these books do not need to be written by someone in any "inner circle," which is a significant advantage. But there is no organized evangelism effort to ensure that the whole system is documented to a certain level, or to encourage software developers to port their applications to Linux, or to provide them with a lab where they can come to get help with their Linux work.

*   *   *

How else does the Linux community differ from Microsoft? Microsoft spends a lot of resources combating software piracy and coming up with licensing schemes that will ensure that everyone who uses Microsoft software pays for it. Despite this, piracy is still rampant. Since the core Linux team does not make any money from the software, it is not concerned about licensing issues. This does not necessarily mean that piracy won't affect the Linux community. Companies like Red Hat make their Linux distributions available for free, but also sell copies that include technical support. It is easy to imagine someone making pirated copies of the Red Hat package and selling them, which would rob Red Hat of revenue and might generate expensive calls to Red Hat's support phone line for a copy of the package that the company didn't make any money on. Currently people pay Red Hat to get an actual CD-ROM as opposed to waiting for a free copy to download over the Internet, but if Internet infrastructure keeps improving, in the future downloading it from the Internet may become faster than copying it off a CD-ROM.

Is the Linux development model superior to the one used by Microsoft? In his book of essays *The Cathedral and the Bazaar*, Eric Raymond, who is the closest thing the open source community has to a chief advocate, argues that Microsoft's code is "built like cathedrals, carefully crafted by individual wizards or small bands of mages working in splendid isolation," whereas open source is developed by "a great babbling bazaar of differing agendas and approaches out of which a coherent and stable system could seemingly emerge only by a succession of miracles." He also argues that

Microsoft is based on an exchange culture, in which "social status is primarily determined by having control of things (not necessarily material things) to use or trade," whereas open source is based on a gift culture, in which "social status is determined not by what you control but by *what you give away.*"

I think the exchange/gift comparison is an interesting analogy run amok. Raymond is confusing the motivations of Microsoft the corporation with the motivations of its employees. If you want to compare something to Microsoft, compare an actual company like Red Hat. Both are publicly traded companies, seeking to provide financial return on their shareholders' investments. Does Red Hat have a mandate to participate in the gift culture? If Red Hat decided to give away all of its profits, would this increase its status in the eyes of its shareholders?

The view that Microsoft employees are faceless robots under the iron control of Bill Gates is a common misconception in the open source community, whose members like to refer to Microsoft as "the Borg." Linux programmers write cool code and get respect from their peers as a result; in point of fact, Microsoft developers also write cool code and get respect from their peers. It's true that at Microsoft your "peer" might also be your boss, who has the power to command mighty stock options from above. But I do not think most Microsoft developers are mercenaries only out for the financial rewards. One of my favorite memories of Microsoft is the time that Dave Cutler came into my office ranting about how some code in a network-card driver I had written was broken. He hauled me back to his office and we started debugging it. After a while it became obvious that the bug was actually in his code, and he later sent me email thanking me for helping him debug it. I was excited not because Cutler, at the time, was my boss's boss's boss; it was because he was a universally known and respected member of the Microsoft community. I don't believe that the motivation of Microsoft developers is nearly as different from those of Linux programmers as a lot of open source advocates claim. Certainly the long-term exposure to money may displace some of the "coolness" motive as a reason for working at Microsoft, but I know several people who have left Microsoft and now work on open source projects, and as far as I can tell they did not undergo any cultural epiphany in the interim.

This reflects a general lack of understanding in the open source community about how Microsoft works—theoretically a strategic disadvantage for that community, in that it is failing to follow the maxim "know your enemy." One aspect of this is the common assumption that Microsoft software is on a path of unending bloat, and will eventually fall apart under its own weight—that on some future version of Office or Windows it will become impossible to fix a bug without introducing at least one other one, the code will never converge, and ultimately will fail to ever ship, thus ending the life of the product. In an essay written for the book *Open Sources* in December 1998, one year before Windows 2000 was completed, author Raymond predicted, "Windows 2000 will be either canceled or dead on arrival. Either way it will turn into a horrendous train wreck, the worst strategic disaster in Microsoft's history." It is safe to say that this vision of horror did not come to pass, and Windows 2000 is doing just fine. In his book *Free For All*, about the open source community, author Peter Wayner spends some time discussing how Microsoft will compete with Linux. He mentions that it might leverage its Windows installed base, or use its patent portfolio as a weapon. The notion that Microsoft might simply make a product that is more compelling to users is never seriously entertained.

I would not say that Microsoft understands the open source community much better, even though most of its dealings take place in public. Many people at Microsoft have a similarly snide view in reverse, that because of how open source software is developed, it is eventually bound to crack in some way—it will start to be buggy, or it won't scale to larger system. Nobody thinks this about other competitors; they plan strategy on the assumption that Sun and Novell and Oracle will continue to execute and ship good software. This bias against open source software is preventing Microsoft from attacking Linux the way it does other competitors, by evaluating the product, determining why people use it, and deciding what should be done to compete against it. In late October 1998 two internal Microsoft memos discussing open source—which became known as the "Halloween Documents" because of the timing—were leaked outside the company. One of the main points they made was that some out-of-the-box thinking was needed—open source and Linux needed to be addressed as a movement, not as a specific company. In February 2000 I attended an internal Microsoft briefing on Linux at which 850 people showed up, an astonishing number, and encouraging for Microsoft. But from talking to people at Microsoft, it appears that people are still relieved to be able to focus on how to compete with a single company, such as Red Hat, rather than having to treat open source differently from other competitors.

Microsoft has talked about opening the source code for NT, but to really open it—that is, to allow anyone to see it and make changes that become part of the project—would be anathema. What Microsoft would really want is for people to look at the source code, suggest changes that the company could use, and then go away quietly, thank you. Open-sourcing the code under such rules would not generate very much useful feedback.

I find Raymond's first point from *The Cathedral and the Bazaar*—that Microsoft code is crafted by wizards—more compelling than the exchange versus gift culture idea. First of all I always love it when someone uses the word "craft" to describe what I do, and I think I'd look good in a pointy hat. More importantly, there are some real differences between the development of Linux and the development of Windows NT (a.k.a. Windows 2000), the project I am most familiar with and the one that competes directly with Linux. Is the Linux method of natural selection better than Microsoft's program of directed breeding?

The difficulty of the task—writing an operating system that runs on a PC and supports a wide variety of hardware—is similar for NT and Linux. However, the nature of Linux development enforces some desirable behavior that the NT team recognizes as desirable, but does not follow. The fact that the Linux work is so geographically distributed means that interfaces between components—the internal APIs that they export and call—need to be well defined early on, because once the APIs are set it becomes very expensive to track down everyone who is using a particular API and notify them of a change. People recognize this fact and engage in a lot of discussion of API definitions before any code is written, to make sure they are right. For example, in the car door illustration I used previously, there would have been a lot of discussion about both the design of the car door and the color of the car before the car was built, so the likelihood of two conflicting changes being made later would be much lower.

In the NT group, by contrast, people generally define internal APIs on their own. They do send the definitions out for review within the group, but reviewing other people's API definitions is not high on anyone's list of priorities. In particular, unless you know your code is going to be using that API and think through all the possible scenarios in which you will do so, it is hard to know whether it will work for you. To the person defining the API it may seem perfect ("It's just the way I would have defined it!"), but in some cases, what is the ideal API from the point of view of the person exporting it is not necessarily perfect from the point of view of someone calling it—the API "consumer." In any case, someone defining an API will generally send it for review to the people they work with, who tend also to be on the exporting side of the API. Consumers of the API within the NT team may not find problems until they really start writing code that calls it, either because they were not asked to review it beforehand, or because they reviewed it but did not analyze it well enough. The feeling is that if people in NT find problems once they start using the API, it can be changed then—which is true, but this requires locating and changing all the source code that has been written based on the original version. Nonetheless the hubris exists that this isn't a big deal because all the code is being written within Microsoft.

In the open source world, someone who is going to be consuming an API will likely get a chance to review it in an Internet discussion and will recognize the advantage of doing so quickly and conscientiously. So the open source model forces much earlier and much better review of internal interfaces, which is a good thing.

Linux also depends much more on standards than NT does. This follows the unwritten Microsoft rule that APIs should be owned by Microsoft whenever possible—which means that Microsoft tends not to use standards unless it has had a hand in designing them. Using someone else's standards can be considered lazy, but in a good sense of the word: it saves you time—development time, testing time, and evangelism time.

Furthermore, the reward system for a project like NT is out of whack. In both the Linux and NT worlds you get respect for "owning" a chunk of the project—being the main architect or technical contact. But in NT, it is as easy to do that by starting up a new subproject as by taking over an existing one, and new projects are viewed as sexier. So the incentive is for developers to ignore what is there, start over, define a new API, and start coding. If someone in management complains, it is highly likely that you can come up with technical justification for why the old way was flawed—which can be hard for a manager to refute without expending a lot of effort to really understand the issues.

In Linux, any attempt to do that would be met with a demand that you prove why it is necessary to replace the existing work. So the tendency is to keep things as they are, refining and stabilizing them, as opposed to throwing things away and starting over. In addition, since the people working on the software are generally not being paid for it, there is no requirement to keep adding features in order to encourage upgrades from previous versions. This reduces "feature creep," which means more time can be spent fixing bugs instead of introducing new ones. It also cuts down "API creep," the tendency to throw away the API for some set of functionality and replace it with a redesigned one that is arguably "better," but also incredibly disruptive to software developers using the old one. Once again, Linux is encouraging practices that Microsoft should be following, but isn't.

Once you have your source code changes done in Linux, it is relatively easy to "check them in" to the project once you have established yourself. The nature of the actual code changes you want to check in figures heavily in the decision to accept them. While the NT group was working on Windows 2000, it was very hard to check in any changes. You had to show that they have been exhaustively tested, and even then the final decision on whether to check them in was often made by people in upper management, who did not understand the details of the code. It was as hard to check in a trivial code fix as a complicated one, and it was easy (and, because of all this, often very tempting) to sneak in other fixes and changes while checking in fixes for an approved bug.

I once had a dream where I had an approved checkin I was trying to make to the NT source control server, and I kept running around to different offices trying to do it, but at each office there was some reason why I couldn't do it—one machine was broken, another was being used, the third couldn't connect to the source control server, and so on. What is amazing is that I had this classic anxiety dream not about finding or fixing some particularly heinous bug, but about checking in the fix—a sad testimony to the counterproductiveness of the way the process was constituted. NT management was essentially saying, "Yes, we are paying you a high-five-or-low-six-figure salary to write code for us, but we don't trust you to decide if your code should be checked in or not." This led to a typical case of lack of trust causing loss of confidence, with the result that many NT developers lacked the experience to make good decisions about whether fixes should be checked in. The environment became one of developers against management, with developers trying to sneak in as much as they could and management trying to keep things out. The attitude from above was, "If you don't like the rules, don't write code with bugs in it," which was an absurd simplification of the debugging cycle. All we developers wanted was the benefit of the doubt, to be considered innocent of build-breaking tendencies until proven guilty.

It is not clear whether Linux is a better development model for producing stable code, or a better recruiting model for finding the best people, or a better design model for when your users are more technical, or all of the above. If all the main Linux programmers worked at a company where their job was to develop Linux, and Linus Torvalds was their manager, would the same product emerge? Is there something about management, market research, and schedules that hurts development of operating systems?

I suggested to a few people that NT adopt an "internal open source" model, where any developer on the project could check in any change he or she wanted—at least for short, well-defined periods of time during the project cycle. If you thought some piece of the system needed improvement, you would be welcome to scratch your itch and take a crack at fixing it. I think this would have many of the benefits of completely open source, without any loss of control of the intellectual property embodied in the source code. Unfortunately, nobody thought I was being serious. I asked Eric Raymond about this plan when he spoke at Microsoft in June 1999. His reply was that there were not enough eyeballs, meaning that the number of developers who would be able to participate in internal open source would not be enough to achieve the magic critical mass. I disagree; on NT alone there are hundreds of developers, and if you opened it up to the thousands of developers who work at Microsoft, you would have quite a lot of eyeballs, many of whom probably have some pet peeve about NT that they would love to take a crack at fixing.

The NT project actually used to work similarly to this. Back in 1988 and 1989, before any code was written, the team spent months and months coming up with exhaustive, carefully reviewed documentation on many of the internal and external interfaces in the system. (In the summer of 1999, a copy of this 10-year-old spec was added to the Information Technology collection at the Smithsonian Institution's National Museum of American History.) When I joined the NT team in 1990, coding had begun, but team members—fewer than two dozen developers—thought nothing of reviewing other people's code and sending nasty comments about it. People did their own builds of the source code, like in an open source project. If someone noticed the build was broken, they fixed it themselves. Dave Cutler ruled the roost technically in much the same way that Linus Torvalds does for Linux, having written the core of the kernel himself, and being the final arbiter of any disagreements between his handpicked lieutenants. The NT team even had a bit of an adversarial relationship with the rest of Microsoft. Like the Linux community today, it viewed Microsoft's mainstream operating system product (Windows 3.0, back then) as a toy.

The final point about Linux development is that, by all accounts, it is fun. NT development, circa early 2000 when I left the company, was not fun. It was too hard to check changes in, too hard to get a good build, too hard to get meaningful peer review. People at Microsoft like the benefits and stability that come with having a full-time job, and in fact Microsoft policy prohibits them from contributing to open source projects. But if Red Hat opened a development office in Redmond, I think some of the Microsoft folks would be sorely tempted to jump ship.

The preceding arguments are valid for Linux versus NT, but they may not be valid for the general cathedral-versus-bazaar argument. Linux is one of the most successful and smoothly running open source projects ever, and NT is one of the largest and most unwieldy projects at Microsoft. Open source is not a panacea; not every project can attract enough programmers to make it work. But I have no doubt that right now, a specific instance of open source, Linux, has a development model that works better than a specific instance of closed source, NT.

*   *   *

Linux does have some problems, certainly. One is the lack of an organized evangelism effort. The core operating system is guaranteed to have a certain API set available, including basic graphics support provided by a layer known as the X Window System. More advanced GUI functionality such as toolbars and drag-and-drop between applications is provided by a layer known as a "desktop environment," which corresponds roughly to the Microsoft Windows GUI. Right now there are multiple desktop environments available for Linux, each with its own API. The net effect of this for programmers is that if they want to write a basic application they don't need to worry about which desktop environment the user is running, but if they want their application to run as well as possible and look as good as possible, they need to write extra code to deal with each desktop environment. This is the same argument people have made about Microsoft bundling the browser with Windows; is it better to have multiple desktop environments available, so users can choose, or is it better to have one, so third-party software developers can know what to write for? My belief is that people do not "use" the GUI very much, but are more concerned with how many applications run on top of the GUI, so it would be better for Linux to standardize on one desktop environment and give application writers a single target to aim for.

Within the Linux community the choice of desktop environments is viewed as a *strength* of Linux over Windows. Strong followings have evolved behind several different Linux desktop environments, in particular between one called KDE and one called GNOME. Heavily technical people are among the only ones who care about this issue, because they spend a lot of time futzing with the desktop environment itself. As a result they care about things like whether it has a clean internal architecture and whether the windowing metaphor defined by its exported APIs lines up with their own worldview. Most users don't care; all they see is that there are fewer applications available. Most programmers actively dislike this battle, since it means more work for them. Unfortunately, the heavily technical users are the sorts of people having religious wars about Linux desktop environments right now. Thus the split may continue, which would be to Microsoft's advantage in the mainstream market. By contrast, Windows has only ever had one GUI, the one Microsoft wrote—so that not even in the course of the U.S. Department of Justice lawsuit has it been suggested that Microsoft should be forced to unbundle the Windows GUI from the base operating system.

New PC hardware features are generally supported on Microsoft operating systems first. In a sense, right now Microsoft is providing the "native" operating systems for the PC hardware platform, because it works in such close cooperation with Intel before new features are introduced, while Linux has the flexibility disadvantage of middleware because support will lag behind. It's not quite as bad as that; once new features are supported on Linux it won't have any performance disadvantage compared to Windows, and Intel is starting to work more closely with the Linux community to keep it abreast of new hardware developments.

Linux may also be hampered in the mainstream market by the fact that open source may work better in situations where users are relatively technically oriented—a class sometimes referred to as "power users." Linux manages the neat trick of having simultaneously a reputation for never crashing, and also a reputation for getting quick fixes when it does crash. But it requires a certain level of technical proficiency to be able to determine with confidence that a fix you get is valid, and does not keep the bug around, introduce another one, or act as some sort of Trojan horse that compromises the data on the machine. Microsoft also spends an enormous amount of time on tasks such as ensuring that upgrades from one version of the operating system to another work smoothly. So it is likely that Microsoft will continue its dominance of the mainstream market. But almost every home computer already runs Windows, so Microsoft does not have a lot of opportunity to sell more copies of Windows except as more homes get computers, or people upgrade over time.

Where Microsoft *does* present a huge target is in business environments, where people may have expensive mainframe or mini-computers that they wish to replace with cheaper PCs. Imagine you are a database company, such as Oracle, and you want to ship a bundled "appliance," a device that you simply plug into your network and use as a database server. The appliance needs an operating system, even though the user may never see it. What operating system do you pick? Even ignoring the cost, Linux may be preferable to NT because you can get access to the actual source code and debug it as extensively as you need. Sure, you may need to hire 50 people and have them spend six months learning the intricate details of Linux, but once you have that you are set with a product that you can support much better than one that had NT running inside. Those 50 people are the sort of technical user that Linux is perfect for.

One of the ways Microsoft has responded to Linux is by trying to pick holes in it—pointing out that it is not as reliable or as fast as anecdotal evidence would have you believe. In the case of Linux, such details miss the point. I firmly believe that right now NT is better than Linux, although there are so many ways to define "better" that it is easy to disagree with that. But it doesn't matter if at some point in time Linux is 50% better or 50% worse than NT; if Linux has better recruiting methods, and the development process is truly superior, in a few years Linux will be better no matter where it started out. And if Linux has trouble getting people to continue working on it, and the development process breaks down, in a few years NT will be better.

It is interesting that Linux seems most interested in the mainstream desktop right now, whereas Microsoft is worried about the large corporations—each going after the other one's natural turf. Partly this is the natural desire to get the other guy's clients, but there is something else at work. Linux, being a side project among programmers, is very interested in visibility, and the way to achieve visibility is to be used in the home. Microsoft, being a publicly traded company, is very interested in piles of money, and the way to make piles of money is to sell software to businesses.

One of the lessons that Microsoft has learned is that it is okay to start out having your developers define and test the product, but eventually you need someone like a program manager to start defining it. And then you start to need a test team to test it. And around all this you need an evangelism team to get other developers interested. You need to deal with program managers acting superior, and testers getting looked down on, and nobody having enough time to help with evangelism. Linux has not yet started down this path.

I am not saying that these problems with Linux are insurmountable. It is fashionable these days when writing about Linux to start out the article with some variant of, "Who would have imagined that a bunch of volunteers, few of whom have ever met, could have challenged Microsoft," and so on. This is a vast over-simplification of the process that underlies Linux development. The Linux community, having mastered open source development, may go on to master open spec program management, open lab testing, and open SDK evangelism. Back in the early days of artificial intelligence, there was a lot of sneering about what artificial intelligence would never be able to do: a computer could never beat a human in chess, never correct English grammar, etc. As each of these milestones was attained, the naysayers raised the bar higher, claiming that they had been confused before—"Beating a human in chess isn't really artificial intelligence." Although nobody would say that computers now have the intelligence of a human, as each artificial intelligence milestone is reached the possibility becomes less remote. A similarly dangerous attitude exists at Microsoft about Linux: it will never be used in the home, it will never be used to run a business. As each of these milestones is achieved, the bar is again revised upwards, but each time you have to wonder a little more about when exactly the Linux open source community is going to reach its peak—and whether that peak will be lower than Microsoft's.

*   *   *

One thing that has intrigued me about the rise of Linux is the refusal of almost everyone in the open source community to acknowledge the contributions of Microsoft. Microsoft did a lot of work designing and evangelizing Windows, whose accessibility to novice users and vast application support caused an explosion in the amount of hardware sold. This allowed hardware vendors to keep driving prices down to the point where the hardware used to run Linux became as affordable as it now is. In the mid-1990s, Microsoft started including TCP/IP with its operating systems. TCP/IP is the fundamental network protocol used to communicate over the Internet, and it is quite a complicated piece of code. The company helped define the winsock API specification, which took the Unix sockets API (which is the standard way that people write applications that communicate over a TCP/IP network) and moved it over to NT and Windows 95. This enabled anybody writing an application that used TCP/IP services—such as a Web browser—to assume that those services were available on any system running NT or Windows 95. This in turn allowed companies like America Online to drive the Internet into the home and create the massive upgrade in Internet infrastructure that allowed the open source movement to prosper. Will hardware functionality keep going up, and prices keep going down, if Microsoft goes away? Despite this, Microsoft is viewed as the great evil by the open source community, and the downfall of Microsoft is one of its goals. (Eric Raymond, to his credit, has consistently stated that all he wants is "software that doesn't suck" and is anti-Microsoft only to the extent that he feels it prevents this; but many other open source advocates are not so charitable.)

As someone who spent seven years working on various versions of Windows NT, what especially frustrates me about Linux is that poor decisions by Microsoft led to its rise. First there was the basic decision to ignore Unix and focus on OS/2 and Novell. Way back in 1994 Gordon Bell was warning the NT team that Unix was the real operating system competition. In October 1997, after being prodded by my father who was having trouble getting his NT machine integrated into the mostly Unix network at McGill University, I sent email to the NT marketing team asking how come NT had such lame network interoperability with Unix. The answer was that it just wasn't worth the expense of improving it (to which I responded, in a rare moment of prescience, that my father and other university types "were seriously thinking about Linux").

Worse, the marketing message that Microsoft concocted about Windows 95 and Windows NT being part of the same family (and later, about Windows 98 and Windows 2000 being part of the same family) obscured the underlying strength of NT. As someone who spent many years working on the core components of NT, I find this annoying. The core architecture of NT is arguably superior to that of Linux—it is certainly no worse—but Microsoft's marketing has completely hidden this fact. Instead the marketers go on about new features added with each release, which have actually destabilized the product because of the amount of new code required. Somebody in marketing heard that Windows 2000 had 31 million lines of code in it and decided to start trumpeting this as a feature—until competitors began playing that up as 31 million chances for bugs in the code.

Another bonehead move, in my book, was the renaming of Windows NT to Windows 2000. Windows 2000 is nothing more or less than Windows NT, version 5.0, with a new name. To fit it into the Windows "family," the name was changed to "Windows 2000, powered by NT technology." The idea was to present Windows 2000 as just another upgrade from Windows 98, but it winds up making it sound like some unholy merger of Windows NT and Windows 98, which is not a great thing given the reputation Windows 98 has for crashing. Moreover, if someone is trying to find a third-party driver for some new hardware, and they have one diskette with Windows 98 drivers and one with Windows NT drivers, which one will they assume works on Windows 2000? Probably the Windows 98 one, which will lead to a frustrated customer and likely a call to Microsoft phone support.

My greatest peeve with Microsoft's handling of NT concerns the command prompt. Microsoft made a conscious decision to require that many operations be performed only from a graphical user interface instead of from a command prompt. The whole existence of a command prompt in NT has been downplayed. I personally prefer using it for most operations, as do many power users. Just as one example, when my kids play on the computer, I like to slow the speed of the mouse motion. To do this I click Start, then Settings, then Control Panel, then Mouse (a double click), then the Motion tab, then move the little slider. To put it back, I do the same thing again. If NT had decent command-line tools, I would be able to type a single short command to set the mouse speed.

Beyond emasculating the command prompt, Microsoft went out of its way to belittle it. In Windows 3.1/95/98, there is what is known as the "DOS box," which lets you run DOS applications using the DOS command-line interface. The NT command prompt uses an extension of the command set of the DOS command line. It also does a lot more: It can launch Windows applications, and more importantly it can launch Win32 "console mode" applications, which use an NT-specific API to allow applications that are character-based as opposed to GUI-based but that can still take over the full screen of the command prompt's windows. As an example, the editor I use does this. It allows me to bring up the editor quickly without having to jump to a separate graphical window. The editor replaces the command prompt, then when you exit the editor the command prompt reappears in its place. The API is also useful for someone porting an application from Unix, which has console windows that operate in a similar fashion. Unfortunately, a decision was made for the first version of NT that the command prompt would be given the same icon as the Windows 3.1 (and later Windows 95 and 98) DOS box—a small version of the MS-DOS logo. So this extremely slick command prompt got marketed as merely a means to run DOS applications.

In the summer of 1999, author Neal Stephenson wrote an essay called "In the Beginning was the Command Line," which discusses open source and the history of operating systems. In it he describes the perfect operating system:

> The ideal OS for me would be one that had a well-designed GUI that was easy to set up and use, but that included terminal windows where I could revert to the command line interface, and run GNU software, when it made sense. A few years ago, Be Inc. invented exactly that OS. It is called the BeOS.

He later points out that Linux also works like this. He correctly states that Windows NT can't do this. What he may not realize is that NT is about 99% of the way there. The "terminal windows" he refers to are NT command prompts. All that is missing is the "GNU software," which is a set of standard command-line applications that have evolved on the Unix platform (GNU stands for "GNU's Not Unix" and was designed to be a version of Unix that anyone is free to run, copy, study, and change). The GNU tools are available for NT, but they are not bundled by Microsoft. But the GNU stuff is the little tiny top of the pyramid—everything else he wants is in NT. Now, if Stephenson, who is a smart guy and an experienced user, can't figure out what your product does, you have to wonder about the job your marketing team is doing.

I'm not the only NT developer who complained about design decisions like this, but the answer from program management was always that we were not the typical user and we should pipe down. This was probably why my "internal open source" idea never got any adherents in management—heaven forbid if the user interface was modified to suit the warped needs of developers!! Never mind that the most important audiences for Microsoft's software—the third-party software developers it is trying to get to write applications for the NT platform, the college students it is trying to hire, the current Microsoft developers it is trying to retain, and the technical people who advise regular users on what software to buy—are also warped in the same ways.

* * *

The big new concept for Microsoft's software is that it should "just work." If the user plugs in a new piece of hardware, the system should automatically detect it and start using it (so-called "plug and play"). If the user wants to do a complicated task such as setting up a Web server, there should be a simple program (known as a "wizard") that asks a few questions and then does all of the detailed configuration work for them. On Linux, on the other hand, such operations may require many distinct steps, each of which accomplishes a small part of the task.

The "it just works" idea works well for novice users, who need to be given simple task-based choices. On the other hand, for a more sophisticated user who is trying to run a business, "it just works" is nice when it works, but awful when it doesn't. If you have one big wizard to configure your Web server, and after you hit the "Finish" button it pops up halfway through with some obscure message such as "Could not contact primary DNS server," what do you do? Do you try the whole operation again? Is it okay to redo the first half of it? What part failed, and how do you fix it? In the same situation using Linux, you are probably following a list of distinct actions that someone else figured out. It is not obvious why you have to do each one, but you don't care. If a particular piece fails, you know exactly where things went wrong. And when you get it working, you know exactly where in the set of steps you need to pick up again.

Consider the "TV/VCR" button on the remote control of a VCR. Do most people know what this button does? Do they know why the TV/VCR button is associated with the VCR, not the TV? All they know is that if they are trying to watch TV and the channel is fuzzy and the VCR is on, pressing TV/VCR usually fixes it.

Now consider a TV/VCR combination unit. These do not have a TV/VCR button. Why? They don't need one. Because everything is integrated, a combination unit can figure out that when a tape is playing it should show the tape output, and when it isn't, it should show the TV. When the TV and VCR are separate devices, there is not enough communication between them to allow the VCR to tell the TV whether it should be tuning a signal onto channel 3 or 4 of its output, or passing the input cable signal through unchanged (which is what the TV/VCR button actually controls). So the integrated TV/VCR is better because it removes the need for the TV/VCR button. But imagine that it stops working in some way: say that when you press record, all you get is fuzz. With a separate TV and VCR, you can do some debugging yourself; you can swap in a second VCR, or try a different TV, or replace the cables, and so on, to at least narrow down what is going on. With the combo unit, all you can do is bring the whole thing in to the shop.

Now imagine a TV that has a cable box, a satellite dish, and a VCR hooked up. You want to record a satellite program on the VCR while watching a cable channel on the TV. Do you know how to set this up? Is it even possible? There exist fancy remote controls that let you select a task, such as "Record from satellite to VCR," with a single button, and then emit the correct codes to tell all the different components what to do. When these work, they are very nice, but they tend to be very dependent on starting in a known state—if the VCR is on rather than off when you press one of the magic buttons, it may not work. Then what do you do? If you control each component individually and are aware of what signal is flowing down each cable, it may take a little more work to set up each task. But at least when something goes wrong you have a prayer of figuring out why.

The NT model is the one using the magic buttons on the remote, and the Linux model is the one where you do each task by hand (at least as Linux is currently designed; this distinction is not due to Linux's status as an open source project, but rather to the fact that the "designers" of

Linux—to the extent that it has any—are the programmers who are writing the code). You trade off ease of use in most cases against a much harder time when things don't work. In the case where the user of the system is a computer person as opposed to a novice, and the system needs to have problems fixed as soon as possible, the Linux model—in which you have a TV/VCR button *and* know what it really does and when to press it— works much better.

12

Evil Empire

For as long as I worked at Microsoft, there were people out there who hated the company with a passion. In 1992, in a discussion in the Usenet newsgroup comp.os.os2.advocacy, someone wrote:

> Personally, I'm starting to care less and less who wins the PC OS war, but with every passing MS message I receive I hope more and more that it's IBM for no other reason than to put MS out of business. Tell me, do all of you go to the same arrogance school? (where the hell you get this arrogance from after producing shit like DOS and Windows is far beyond me).

In 1995, in the same newsgroup, someone wrote:

> No, I have NEVER expected to see innovation out of Redmond, I don't ever expect to see innovation from there either.

And another person complained:

```
I have to work all day long with some of
these members of the Microsoft cult and some
of them are just: Damn stupid arrogant
pseudo computer-literate weenies who think
they know everything about computers.
```

In Hadi Partovi's 1994 internal memo about university students' attitudes towards Microsoft, the standard diatribes were heard: "Microsoft is not making any cool products," "Microsoft isn't doing what's best for technology per se, but only what's best for them," and the inevitable "Microsoft's success has been, and continues to be, based upon marketing and timing superiority, not technical superiority" (and that was from a professor!).

Today the Web is crawling with anti-Microsoft sites. It is easy to find them; you need only do a search for strings like "Micro$oft," "Mickeysoft," "Microshaft," "Microsloth," "Windoze," "Winblows," and so on. These pages repeat the same accusations, and as a Microsoft employee you mostly laughed at them. These people don't merely "dislike" Microsoft; they hate it with a passion. They hate Microsoft products, and if they met you and found out you worked for Microsoft, they would probably spit in your drink and kick your dog for good measure. Above all, they hate Bill Gates and dream of a day when he is forced to live in poverty as payment for his alleged sins.

What is causing such venom?

It has been strange watching from within as Microsoft's reputation has evolved over the last decade. Back in 1990 when I first started working there, the general public was completely unaware of the company. Within the computer software industry, Microsoft was seen as having a very solid niche in operating systems, and competing fitfully in various other areas. There was very little of the "big bad Microsoft" sentiment that exists now. Some people liked OS/2 better than DOS, but there was not a sense that DOS was an abomination that was preventing something better from being used. The Macintosh had its faithful adherents, who considered their operating system vastly superior to DOS (which it was), but Microsoft made a line of successful applications for the Macintosh (in fact Microsoft enjoyed a dominant position in Macintosh applications, in contrast to PC applications), so Mac users generally were not anti-Microsoft, just anti-DOS. People who used Unix systems sneered at the entire personal computer industry, not at Microsoft specifically. In areas such as databases and networking software, Microsoft was the scrappy upstart, not the entrenched monopoly.

So why nowadays is Microsoft referred to as the "Evil Empire"—and why are there so many detractors to begin with? The main arguments against Microsoft can be summarized as follows:

- Microsoft makes bad software.
- Microsoft doesn't invent anything.
- Microsoft's success is based purely on marketing, not technology.
- Microsoft's success is based entirely on momentum from IBM's choice of DOS back in 1982.
- Microsoft misled software developers about OS/2.
- Microsoft is an unfair, unethical company.

Let's discuss each of these.

Microsoft makes bad software. This can be split into three sub-arguments: (1) Microsoft makes software that crashes a lot, (2) Microsoft makes software that is big and slow, and (3) Microsoft makes software that people don't like.

Microsoft software *does* crash. People who are critical of the way software works like to make analogies, for example claiming that if Microsoft made cars, the steering wheel would randomly come off, the radio would work intermittently, and the hood would fly open on the highway.

As a programmer, it is hard to defend buggy software without sounding guilty. Software people like to think that they are smart, and it is likely that most of them are; I don't think that software is buggy because programmers are bad at what they do. When you get right down to it, all you can do is wave your hands and sputter that software design is difficult in ways unlike other consumer products.

Many bugs in software do not occur in the individual components that each developer writes, but rather in the interactions between different components. This is because it is much easier to test individual components than to test the interactions, which are so complex that the only way to test them effectively is to actually use the program under real-life conditions. If you are designing a piece of code that exports an API, you can write another piece of test code that calls your API in various ways. When you run that test code, you will probably find bugs in your real code, but you can fix those before you declare that your code is done. As more and more pieces of code are merged together and need to be tested as a unit, the amount of work you need to do to create a valid test for them becomes much larger.

In the real world, you can make things stronger than they need to be. If you are designing a bolt to hold two pieces of car together, you can make it twice as thick as it needs to be. This notion of "twice as strong" doesn't exist in software the way it is written right now. You could try to add some more code to make it "stronger," but then you have more software that might have its own bugs. Problems in car design boil down to the properties of well-known components like steel and rubber.

Certainly cars do have bugs that appear during testing. New engines blow up when they are stressed the first time. When this happens with physical products, you can go in and see what failed, what is bent or burned or broken. Software often fails in ways that leave very little information about what happened. So even when you have a good test set up that does catch a problem, you might not be able to figure out what happened and prevent it from happening again.

Software is a young industry. It is possible that in the future it will become more like engineering and less like art, and thus more reliable.

The fact remains that you can write software that does anything—the thing you want to do, and everything else that you don't want to do.

There exists complicated software that does have high reliability. The software controlling telephone systems rarely fails. Software controlling spaceships rarely fails, although when it does, as with the Mars Climate Observer, it is spectacularly obvious. Microprocessor chips, which to my mind are even more complicated than software, generally work. This amazes me, because in addition to software-like complexity, microprocessors also have the possibility of physical failures—a bad batch of silicon may cause a good design not to work, just like a bad batch of steel may make a well-designed car fail.

What successful software like this has is a very long period of testing before it is installed on the real phone network or launched into space. Now you get into the realm of Microsoft's practices, in particular the question of whether the company tests its software enough before it ships. People hear that Microsoft's software ships with hundreds or thousands of known bugs and are appalled by this. Can't the developers just fix them all from the get-go?

People say that they would rather wait to get their software if it will mean fewer bugs. What they mean is, fewer bugs *that will affect them*. They don't care about bugs they never come across. When Microsoft ships software, it is making a calculated decision that the bugs that exist are less important than the benefits of shipping then—that Microsoft will make users more unhappy by delaying the software than it will by shipping in its current state. This means the bugs that exist are either so minor that they won't affect people, or they are so esoteric and hard to reproduce that users are unlikely to be affected.

This is a judgment call. I think it is true that Microsoft often devotes too much time to adding features and not enough to ensuring software stability. Unfortunately this is something you can only know at the end of the development process, when you see the ship deadline approaching and the product is not ready. There is something about the nature of software and the attitude of developers that makes this happen over and over, as if the lesson is never learned.

When Windows 95 shipped, everyone at Microsoft was worried about a "killer bug," something the press would play up to emphasize the flaws in the new operating system. The assumption inside the company was that the press would pick some bug and label it a killer bug, just to have one to talk about. But Windows 95 shipped with no killer bug, real or invented. It had flaws, but there was no easy way to lose data, no entire class of machines that it wouldn't install on, no common scenario that it failed to handle. The visibility of Windows 95 forced Microsoft to be extra careful and lock down the feature set earlier, and the results showed.

This is the key. If you don't add too many features, you can stabilize your software with each successive release. Unfortunately, Microsoft has demonstrated an addiction to making wholesale changes to things that are not broken. For example, the user interface of the operating system changed dramatically with Windows 3.0, in 1990. It changed again completely with Windows 95, in 1995. It changed again with Windows 98 when the browser was integrated (although in a way that was less evident to the user), and when I left Microsoft in the spring of 2000, plans were afoot to completely redo it again for a future release.

This constant changing annoys users who are used to the old way. Microsoft will solicit user feedback on a new UI, see that people like it, and decide to change to it. To the people pushing the new UI, it seems natural and much more user-friendly than the older version—the perfect UI that they've always wanted (naturally, since they designed it)! This is like making API changes, where the cost of getting rid of the old way is not considered. People liked New Coke, until they realized that Old Coke was going away. Users perceive this sort of gratuitous change as arrogant, suggesting that Microsoft's attitude is that it knows what is best for users and if they like their old UI, it is because they are Luddites who don't know any better.

Worse, a major change like this throws away all the work that has been done stabilizing the old code and brings in a whole new set of bugs. The statement has been made that it takes Microsoft three tries to get something right—that the third release of a product will be the first one that works well. This is not a hard-and-fast rule, but there is a lot of truth to it. In the first release of a product, you need to make it work; there is no simple "feature" that can be cut, so you wind up rushing to finish and seeing your schedule inevitably slip and leaving out all sorts of minor things. In the second release you can finish up all the things you left out of the first. Finally, in the third release, you can add features that users have requested from their experience with the first two versions, and since you have a stable base to begin with, you can be much better about cutting features in order to ship on time. So the third release can be nice and stable and also have added features that users want. If Microsoft never lets its software get to a third release without major changes, it will never reach this stage.

Microsoft has to make a call about when to ship a piece of software, balancing bugs against delays. The results were sometimes embarrassing to me, as an employee. But what really frustrated me was when users complained that Microsoft did not care about buggy software, that developers didn't take pride in their work, that Microsoft was arrogant and thought it could force-feed users inferior software.

Sometimes, however, I wonder if users have a point. When Microsoft shipped Word 97, it changed the file format from what it was with Word 95. So a file created by the new version could not be read by the old version, and there was not even an option to save it in the old format! The explanation given was that the old format had some fundamental flaws that prevented new functionality that was desired in Word 97. I have no reason to doubt that. What worries me is that nobody seemed to realize what an issue this would be for users. The effect of the change was that once an organization started rolling out Word 97 to some users, it had to roll it out to all of them quickly, or half the people wouldn't be able to read files from the other half. This happened within Microsoft first, when people started running betas of Word 97, but at Microsoft, Word 97 was free and easy to install off the corporate network. A cynic would claim that when this decision was being debated, the fact that it would hasten adoption of Word 97 was a major factor in deciding to go ahead with the plan. It is hard for me to argue against that. This lack of empathy with real-world users is startling, depressing, and worrisome.

People should also understand that the openness of the Windows platform, the driver support for the wide variety of hardware, the plummeting price of computers, the wide variety of applications, and the slight instability of the result are all tied together. Think back to Comdex/Spring in 1982, when everybody sold complete systems. I'm sure they were stable, because the testing matrix—the number of possible different configurations of hardware and software that had to be tested—was so small. Relative to today's machines, they also cost a fortune for the performance they provided. Microsoft expends a huge amount of energy before an operating system ships making sure that every application and every driver work on it. But inevitably, with such a huge, loosely controlled variety of software out there, there will be some that don't get tested, or that can't be made to work.

The second claim about Microsoft making bad software is that its products are big and bloated. DOS 1.0 fit on a single 160K floppy; Windows 2000 is having trouble fitting on a single CD-ROM, which holds more than 4,000 times as much data. In an interview in the very first issue of *PC Magazine* in 1982, Bill Gates predicted this:

> In five years the cost of computation will really be effectively decreased. We'll be able to put on somebody's desk, for an incredibly low cost, a processor with far more capability than you could ever take advantage of. Hardware in effect will become a lot less interesting. The total job will be in the software, and we'll be able to write big fat programs. We can let them run somewhat inefficiently

because there will be so much horsepower that just sits there.

I don't consider that to be bad. Windows 2000 may be 4,000 times as big as DOS, but the size of a standard hard drive has grown by the same amount. People who get misty-eyed for the "good old days" of DOS probably don't remember what it was like. When applications for DOS first came out, one of the questions reviewers had was, "If I go to save my file on a floppy, and there is no floppy in the drive, will the program prompt me to put in a floppy, or will it crash and lose all my data?" It took a few years before users could stop worrying about that. When buying an application, you had to check whether the application supported your printer, because there were no generic printer drivers in the operating system (not to worry: most application manuals included handy documentation on defining your own application-specific printer drivers, if you had a spare afternoon). People using modems had to remember the Hayes modem command set (all together now— "ATDT,5551212") to make calls.

Software is a lot bigger now, but it does a lot more. When the first version of WordStar, the most popular word processor of the day, came out, it literally took a few seconds to scroll down each time you hit "Page Down," and all the program displayed was plain text characters. Nowadays Word can scroll so blindingly fast that it annoys me, and that is while doing onscreen "what you see is what you get" formatting, and also occasionally displaying the annoying wiggling paper clip.

People claim that Microsoft is doing this to force people with old computers to buy new ones, with faster processors and bigger hard drives, which will generate at least a new sale of the operating system. Or that the company is ignoring folks who have old computers when it piles on new features. They claim that since you can use a car for 10 years, why not a computer? But while cars may get a little better with each model year, computers are doubling in capability every few years. If you aim your products at people with computers that are five years old, you are cheating the users of new ones of features they could have. There are good reasons to stop stuffing in new features—they can make new versions slip past their planned ship dates, they can destabilize the software—but in this particular case I agree with what Microsoft has done. In any case, it appears that the limit on how many bells and whistles you can stuff into a word processor or spreadsheet has been reached, and the focus now is on collaborative features and the Internet. Of course, major advances such as speech recognition may cause program sizes to balloon again in just a few years.

As an aside, Bill is often quoted as having said, back in 1981, that 640K of memory—roughly 1% of what a typical computer has now—ought to be enough for anyone. This would have been a very shortsighted opinion, but in fact nobody has ever provided specifics on when or where he said it, and he himself denies saying it. I think the *PC Magazine* quote about "big fat programs" makes it unlikely that he ever said it. In the same article he does say, talking about the 8088 microprocessor found in the original IBM PC, that it is a 16-bit microprocessor, as opposed to the 8-bit ones of the day, and that "16-bits is extremely important, and it is not because of speed…the main reason for the 16-bit micro being advantageous is its increased address space," meaning how easy it is for programmers to use more memory. Later he says, "The logical address space limit…is for all practical purposes gone away. The chip is designed to address a megabyte." Thus you could argue that he felt that one megabyte (which is 1024K) was enough for anybody, but he never explicitly said that.

The final rant against Microsoft software is that people don't like the way it works. They point to things like the paper clip assistant in Office. That paper clip annoys me too, but I figure I am a more technical user, like most of the people putting up anti-Microsoft Web pages. I have, more or less, complete confidence that the people who designed the paper clip did studies and determined that this was something users liked. There are reasons not to change things like this, since every time you change your user interface too much you confuse people who were used to the old way.

But I trust (I think) that such concerns were also taken into account when deciding to make a change. Matters of taste are hard to debate.

Microsoft doesn't invent anything. The argument is that Microsoft is merely a "fast follower" that takes the ideas of others and improves them. I have a hard time seeing this as anything more than an excuse to complain. Did Ferrari invent the car? Did Sony invent the television? Did Dell invent the personal computer?

In most industries, people accept that there is one standard, *somebody* invented it, and everyone else uses it and competes on other merits. The standard has weight, and people don't try to overcome it. Only in the computer industry do people try to reinvent everything and then claim that this is a good thing and they should be applauded for all their inventiveness.

This argument can be shot down without even getting into the issue of whether any of the myriad things Microsoft has done over the years qualifies as an "invention," whatever the boundary of that is. Look at all of Microsoft's competitors. Take Netscape in particular, which briefly was considered the leader of the anti-Microsoft forces and its leader, Marc Andreessen, the boy wonder of Silicon Valley. What did Netscape invent? Netscape is remarkable for having, in its admittedly short lifetime, invented absolutely nothing at all. It didn't invent the Web browser, or the HTML language, or the HTTP or TCP/IP network protocols, or the winsock API, or open source development. It certainly didn't lay any cable or phone lines, or write any operating systems, or design any hardware. It did not do any of the work on the software and hardware that is the backbone of the Internet. It took advantage of all those things to make some good products—which to me is just fine; but how come the people who complain about Microsoft are silent on the subject of Netscape?

A search of the U.S. Patent & Trademark Office's online bibliographic database in August 2000 reveals that since August 12, 1997 (the date Netscape first had a patent granted), Netscape was granted 34 patents.

Microsoft was granted 1,041. Now, many software patents are dubious, and consist of simply patenting whatever logic is in the software you worked on, instead of some breakthrough. Some companies may refuse to file patents unless they cover "real" inventions. But a quick perusal of Netscape's patents reveals no particular nobility of this sort. It's not like Netscape was patenting the wheel and fire and Microsoft was patenting a new mouse cursor.

Netscape did invent one great thing, which was its name. Because it was repeated so often, nobody stopped to marvel at what a great word it was. If the company had not glommed it, it could easily have entered the language as a cyberspace equivalent of "landscape." Imagine this prose from a techno-thriller of the near future: "Meanwhile, back at the server farm, Abe the admin sharpened his packet filter. He surveyed the glowing netscape and growled, 'I don't like the look of them ICMP redirects!'" Unfortunately Netscape sold out to America Online and the name disappeared.

Sure, Netscape wrote a better browser back in 1994 and did a lot to create excitement about and popularize the Internet. In the process Netscape scared the pants off Microsoft, and more power to it for that. Netscape shipped a lot of software in a hurry and it worked, for the first few years anyway. But the only thing Netscape actually invented was the super-hyped Internet IPO—which is certainly worthy of being considered a major invention, but I don't think it's the kind under discussion here. Oh, and it may also have invented the competitive strategy of ratting on Microsoft to the government.

Did Lotus invent the spreadsheet? Did WordPerfect invent the word processor? Did America Online invent bulletin boards or chat rooms? Did Sun invent Ethernet, or Unix, or middleware, or the childish CEO?

Then there is IBM. Now, IBM invented a ton of stuff. IBM even has people doing pure research. Imagine that, a for-profit company funding pure research. Who else in the industry does that? Besides Microsoft, I mean.

Microsoft's success is based purely on marketing, not technology. This argument is partly meant as a slap in the face to the technical competence of Microsoft, and is often stated as such: "Neener neener, you are a marketing company, not a technology company." Success due to marketing is seen as impure and implies that the company is pulling a sucker job foisting off bad technology on unsuspecting users. I think everyone misstates this argument. Do they really claim Microsoft's success is based on *marketing?* I suppose my opinion of Microsoft's marketing department is tainted by my technical bent, because every time I looked, it seemed marketing people were misstating a technical issue in the press. Marketing was what drove the name change from Windows NT 5.0 to Windows 2000. Microsoft's marketing team does a lot of good work, but it is behind the scenes—making it easier for large corporations to buy software, say. To me the public face of Microsoft marketing is not very impressive.

I think what people mean when they say Microsoft's success is based on marketing is that its success is based on something other than the pure merits of the software. In searching for a name for this nebulous entity, they seize on "marketing" for lack of a better term. What they really mean is that Microsoft's success is based on public relations, OEM sales, and evangelism.

Microsoft certainly is aggressive in its public relations. At conferences, many of the people in the Microsoft booth are just regular employees who worked on the products being displayed. They are under strict orders not to talk to press people, but instead to direct them to the PR folks buzzing about. At one point, the wife of an employee was going to write an article about an online parenting discussion group that I participated in at Microsoft, to be published in a local parenting newsletter. There was a possibility that she might want to interview me. Not the kind of thing that makes or breaks a corporate image—but nonetheless, unbidden, I got a call from a public relations person, spelling out some quick guidelines, and asking if I wanted her to sit in on the phone call (which in the end never happened).

A few years back, a column began appearing in a local paper, *Eastside Week*, offering an insider look at Microsoft. The author was understandably anonymous, appearing under the byline "Fenster Blick," which means "windows view" in German. The material was pretty tame—a typical column considered the brand of toilet paper used in the bathrooms at Microsoft—but the fact that raw facts were escaping from Microsoft got some people in a tizzy. A mad hunt was launched for Mr. Blick, and within a month, his column mysteriously disappeared. You have to assume that the real Fenster also disappeared from Microsoft's payroll, although nothing was ever revealed. *Eastside Week* itself folded a few months later; a coincidence, I'm sure.

Sales to Original Equipment Manufacturers, or OEMs—companies such as Compaq and Dell that build computers—are another of Microsoft's strengths. When you buy a computer, it almost certainly is running Windows, probably Office, and may have other Microsoft software on it. Microsoft made its money before you even opened the box. When something new like Windows 95 comes along, the battle is won before it ships, when the OEM contracts are signed.

Then there is evangelism, which in my mind (in case you haven't been paying attention) is the single most important thing that Microsoft does. If you win the minds of third-party hardware developers and third-party software developers, so that you are their first choice when they write hardware drivers and applications, you have won the battle to establish your operating system as a standard. If you lose them, you have lost.

What I don't see in all this is what is wrong. Is a company not supposed to market and do PR? Just because the rest of the industry seems to be oblivious to the value of OEM sales and evangelism, should Microsoft stop doing them?

As I said above, there are other reasons beyond technical merit that Microsoft succeeded. But it is false to claim that this automatically negates any claims of technical merit. It is true that, in this day and age, people don't necessarily have the opportunity to choose what operating system, word processor, and so on to use based simply on the intrinsic merits of a bunch of possibilities. But you can't thank or blame Microsoft's alleged marketing machine for this. There are very strong forces (weight, convenience, and so on) pushing toward the rise of one standard operating system to the exclusion of others. Only in a few fairly specialized areas can users "afford" to pick Macintosh over Windows (graphic design, some parts of publishing, some scientific work), or Unix over Windows (some academics and some programmers). For most people the inefficiencies of doing so are too great. Sure, Microsoft worked hard to ensure that this one standard turned out to be its standard and not somebody else's, but it didn't create the standardizing forces, which are way beyond any one company's control. And even if you buy the arguments made in the Justice Department lawsuit about how Microsoft allegedly maintained its monopoly illegally, none of them have to do with how the company marketed its software.

Microsoft's success is based entirely on momentum from IBM's choice of DOS back in 1982. Essentially, this means that IBM helped Microsoft get a lead and grow into a big company, and it has been living off its sheer size ever since.

First of all, Microsoft was a successful, five-year-old company before IBM chose it; that's why IBM did so. There is no reason to suggest Microsoft could not have continued being a successful vendor of language products, and later branched into operating systems and applications. IBM had originally approached Digital Research about making CP/M the standard operating system for the IBM PC, but Digital Research turned down the offer (the story is that the legal agreement IBM wanted Digital Research to sign was too strict for its tastes).

Microsoft certainly jumped on that opportunity with both feet, as it has many others. But Microsoft also made moves to aggressively evangelize the platform, a strategy that nobody else understood at the time. If

Microsoft had simply sat back and coasted after getting the IBM contract, it would never have reached the size it was by 1990, when Windows 3.0 came out.

Was it just pure size after that? Does Microsoft stomp in and crush everyone? An August 23, 1998, article in the *Seattle Times* newspaper is typical. Discussing Microsoft's travails with the Microsoft Network (MSN) Internet access service, it starts out, "When Microsoft eyes a new business, it typically swoops in with unparalleled technical and marketing muscle, and swiftly takes over." Later in the article, the vice president of marketing for the Internet portal Lycos, Jan Horsfall, is quoted as saying, "I think Microsoft gained an appreciation that the Internet is not the same thing as the software business. This is about more than simply throwing a lot of money at something, or throwing a lot of people at something."

Both these quotes reflect the belief that the standard Microsoft play is to move in with a lot of resources and quickly dominate. The only problem with this attitude is that it is exactly wrong. Look at all the areas where Microsoft has been successful: word processors, spreadsheets, database software, networking software, software development tools. In *every* one of those areas, Microsoft took on entrenched competitors and worked hard for years and years to win the battle. At the core of any of these victories was the actual software that was shipped, not the size of the company.

MSN was a situation where Microsoft got stupid, did not do its homework, and tried to swagger in and take over quickly with mediocre software—and promptly fell flat on its face. As a result of this lack of preparation, MSN missed a golden opportunity in early 1997, when America Online switched from charging an hourly rate to charging a flat monthly fee and could not handle the load, leading to class-action lawsuits. Unfortunately MSN was not able to extend the welcome mat to those disgruntled users. So the analysis quoted above is correct in its take on MSN, but the parallel with Microsoft's other successes is false. The problem was not that Microsoft's behavior with MSN was like its behavior with packaged software—the problem was that its behavior was so different.

In operating systems, Microsoft certainly got a gigantic boost from IBM's choice of DOS. But it has had many competitors over the years in operating systems alone, and has fended them all off. Microsoft engineered two shifts in programming paradigm, to 16-bit Windows and then to 32-bit Windows, in direct competition with IBM. At this point I think it is safe to say that Microsoft is maintaining its momentum on its own.

Microsoft misled software developers about OS/2. The 1990 "divorce" from IBM seemed to create the first batch of rabid anti-Microsofties. Microsoft was viewed as abandoning a superior technology, OS/2, in favor of an inferior one, Windows. In addition, the company was accused of having intentionally misled software developers down the OS/2 path—the ultimate crime of bad-faith evangelism. This led to a raging battle in the Usenet newsgroups between the OS/2 and Microsoft faithful (examples of which were quoted at the beginning of this chapter). As a Microsoft employee (and occasional contributor to this debate), this didn't bother me very much. The OS/2 debacle was not the result of any master plan of Microsoft's.

When I started at Microsoft I was working on LAN Manager, which was a networking product that ran on top of OS/2. I can truthfully testify that the LAN Manager team was genuinely aligned with OS/2 at the time, and thought Windows was some annoying product that wouldn't go away. (LAN Manager was co-developed with IBM, and I can also testify that working with IBM was a nightmare.) The Systems group at Microsoft was investing heavily in OS/2, and dropping it was traumatic. It wasn't just losing OS/2 itself, but the effect this had on products like LAN Manager and SQL Server, which ran on top of OS/2.

When I started working on NT in early 1990, before the divorce, it was being called "NT OS/2"—the plan was to sell it as a more robust version of OS/2, not a more robust version of Windows. The internals of the system were new, but the user interface and API were meant to mirror those of OS/2. Only after the split with IBM did it get recast as "Windows NT," with the UI and API changed to follow Windows 3.0. Luckily, at that point the internals of the system, which didn't need to change, were the only parts that were far along in development; not a lot of UI and API work on the OS/2 path had to be scrapped, because not a lot had been done. A lot of the former OS/2 developers came over to the NT team, and they were genuinely unhappy with the strategy of dropping OS/2 (although they also knew that the split development between IBM and Microsoft had not been going well).

After the divorce, IBM decided to spruce up OS/2, primarily by announcing support for the Windows API, something that Microsoft had been trying to get IBM to do all along. Now Microsoft really looked guilty. After all, right after the divorce, IBM suddenly announced a bunch of improvements to OS/2—so it must have been Microsoft that was holding OS/2 back, right? Thus the debate about OS/2 versus Windows raged on. Of course I was working on NT, which I considered to be superior to *both* Windows and OS/2, so I felt that Microsoft as a whole had nothing to be ashamed of.

Microsoft is an unfair, unethical company. One of the main complaints about Microsoft in the computer industry is that it practices FUD, short for Fear, Uncertainty, and Doubt. According to industry lore, the term originated after the principal architect of the IBM System 360 mainframe computer, Gene Amdahl, left IBM and in 1970 founded a company called Amdahl that made clones of IBM mainframes and parts. IBM salesmen, when asked about Amdahl equipment, would not lie and say it wouldn't work. What they would do was roll their eyes a bit and say, Well, Amdahl makes fine equipment, but you know, IBM doesn't test its stuff with Amdahl's stuff, and it might work now, but who knows if it will work with something later. So, in the customers' own best interest—which was near and dear to the salesman's heart—wouldn't they sleep easier if they had genuine IBM equipment all across the board?

What they were doing was creating fear, uncertainty, and doubt that the Amdahl equipment wouldn't work, and ultimately, that the person who chose Amdahl over IBM would get fired when things went wrong. There is an old saying, "Nobody ever got fired for buying IBM." Still, you can only FUD for so long. Eventually *someone* was going to buy an Amdahl machine, if only because it was so much cheaper, or perhaps because they didn't like their IBM salesman (although IBM had a very, very good sales force). When it worked, they might tell a friend, and soon the inevitability of IBM would begin to be chipped away. Amdahl did in fact prosper and survives to this day, although not as an independent company. In 1997 Fujitsu, which already owned 42 percent of Amdahl, acquired the rest of it.

There is an offshoot of FUD called vaporware, in which you announce products before they are ready. The idea is to freeze out competitors who have already shipped by promising that something better is coming soon, so users should wait to buy it and avoiding committing to a competitor's product in the meantime.

Look back at what Chris Larson said about DOS in *PC Magazine* in 1982. He made some extravagant claims about the product, but he didn't make any claims about its competitor, CP/M-86, being unstable or risky. It doesn't sound like FUD to me, just evangelism. Since he was talking about DOS, which had been available for sale for six months, you can't accuse him of discussing vaporware. He did point out that Microsoft wouldn't port its languages to CP/M-86, but that was an actual fact—he was not rolling his eyes and saying, "Gee, I can't guarantee that Microsoft will port its languages." He was flat out saying it wouldn't.

That later article about the Microsoft/Lifeboat announcement (concerning their anointment of MS-DOS as the 16-bit standard) contains the following, which is not a quote but the author's own analysis: "In truth, both PC-DOS and CP/M-86 are souped-up versions of CP/M-80, enhanced to take advantage of 16-bit microprocessors. However, neither is compatible with CP/M-80 as many are misled into believing. Without translation, CP/M-80 will not run on either CP/M-86 or PC-DOS."

The key points about this are that it is a technical statement, it is not based on anything the people he was quoting said (in fact it contradicts them), and it is 100% correct. This highlights a big change that has come over the mainstream personal computer press in the 1990s.

When you buy a car magazine, you get a sense that the writers are car people—they change their own oil, know what tire size markings mean, probably drive a little too fast. They may not build cars themselves, but they could certainly tell you what each small piece of a car does.

When you buy a personal computer magazine, you get a sense that the writers are not programmers. They are experienced users of computers, and they are intelligent people, but by and large they don't know a lot about how software really works. It's as if you had a car magazine written by people who drive a lot, but don't ever look under the hood.

What this creates—and this is not a justification, just an explanation— is a gigantic opportunity for computer companies to spin the computer press with FUD and vaporware. If Ford issued a press release stating that that they had a new car that would get 150 miles to the gallon and deliver 500 horsepower, the response from the automotive press would be, "Yeah, right! Let's see one." Those writers have enough experience to be skeptical. In the computer industry, you see press releases like that all the time, and they are quickly followed by a rash of articles that are nothing more than restatements of the press release.

I hope I'm not insulting the press too much here. As I said, these writers are smart people, they write well, I'm sure they play games with their kids and give generously to charity. They certainly know more about users' needs than we programmers do. But they are not programmers. The temptation to feed them a line is overwhelming. I recall one column comparing the multi-processor scalability of NT to OS/2. When you upgraded an NT machine from having one processor to four, it ran only 2.8 times faster (or whatever). This information was based on actual tests someone had run on a shipping version of NT. OS/2, it was reported, would run four times faster with four processors. What was the source for this? An IBM press release about a future OS/2 release. I can picture an IBM PR person, writing the press release, weighing the idea of claiming it ran *five* times faster with four processors, to see if anyone noticed.

Even the techno-savvy magazine *Wired*, which you would think would be a little more hip to this sort of thing than most, can be buffaloed this way. In the July 1995 issue, *Wired* had an article discussing the various interactive television trials going on at the time, including Microsoft's. The writer talks about seeing the cable head end that Microsoft has built—which was authentic and was eventually used in a real trial. He is then shown a demo of what the service was supposed to be like for users in their homes. The demo is actually a Visual Basic application, running on a standard PC. It has nothing to do with the code that will eventually be used in the trial. The only "television" aspect of it is that instead of displaying the output on a standard monitor, it is piped into a 50-inch television set. It's not that the author isn't skeptical—the title of the article is "People Are Supposed to Pay for This Stuff?"—it's just that it was shockingly easy to make this Type 4 demo seem like the real thing.

This is not meant to justify FUD and vaporware but to explain why it seems so prevalent—because almost every instance of it is immediately given credence by the press. Is Microsoft guilty of pre-announcing products and then having its plans change later? Sure. Is it more guilty than anybody else in the computer industry? This is a hard question. There are two particular incidents that trouble me about Microsoft: The DR-DOS incident, and the GO incident.

DR-DOS was a clone of MS-DOS, written by Digital Research after it gave up on CP/M-86, which was later sold to Novell. Early versions of Windows ran on top of DOS; the user first booted up DOS and then ran Windows by typing a specific command. Thus, Windows could theoretically run on top of DR-DOS also. In a beta version of Windows 3.1, Microsoft apparently put code in that explicitly checked to see if the user was trying to run Windows on top of DR-DOS, and when it detected this, it put up an ominous error box that stated "Non-fatal error detected, please contact Windows 3.1 beta support." The user was given the option to continue to load Windows, although the default was to stop.

I say "apparently" to avoid prejudgment, because a company called Caldera is currently suing Microsoft over this very issue. (Caldera is none too saintly itself; it did not develop DR-DOS, but rather bought the rights and then used them to sue Microsoft.) I have no special Microsoft-insider knowledge of the details; everything I know is from reading publicly available information. Nonetheless, this looks suspiciously like classic FUD. The code, I will point out, was removed from the shipping version of Windows 3.1. Thus you could argue it was never released to the public.

In the case of GO, a company making a hand-held computer controlled by a pen, Microsoft quickly followed up GO's early 1991 announcement of its Penpoint operating system with an announcement of Windows for Pen computers. This looks like Vaporware 101, since Pen Windows at the time only existed on a few slides. Again, I have no internal knowledge of this. GO CEO Jerry Kaplan documented his side in his excellent book *Startup*. Interestingly, Kaplan viewed Microsoft's vaporware tactics as the #1 problem his company hit, and groused about them repeatedly, even though in my opinion, from reading his book, the main problems were his selection of IBM as a hardware partner, and the fact that the industry wasn't ready for pen computing back in the early 1990s. (When Microsoft did eventually ship Pen Windows, it went nowhere.)

Cases like this make me extremely uncomfortable about proclaiming Microsoft's unconditional innocence. But does this make Microsoft an unfair, unethical company? It was somewhat bothersome to me that when people saw @*microsoft.com* in my email address, they might think that I was unethical. What I would like to believe is that Microsoft is fundamentally good, but (like most companies) has some people who take aggressiveness too far. I never felt that Microsoft was so revolting that I must resign on general principle. I don't think Bill Gates personally ordered that a FUD-y message be put in the Windows 3.1 beta. If it was done, it was done by people who were trying to emulate Bill, but lacked his experience and judgment and crossed the line. I sincerely do not believe that Microsoft is intrinsically a "bad" company. The only person whose motives I can truly know is myself, and I believed that I was writing code to help customers solve problems. It is hard to know what evil lurked in the heart of the guy down the hall, however.

In any case I see no moral superiority in Microsoft's competitors. My father, who used to use Sun hardware, reported that Sun would not repair his Sun workstation unless he had a service contract from Sun, nor would it sell parts to the third-party company that normally serviced his computers. Despite its claims about Java, Sun did not start out in business with a goal of write-once, run-anywhere software (it *did* emphasize networking from the beginning, which was far-sighted and contributed heavily to its success, and it deserves credit for that—but that is a separate issue). Sun recognizes Microsoft as a competitor, and when it discovered Java within its own company it decided to run with it. But it intended to use Java to destroy Microsoft just as much as Microsoft wanted to use Windows to destroy Sun. Both companies wanted software developers to use their platforms, to create weight in applications towards their platforms, at the expense of someone else's.

Nonetheless, Microsoft currently has an image problem. Like Caesar's wife, who had to not only be pure but be seen as pure, Microsoft has to not only be honest, but be seen as honest. Microsoft's bad image has led to several lawsuits, including the massive one by the Justice Department and 19 states.

It has motivated competitors. It has spurred the development of Linux, currently the only credible alternative to Microsoft's operating-system dominance. And it has hurt Microsoft among two key constituencies— college students and developers at other companies—which is hurting it in the two areas that matter most of all: its ability to recruit, and its ability to evangelize.

13

Justice

Despite, or perhaps because of, its success in the market, Microsoft in the 1990s has been under fire repeatedly in the legal arena, causing some Maalox moments for employees.

The first of these was caused by the Apple lawsuit, which was in progress when I joined the company. In 1988 Apple sued Microsoft over the "look and feel" of Windows, claiming that the use of windows, icons, the mouse, and so on was copied from the Macintosh OS. The case hinged on a license that Microsoft had signed in 1985 to use that look and feel in Windows version 1.0. Microsoft was claiming that the license covered future versions of Windows (including the soon-to-be-extremely-popular Windows 3.0), while Apple disagreed. Microsoft had a legal defense, that the agreement was valid, and a moral defense, that both systems had borrowed their look and feel from an earlier system developed at Xerox's PARC research lab, which Xerox had not patented but instead put into the public domain.

This case was worrisome because Windows sure did look a lot like the Macintosh OS, and nobody was familiar with the exact details of the licensing agreement. Had Microsoft really been clever enough—and/or had Apple really been dense enough—to sign an agreement that extended to all future versions? Apple had "home field advantage" because the case was being tried in California. Upper management was reassuring everyone that the case was without merit and Microsoft would win (I was a new, un-cynical employee at the time, so I believed them). In addition, there wasn't the same feeling that Windows was so crucial to Microsoft's success—it had its applications and so on to fall back on, and Windows could perhaps be modified to comply with whatever judgment was handed down. Also, in those days most people were not watching the stock price on a daily basis to see how much their options were worth. This (in retrospect naive) sense of not having that much to lose made the prospect of the lawsuit less terrifying. Ignorance was bliss in this case, although in fact losing this suit could have short-circuited Microsoft's success in the 1990s before it ever started: Apple wanted more in royalties for each copy of Windows sold than Microsoft was earning.

After more than four years, the judge ruled in favor of Microsoft, much to the surprise of some people (particularly people inside Apple, who were reportedly basing their future plans on the assumption that they were going to win). Apple appealed, and the case officially dragged on until Apple got into such dire straits that in 1997 the company needed a $150 million investment from Microsoft to bail itself out. One of the conditions of that investment was that the appeal be dropped.

On the day after the verdict was announced, April 15, 1992, there was a palpable sense of relief around the company. Not veering-away-from-the-precipice relief, more like avoiding-something-that-could-have-been-annoying relief. That day the stock jumped from $117 to $128 7/8 a share, the largest one-day jump since I had joined Microsoft. This was the first time I clued in to the way good news for the company could affect the value of my stock options. A co-worker announced that he was sure the stock had peaked and he had exercised all his options. Of course the stock split two months later, and adjusted for subsequent splits the stock is now trading around $1,700. So locking in an $11 gain looks a little short-sighted in retrospect.

While the Apple lawsuit was still in progress, the U.S. government began its decade-long interest in the doings of Microsoft. First up was the Federal Trade Commission (FTC), whose investigation became public in March 1991. It started from a claim that Microsoft and IBM had conspired back in 1989 to limit the features in Windows, in order to allow OS/2 to succeed. In the interim Microsoft had split with IBM, dramatically enhanced the feature set of Windows, and was in the process of beating IBM over the head with it. The general reaction inside the company was, "What the #@*&?!?" Why would the government care about such an obvious non-issue? Didn't these people understand the software business?

The FTC kept poking around, making employees nervous, because it became apparent that government bodies like the FTC could arbitrarily extend their investigations, once they had started, in any direction that struck their fancy. Then Microsoft's competitors started repeating in public what they told FTC investigators in private. For the first time the press was giving widespread coverage to gripes about Microsoft competing too hard, stealing ideas, and generally playing the heavy in the industry. For me personally, head down trying to ship the first version of Windows NT, this was no big deal, but it made me wonder who had hired the other employees who had supposedly misbehaved so badly.

In February 1993 the FTC decided to take no action. The vote was 2 to 2 with one person not voting—not exactly a ringing endorsement, but a tie in this case went to the runner, and it was back to business as usual.

In January, right before the FTC vote, a company called Stac Electronics sued Microsoft. Stac made a product called Stacker, which allowed users of DOS to compress their disk data, increasing the amount that could be stored on a hard drive. In version 6.0 of DOS, planned for release in early 1993 and already in beta testing, Microsoft had included similar technology to compress the files on a disk, which it called DoubleSpace. Stac claimed that this infringed on its patents.

What was new in this case was that Microsoft took a massive public relations hit. In the Apple case there had been Microsoft detractors making noise, but it had been viewed as a battle among equals, Apple defending its Macintosh franchise against Microsoft. Although the PC market was larger than the Macintosh market, Apple was a bigger company—1990, my first year at Microsoft, was also the first year Microsoft sales exceeded $1 billion, while Apple pulled in over $5 billion that year. There was no disputing that Apple had licensed the look and feel to Microsoft for at least *some* versions of Windows, so the lawsuit seemed to be based on who wrote a better contract, as opposed to outright thievery. And the press was consistent in reporting that the general look and feel had come from Xerox PARC, predating both systems.

The Stac case, in contrast, was immediately played in the press as Microsoft blatantly ripping off technology from a much smaller company. Interestingly, the issue of Microsoft including, for free, a technology that another company was selling—which would be the crucial issue in the Justice Department's 1997 lawsuit against Microsoft—was not the focus of the complaint. It was the reason Stac was suing, but the lawsuit only spoke of the patent issue. And the Justice Department was mum on the whole situation.

As it happens, I was working closely at the time with people involved in the disputed compression code, and I can say that Stac's public relations spin on the case was 100% bunk. Compression technology was a clever idea but it had been around for years, first described in papers by theoretical computer scientists who were not inclined to patent their work. Eventually patents were issued covering the application of the technology, but nobody paid much attention to them. Both Stac and Microsoft went on after-the-fact patent searches to back up their technology, and unfortunately the patent Stac bought was older than the one Microsoft bought.

So even though Microsoft was (in my opinion) completely in the clear morally, Stac had Microsoft dead to rights on the legal issue. In February

1994 Microsoft was ordered by the U.S. District Court to remove the compression technology, leading to the shipment of DOS 6.21 with DoubleSpace removed (with the company all the while loudly proclaiming its innocence). Microsoft began readying a new version of DOS, DOS 6.22, which had compression technology called DriveSpace that was different enough (so Microsoft claimed) that it did not infringe on Stac's patent. Before Stac had a chance to dispute this in court, Microsoft settled the case, buying $40 million in stock and paying $43 million in royalties to make Stac and its lawyers go away. The story I heard was that the OEMs who included DOS with their computers were complaining about the proliferation of multiple versions of DOS, and wanted to know which single operating system they should preinstall on their systems. With OEM sales already a huge business for Microsoft, the payoff to Stac seemed like a pretty good deal to make the OEMs happy, and also prevent future black eyes in the press on this issue.

By then I understood that DOS was Microsoft's cash cow, and that small changes in DOS sales could have a big effect on the company's bottom line— and thanks to the magic of stock options, the company's bottom line had a big effect on my personal bottom line. Still, Microsoft supposedly had a new, non-patent-infringing version of DOS ready to go if it lost its appeal, so what was there to worry about? More grating was watching the press continually paint Microsoft as the big bully picking on small companies. Imagine going to work each day with the faint sound of metal scraping on a blackboard in the background, and you get an idea of what it felt like. Didn't the press understand the software business? Or (more cynically), did it just like picking the angle that made Microsoft look bad?

The Stac suit went away, but the image that lingered on in the collective consciousness was of Microsoft ripping off technology from Stac, directly and intentionally violating a patent on technology that Stac had invented. An article in the business section of the *Seattle Post-Intelligencer* newspaper on March 31, 1999, described the Stac lawsuit as a result of Microsoft "illegally bundling a competitor's technology into its dominant computer operating system." Paying Stac off was proof that Microsoft was guilty as sin. For the first time the image of "big bad Microsoft" had made an appearance. And this incident figures strongly amidst the litany of misbehavior that festers in the minds of Microsoft haters.

Proving that people don't sell stock prematurely only on good news, a co-worker on NT exercised all his options the day the Stac settlement was announced. He had been responsible for writing the DoubleSpace support in Windows NT, and had therefore had the honor of ripping that same code out. When I ran into him years later, he was no longer employed full-time at Microsoft but was back on a part-time assignment, haunting the hallways like the ghost of stock options past. I last saw him leaning his head forlornly against a wall, repeating the price at which he had sold his shares (which was, adjusted for splits, about $5 per share).

Continuing the trend of overlapping private lawsuits and government investigations, in August 1993 the U.S. Department of Justice took over the investigation that the FTC had dropped earlier in the year. To me, this seemed like double jeopardy—being tried twice for the same alleged crime. The main complaint involved how Microsoft sold Windows to OEMs—not the focus of the FTC investigation, but something that had surfaced as part of the general bitching that the FTC dug up. Normally an OEM would sign a license that had them paying Microsoft a certain amount for every computer it shipped with Windows on it. Some OEMs had signed contracts that had them paying a slightly lower amount, but then they were charged for each *computer* they sold—whether or not it had Windows. This gave them a financial disincentive to offer anything other than Windows, since they would be paying for Windows anyway.

I thought those contracts were very clever, to say the least. Did they go a bit too far beyond clever? It seems such arrangements are not uncommon. For example, in the spring of 2000, AT&T used the threat of delayed service and litigation to force King County (which includes Seattle) to allow AT&T to require all customers of its high-speed Internet access in unincorporated areas to pay $39.95 to AT&T's own

Internet Service Provider (ISP), Excite@Home, even if the customer chose a different ISP that charged its own fees. Keep in mind that AT&T was taking advantage of a cable monopoly that was granted, not built up, and was offering no alternative (such as a plan where everyone paid $44.95, say, but only if they actually chose Excite@Home). Microsoft hadn't forced any OEMs to sign the per-computer licenses; the OEMs had signed because at that point in time there was no viable competition to Windows that the OEMs wanted to sell instead, and they were interested in saving a few bucks. In any case the press got up in arms about this, and labeled the consent decree that Microsoft signed to settle the case in July 1994 as a slap on the wrist; the per-computer contracts with OEMs were terminated, but since there was no other operating system that customers wanted, the OEMs all immediately re-signed deals for per-Windows royalties. The consent decree also prohibited "bundling"—OEMs could not be forced to license any other products as a requirement for licensing Windows. Microsoft would still be allowed to develop "integrated" products—wording that became very significant later on.

In October 1994, Microsoft entered into an agreement to acquire Intuit, maker of the Quicken home finance software, among other things. This was one of the few areas where a competitor had been able to stand up to Microsoft; Microsoft had a similar package called Money that was running a distant second in the market. As part of the deal, Microsoft agreed to sell Money to Novell. The Justice Department objected to the deal, claiming it would reduce competition in the software industry.

The feeling inside Microsoft was that the Justice Department was stalling, recognizing that delaying the merger too much would make it fail without ever having to prove the case. Intuit and Microsoft nominally were continuing development on their respective products, but how motivated could Microsoft employees working on Money be, knowing that if the deal went through their work would be sold to Novell (a sworn enemy of Microsoft), and that the lack of success of previous versions of Money was the reason for the deal in the first place? Microsoft attempted to compensate for this by throwing large amounts of morale budget (T-shirts, parties, and whatnot) at the Money development team. Then in May 1995, Microsoft gave up and abandoned the deal, citing the delay as the reason. The feeling internally was that Microsoft had been hosed by the Justice Department, which had it in for Microsoft because competitors were complaining that the July 1994 agreement had been too weak. This was the start of the feeling of martyrdom—that the Justice Department was out to "get" Microsoft—among the company's employees.

Then, in February 1995, U.S. District Judge Stanley Sporkin threw out the consent decree, stating that it was too easy on Microsoft. Loud cheers from the anti-Microsoft forces ensued, but in June, an appeals court reversed Sporkin's decision. A new judge, Thomas Penfield Jackson, was appointed, and in August 1995, three days before the launch of Windows 95, he approved the consent decree. Judge Jackson, of course, was seen as a hero within Microsoft. Finally, a judge who understood the software business!

*   *   *

Imagine what it was like to be at Microsoft as Windows 95 was launched. The company was at the eye of an incredible hurricane of hype. It had just survived two government investigations. The Intuit acquisition had fallen through, but who really cared about that? All systems were go to release Windows 95 and usher in a new age of technology. The company was surfing the crest of the Win32 API paradigm wave, with Windows 95 versions of its main applications ready to roll, and major support from both software and hardware vendors.

Of course, lurking around the corner was the Internet, and its most visible success story, Netscape, which went public two weeks before Windows 95 shipped. Netscape made people at Microsoft nervous, not particularly because of the browser itself, but because of the excitement the browser was generating. Netscape seemed to have understood the lesson that Microsoft had learned—that the critical tasks were to create a platform, get developers (in this case the "developers" were Web page designers) excited about it, and start creating weight for your platform. And suddenly Microsoft was no longer the "cool" place to work. People talked about how Bill Gates wanted to be the next Marc Andreessen, to which everyone at Microsoft thought, "Har de har—I think."

Was Microsoft going to lose its place atop the industry to this scrappy upstart that, when you looked at its products, didn't seem to have done all that much? There was no time to dwell on such mundane matters as competitors, because things never stayed quiet for long around the Microsoft legal department. In September 1996, the fax machines were cranked up again as the Justice Department launched another investigation, claiming that Microsoft was using its monopoly to compete unfairly against Netscape. In October 1997, the department sued Microsoft, claiming the company was violating the 1994 consent decree by requiring OEMs to bundle Internet Explorer with Windows 95. The attorney general, Janet Reno, asked for $1 million in damages per day. In December 1997, Judge Jackson, so recently viewed as a genius, issued an injunction requiring Microsoft to stop bundling Internet Explorer. Now the heat was being turned up a bit more. Microsoft had billions of dollars in the bank, but still, $1 million a day wasn't peanuts. In addition, it looked like this might affect the upcoming launch of Windows 98, the successor to Windows 95, which had the browser built right in.

By April 1998, attorneys general from 13 states were trying to get an injunction to prevent the shipment of Windows 98 (leading to a bumper sticker that appeared around the Microsoft campus: "Windows 98: So Good, the Feds Want to Make it Illegal"). From inside Microsoft, I watched all this legal maneuvering while also keeping tabs on the impending shipment of Windows 98—monitoring the internal bug database to see how close the team was to being done. It appeared that if Microsoft could only get Windows 98 out the door before any legal ruling against it came down, it would be impossible to stop it later. But the release date for Windows 98 slipped, as seems to happen with all operating systems. Panic! The temptation arose to run over to the Windows 98 build lab and try to fix all the bugs myself.

Finally, in May 1998, an appeals court ruled that any antitrust restrictions placed on Windows 95 would not affect Windows 98, and right around that time the new operating system finally shipped. Everyone breathed again, and in June, the preliminary injunction against shipping Internet Explorer with Windows 95 (which was irrelevant by then since Windows 98 had shipped) was also lifted, which was viewed as a rebuke of Judge Jackson.

There was no time to celebrate, though, because also in May, the Justice Department and 20 states had filed a massive antitrust case against Microsoft, claiming that Microsoft was using its Windows dominance to gain market share in other areas and drive competitors out of business.

In addition, Microsoft was being sued by Sun Microsystems over its use of the Java language. Microsoft had signed an agreement in March 1996 to include Java in Internet Explorer, and in October 1997 Sun sued, claiming that the version Microsoft delivered was not compatible with Sun's version as specified in the contract.

I see no reason why the Java language could not be separated from the Java machine abstraction, and people allowed to write Java software that is optimized for Windows. But the case deals with a contract signed at the last minute by two parties who were unsure which one needed the other more, and it is not clear whose side the legal language favors. Sun is certainly no paragon of virtue, and makes no secret of its desire to destroy Microsoft, and it is unfortunate that it may have found a valid legal attack. Sun tried various tactics, such as trying to get an injunction to delay the launch of Windows 98. This failed, but in November 1998 Sun did get a judge to ask Microsoft to remove the offending code from future versions of Windows 98. The case is currently dragging on. Since Java has not taken over the world as Sun hoped, the feeling at Microsoft is that when the case eventually plays itself out, the results won't matter much.

In the Justice Department trial, the department's lawyers were trying to prove that the inclusion of Internet Explorer was done to hamper Netscape, and Microsoft was trying to claim that it was done to help users. They also attempted to show that Internet Explorer was bundled, rather than integrated. Both arguments are missing the point.

The situation is similar to Microsoft's inclusion of TCP/IP in its operating systems. This unquestionably hurt other vendors who were selling TCP/IP implementations, but at the same time, it helped users tremendously: the availability of TCP/IP and the winsock API on hundreds of millions of PCs was one of the causes of the rise of the Internet. The fact of the matter is that including Internet Explorer accomplishes what *both* parties claim—it helps users, and it hurts Netscape. Allowing third-party developers to assume that the browsing functionality is always there helps them as well. In any case, every other operating system out there includes a browser, so it seems strange to require that only Microsoft's operating system not include one.

The world would be a simpler place if there were only one dominant browser. It wouldn't have to be Microsoft's—it could be Netscape's or anyone's. Having Windows as a standard platform has been a huge boon to new application developers. In the Internet world, the browser is a new platform—that is why Netscape frightened Microsoft so much. Having multiple browsers out there means that website developers—the equivalent of application writers in this model—need to worry about having their products run well on all those different browsers, meaning they effectively need to write their pages for multiple platforms (although the inter-platform differences are much less than between operating systems). There are advantages to having competition in browsers, but it is not an unalloyed good, as is often claimed. At a certain point the browsers are differentiated by obscure features that are rarely used, and it would be much better to have a nice solid core functionality whose availability any Web page designer could rely on.

People have an idea that if Netscape had continued without competition from Microsoft, it would have ushered in a new era in computing, with its browser as the platform, and that somehow this would be better than having Windows as the dominant platform. Yet Netscape had the same desires as Microsoft: to define a platform, control it, make it proprietary, and use that to its advantage in its other businesses (since the plan was based on middleware—the browser—I believe it was doomed from the start, just like Sun's plans with Java, but in such views I tend to be a minority of one).

The Justice Department is upset because it sees no competition in the Intel-compatible operating system market. Yet consider the market for gaming consoles, which is divided among Sega, Sony, and Nintendo. There is a lot of competition between consoles, and they cost perhaps half of what a PC does. But the games cost $50 each, and a Sega Dreamcast keyboard costs twice what a PC keyboard does. Do people want to buy consoles to own them, or to play games? Similarly, people don't want to buy a computer to run an operating system, they want to run applications. There is much better evangelism, and a much wider variety of development tools, in the PC market than there is in the gaming market. The result is a much wider variety of games, which also cost much less. Is all the competition in the console market actually better for users?

If the Justice Department wants to use a narrow definition of the market, such as "Intel-compatible PCs," then why not look at a similarly defined market like "Sega Dreamcast-compatible gaming consoles"? In this market, Sega has rigid control over everything, and there is absolutely no competition in the operating system market for those devices. With complete control of the operating system, Sega can choose whom to anoint as official third-party hardware and software developers, then charge them a royalty on every product they sell. If Dreamcast ever includes an Internet browser, it will undoubtedly be bundled with the system, and it is doubtful more than one will be written. Yet the Justice Department is complaining that the Intel-compatible PC operating system market has a high barrier to entry and that this is stifling innovation.

On the bundling versus integrated product question, what this shows is the weakness of the original language of the consent decree. Attempting to show that Windows and the browser are not integrated misses the point; it is certainly technically possible to integrate them so that Windows won't work at all without the browser present. The fact that Microsoft may have so far done an incomplete job of integrating them is irrelevant. If the only criteria used involve the level of integration, you completely miss the notion of intent, which seems to be what the Justice Department should be worrying about.

The Justice Department and Microsoft's opponents are saying that a browser is an application, and therefore can't be part of the operating system. The question "What is an application?" is a prime example of "I can't actually define it, but I know it when I see it." As we have seen, all software consists of layers upon layers. When you read a Web page you probably go through at least 10 layers of code. To say, for example, that the first four are in the application and the bottom six are in the operating system is meaningless. Some say that a browser is an application because it calls published APIs exported by the operating system, but there are other parts of the operating system that also call published APIs. You can say that a browser quacks like an application, but there are other parts of the operating system that could easily be called applications, such as the Control Panel. The notion that you can include application-like functionality in the operating system as long as it is not too good—that it is okay to include WordPad, but not full-fledged Microsoft Word—would be difficult to define legally. In the end, the best definition of what is part of the operating system may be that if it ships with the operating system, it is part of it—but that definition supports Microsoft's case perfectly.

The Justice Department is concerned about Microsoft bundling a Web browser with the operating system, when its main competitor is also offering a free browser. Meanwhile the Justice Department is letting Microsoft bundle other pieces that people normally charge for, such as a Web server, with the operating system with no complaints. Microsoft is currently promoting an initiative known as Microsoft .NET, a somewhat nebulous attempt to make the Web into a platform for applications. As usual Microsoft is kicking up the evangelism into high gear, and ensuring that all of its developer tools support writing applications for .NET. This is the same strategy it used for previous initiatives aimed at developers, such as Visual Basic and the Component Object Model. The average user has never heard of those, but they contributed greatly to the wealth of applications that exist for Microsoft's platforms. With .NET, Microsoft has a good shot at taking a large share of the Web applications market. One part of the strategy involves including parts of Microsoft .NET with the Windows 2000 operating system—while the Justice Department continues to obsess over the browser.

An article about Microsoft .NET in the July 17, 2000, issue of *Fortune* magazine has the following quote: "Much of the Microsoft .NET strategy hinges on making...a standard that the company's fiercest competitors also support rather than a proprietary technology to be used against them." This shows the typical misunderstanding of how Microsoft operates within the industry. Microsoft has *always* had technologies—the Windows API in particular—that are supported by everybody in the industry, from its fiercest competitors to its closest friends. The notion that it cannot evangelize a standard to the industry while simultaneously competing with large segments of the industry has no basis in history. Yet the Justice Department is assuming that because Microsoft was competing with Netscape, Microsoft was treating Netscape unfairly in Microsoft's role as a platform provider.

In April 2000 Judge Jackson issued his ruling in the antitrust case: Microsoft had violated antitrust laws, using its monopoly to stifle competition. Two months later he announced the remedy, which matched what the Justice Department and the states had proposed: Microsoft would be split into two groups, one owning Windows, and the other owning everything else including the browser. This despite the fact that the alleged "sins" in the case appear to have been entirely committed by what would wind up as the operating systems company. If the company had been split this way 10 years ago, it wouldn't have prevented any of the supposed misconduct. Whatever your feeling on whether the browser is an application or part of the operating system, it's an undeniable fact that Internet Explorer *was* written by the operating system group.

The theory is that the applications groups will then rush to port their applications to Linux and other operating systems. This ignores the fact that it takes a considerable amount of work to do cross-platform development, and more work to test and support it. Microsoft currently develops its applications on one other platform, the Macintosh, but the middleware architecture that it used back in the late 1980s (which allowed it to port its main applications to OS/2 without entirely rewriting them) has been dropped due to the overhead it imposed. At this point the Office team is more or less maintaining two separate code bases—the last version of the Office suite for the Macintosh, Office 98, shipped only on the Macintosh, and the last version for Windows, Office 2000, shipped only on Windows.

Supporting just a few platforms is a huge advantage for the Office team. Adding Linux support would mean a third platform to worry about, and it is unclear that this would be worth it financially. Going from two platforms to three would probably be more than 50% more work, because Linux has multiple desktop environments that would need to be supported. In this sense, the rise of Linux is a major threat to the Office team also. Contrary to popular belief, application writers don't port to different platforms because they want to, but because they have to.

In fact, the applications groups just might do the port, because it would be considered "cool." At Microsoft it can be surprisingly easy to get 10 people together and start working on a skunk works project. Six months later you have something working, and then you can go to Bill and say, "Isn't this cool, and how could you possibly throw it all away?" It's the same way Robert Moses used to get highways built around New York City—first start bulldozing parks, then get approval later to build the highway. With the trust that people have in the Microsoft evangelism machine, it is amazing how many projects start up because they are "cool" and then wind up with a justification and evangelization story that is reverse-engineered based on the hype that the initial work has generated.

The feeling in the press is that if the company is split into operating systems and applications, the best engineers will flock to the applications company, because it is considered "cooler." In fact I doubt that will happen. Microsoft has always freely allowed transfers within the company, so the people who are working on operating systems or applications have already had the opportunity to switch. In fact, it seems that developers naturally divide into "apps guys" and "systems guys," which wouldn't change if the company were split (I was a "systems guy" myself). Of course the work itself might be less of a factor in which company to choose than the perceived future performance of the stock of the respective companies—but since both companies would have a mix of solid revenue-generating software and newer, riskier work, the winner from that perspective is not obvious either.

Some people feel that merely breaking Microsoft in two is not strong enough. Another plan being bandied about is to split the operating system team into multiple companies, each of which would make versions of Windows. The comparison made is with the 1982 breakup of AT&T into seven regional companies. The theory is that the two (or more) operating systems companies would compete with each other, leading to more features and lower prices. This makes sense unless you know anything about how Microsoft works.

First of all, it assumes that the individual companies could all hire enough people to design, develop, test, document, market, and so on all the different versions, when a single Microsoft can't even hire enough people. AT&T—which, keep in mind, was taking advantage of a government-granted monopoly—was already spread out geographically, and for the most part was simply split geographically into units that could not compete with each other because of geographic limitations. Breaking up Microsoft into multiple competing companies would mean that each company would immediately lose half (or more) of its key technical people to the other company. This would require that more resources be spent hiring people to duplicate their work, people who would also presumably be of overall lower quality. Then there is the necessary duplication of various fixed costs within the company—two operations groups, two human resources departments, and of course, two legal departments. This is supposed to help consumers? What this view reflects is the notion that Microsoft is happily foisting inferior software off on consumers, when in fact Microsoft would like nothing better than to hire more people and put them to work improving the quality of the software—if it could only find enough people to hire.

Even worse would be the effect on evangelism. If multiple operating systems somehow did emerge from this mess, all that would mean is that third-party software and hardware vendors would have to worry about multiple platforms. This would mean that some percentage of their resources—let's say 10%—10% of their resources, across the whole industry, would be spent, not improving their hardware or software or helping users in any way, but simply dealing with the fact that multiple platforms exist. Again, I fail to see how this would help users. It is based on another fallacy, which is that people actually "use" an operating system, as opposed to using hardware and software that works with that operating system. Hey, if two competing companies are so great, why not make seven, as was done with AT&T?

Most people at Microsoft draw a distinction between being found guilty in the case and actually *being* guilty. They don't think they work for an outlaw company that broke the law. The feeling is that the antitrust lawsuit is just another issue the company has to deal with, as it has to deal with its competitors. The assumption is that the case will be won on appeal, or if not, something magical will happen. Few people seriously believe that the company will ever be split up. The punishment does not seem to fit the crime; nobody was doing the things you associate with real law-breaking, like handing over bags of cash in the dead of night.

It also is hard for Microsoft employees to shake the notion that the Justice Department is still out to punish Microsoft for past victories. It seems willing to spend millions of dollars essentially to defend one company, Netscape, that isn't even in business anymore and has essentially abandoned the market that the lawsuit addresses. Is it entirely coincidental that the former CEO of Netscape was a college buddy of the Majority Leader of the U.S. Senate? When your own government—which *does* have a license to print money—is out to get you, it is easy to feel persecuted. I saw Bill Gates at a press conference on November 5, 1999, after Judge Jackson had announced his findings of fact, stating that Microsoft was a monopoly. He had the rueful look of an athlete being interviewed after a game that was lost because of a bad call by a referee. You've spent your whole life training as an athlete, building up to the moment of triumph that was rightfully yours, and the referee—who knows what route they took to get there, but you doubt it was as long or as hard as the one you traveled. You know in your heart that they were wrong, but what can you do about it?

At this point, some people view Microsoft with less esteem than they do the U.S. Department of Justice, for goodness sake. The open source movement has a very pronounced "little-guy" mentality, the notion of showing up the Establishment—and they define Microsoft as the Establishment. These are the kind of people who have no trouble believing that the Justice Department was involved, say, in covering up the details of the assault on the Branch Davidian complex in Waco, Texas in 1993, or of Democratic fund-raising abuses in 1996, or of two decades of Chinese nuclear espionage. Yet when you stack the Justice Department up against Microsoft, they root for the government.

In 1991 the ticketing agency Ticketmaster bought out Ticketron, its main competitor, and in the summer of 1994 the rock band Pearl Jam failed in an attempt to schedule a tour without using Ticketmaster. Pearl Jam was protesting the high transaction fees Ticketmaster charged (Pearl Jam claimed they were almost 30% of ticket prices, Ticketmaster claimed they were 14 percent, but both were above the 10 percent that Pearl Jam wanted). The Justice Department investigated Ticketmaster, but in July 1995 the investigation was dropped, with Attorney General Reno stating that the emergence of new competitors in the ticket-selling industry prompted the decision. It seemed very strange from within Microsoft to see Ticketmaster, which had exclusive contracts with many major concert venues and promoters, get off scot-free while Microsoft continued to be investigated over giving away software for free.

There is a new argument making the rounds about the case: the claim that the entire PC and Internet phenomenon is a result of the Justice Department lawsuit against IBM, which lasted from 1969 to 1982. The case was eventually dropped, but it did rein IBM in. The argument goes that IBM made the IBM PC an open standard in response to the lawsuit, and that this led to the boom that followed.

The timing sounds right, since the IBM PC was being designed around 1980, toward the end of the lawsuit. And the argument serves Microsoft's opponents well, tying in with the notion that throttling Microsoft will usher in the next 20-year boom. But the facts do not support the argument. IBM did choose third parties to supply its microprocessor and operating system, but out of expediency, not any desire to have the PC market develop the way it did (the IBM PC project was initially viewed within the rest of IBM as some weird offshoot that wouldn't amount to anything). IBM viewed Intel and Microsoft as suppliers (albeit important ones), like the companies that made the hard drives or the memory chips. It wanted to make a personal computer like all the others of the time, in which it controlled the design but did not produce all the components. IBM opened the standards for third-party hardware and software developers, but only to increase support for a platform that it planned to control tightly (in 1981 Don Estridge from IBM referred to the hardware companies making expansion cards as a "cottage industry"). IBM didn't publish the *Technical Reference* because the Justice Department told it to; it did so because publishing such internal details was part of the business plan from the start. IBM planned to use its proprietary BIOS to ensure that only it could build PCs.

When this plan fell apart, thanks to Phoenix's heroic cloning of the IBM PC BIOS, IBM stewed for a few years, and then came out with the PS/2, which was designed to restore its control of the industry. If you look at what IBM was trying to accomplish with the Systems Application Architecture, which was to use its strengths in mainframe sales to help OS/2, it does not look like IBM was feeling chastised by the Justice Department. IBM had never intended the PC industry to develop as it had, where it had a small share of a huge industry, and no control over its direction. It did start the process of evangelizing the platform, but it was Microsoft, the alleged monopolist, that really got evangelism going, to the eventual benefit of so many companies in Silicon Valley.

14

Community

One aspect of the wide variety among computers demonstrated at Comdex/Spring in 1982 was that a lot of computer owners expected to write their own software. As the 1980s began there was a nascent community of computer users in every city, who would offer each other advice on using and programming their computers. At first I interacted with this community only in person, and rarely; on weekends my friends and I would go down and hang out at computer stores, and occasionally see the same faces. Computer stores back then were somewhat laissez-faire, more like a hobby club meeting than an actual store, the kind of places that made you wonder how they stayed in business. Someone actually buying a computer was the exception, not the rule. The best of these in Montreal was a store downtown called Futur Byte. ("Futur" is French for "future," while "Byte" is an English-only word, the French translation being "octet." Thus the name managed to make no sense in two languages at once—but still sounded neat.) The store was set up with rows of tables and chairs, with one of every computer it sold arranged on the tables. The computers were freely available to use. One time I saw somebody playing a Space Invaders-type game on a Sinclair ZX-81, and I asked him how long he had owned the system at home. The guy replied that he didn't own one, but had written the game in a series of trips to Futur Byte, each time doing a little more work, then saving the results until the next time he returned. The machine had no floppy drive, so programs were saved on cassette tapes, which transferred data at 300 baud.

IBM eventually opened a Product Center not too far from Futur Byte. That store had all the latest IBM equipment. But it wasn't very friendly to curious folk like us. The goal was to sell computers, and the salespeople frowned at acne-faced teenagers who appeared unlikely to have the financial wherewithal to afford one.

In the fall of 1981 my father brought home a line terminal and a modem. The modem was an acoustic coupler, meaning that after dialing the phone by hand, you would insert the handset into two padded collars on the modem. The collars would seal around the mouthpiece and speaker, more or less, insulating enough outside noise that communication could happen over the phone line. The modem would transmit tones out the collar that the mouthpiece was in, which would be picked up and transmitted over the phone line. Sounds coming in from the phone line would be transmitted out the speaker, and picked up by a microphone in the other collar of the modem. The contraption had a Rube Goldberg feel to it—in particular, if you put the handset in reversed 180 degrees, it wouldn't work. It also assumed that your phone was a standard-order Bell one with big round mouthpiece and speaker parts connected by a thin handle; otherwise it would not fit into the collars correctly. Luckily that was all most people had back then.

You would dial in to another computer using the modem, much like the way you connect to an ISP today. At first we dialed in only to the main computer at McGill University. Instead of all the capabilities of a Web browser, all you had was text on the line terminal. Each connection would start with the computer prompting you for a command, which you would then enter. The computer would then print the results of that command, and then prompt you again, and so on. The acoustic coupler modem we had ran at 300 baud, which was standard at the time. That is nearly 200 times slower than today's 56K modems. 300 baud translates to about 30 characters a second, which means that a single line of 80 characters would take almost 3 agonizing seconds to print out. Some more advanced systems supported 1200 baud, considered quite speedy, but at that point you had to be concerned about whether your phone handset fit snugly enough into the modem.

In the fall of 1983, a year and a half after my family got our computer, I found something new to dial in to—an online community that was thriving in Montreal. This was a group of computer bulletin board systems, or BBSs. They were way, way, primitive combinations of today's Internet email and newsgroups, with the emphasis on "way, way, primitive."

You connected to a BBS using a modem, much as home Internet users connect to their service provider with a modem. However, most BBS systems had only one phone line; if someone else was connected, you got a busy signal. And people tended to stay connected for a while, because of the difficulty of getting in. This could be quite frustrating, especially since the first acoustic coupler modem we had did not dial the phone itself; you had to dial the phone by hand (and our home phones were rotary dial, not touch-tone), then when you heard the phone ringing, you would stick the phone into the acoustic coupler and wait for it to be picked up by the computer on the other end. We soon got a modem that could dial itself, but you still had to repeatedly tell it to dial, then wait to hear if the phone was ringing, and if not, tell the modem to hang up and start over. There did exist hardware that would redial automatically (known among other things as "demon dialers") which other BBS callers owned—which made it even harder for us poor normal dialers to get in.

But we did keep trying, and eventually would get connected. What awaited us then? Not much that would keep a current World Wide Web user awake. You were connected only to the specific BBS you had dialed in to; to get to any other, you would have to disconnect and start repeatedly dialing the number of the other BBS. The BBSs were designed to work on line terminals, so they had no graphics, just text scrolling upwards. The system was built around "bulletins," which were like messages on Internet newsgroups (bulletins were referred to, apparently with no trace of irony, as "bulls"). After entering your logon id and password, you would be prompted with a main menu, each item identified by a single letter. So you might choose "S" to scan the existing bulletins, "P" to post a new one, and "E" for electronic mail. Each bulletin was identified by a number; you read one by entering the number in response to a prompt from the BBS.

Email was similar to bulletins, except it was visible only to you. If you selected the "E" option from the main menu, a list of the emails in your inbox would be shown, and you could view or delete them by number. You could also post bulletins, or send email to other users.

Because you were the only one logged on to the BBS at this point, nobody else was going to post or email until you disconnected and hung up the phone. Thus, bulletin conversations or email exchanges could take a while, since one person would post or email, then would have to check back at some point in the future, and hope that the other person had been able to log on and respond in the interim. To keep things fair, the systems would usually have a time limit for a single user to stay logged on, after which they would throw you off (30 minutes was typical). There were also limits on how much email you could have in your mailbox (something really low, like 5) and how many bulletins you could post in a single session (again, a really low number like 2).

Despite all these restrictions, the result was incredibly compelling. What would the bulletins be about? Basically the same things people talk about today on the Internet, except that back then there was a significant computery tilt to everything, since few non-techies were active on the BBSs. A lot of the talk involved computer games, and trading pirated games for other pirated games. Discussions about programming and computers for sale would be mixed in with arguments about politics and sports. People would post intentionally annoying nonsense. Flames would be sent, in public and in email. The current online culture and the "netiquette" that governs it have their roots in these primitive systems. We even had in-person get-togethers of BBS users (which I went off to—tra-la-la—without even thinking of the ominous possibilities involved).

Today people flit through the Internet and email, and this archaic stuff sounds dull. But the key is the ability to interact with people with similar interests whom you never would have met otherwise. This exists even if you are calling in at 300 baud on a line terminal and the people you talk to all live in the same city (there were bigger BBSs with multiple lines in other cities, but since it took a long-distance call to reach them, the people who did tended to be those who knew how to illegally make long-distance calls for free—which was one of the main subjects discussed on those BBSs). Later on, I remember reading *Wired* magazine back in 1994 and it would sometimes print a URL and would have to emphasize that you needed a Web browser to view it—something that would be completely unnecessary today. But *Wired* was already in its second year of publishing back then, because the essential coolness of all this predates the Web browser.

If you go into an Internet chat group today, you get a fairly standard cast of characters—a few people having a serious conversation, a few people asking where everyone else is from, someone who ritually greets every new entrant to the chat room, and someone who is typing in the lyrics to a song by some obscure rock group. If you imagine this same chatter stretched way out across the time it takes every participant to get through to the BBS, you have a pretty accurate idea of what the environment was like back in 1983.

There were a series of these BBSs in Montreal, with names like Micro-Dial, Omega Online, and SABATION (let history record that SABATION was an acronym for System Accessible Bulletin and Telephone Input Output Network, except that both "accessible" and "bulletin" were misspelled in the introductory message that announced this). The various BBSs were silently ranked by participants in terms of how cool they were, which meant how interesting the other users were, and the quality of the pirated games discussed on them; being cool also meant that the phone was busy more. But it was hard for a user to keep current on more than a few BBSs, since it could take an hour or more to get through to any given one. I had a list of three or four that I would connect to regularly; I would start out dialing each of them in a round-robin way, until I got through to one. Once I had reviewed any new bulletins, posted any I felt like, and handled my email, I would hang up and start dialing the remaining ones in my list, until I had hit them all, or my parents threw me out of their bedroom (where our computer was set up). This attribute of a BBS—that I would go to the effort to try to keep current with the bulletins and email—is today referred to as "stickiness."

Because this was Montreal, there were some primarily French-language BBSs also, although there was opposite-language posting on both the English and French systems. And it should come as no surprise that there was a BBS called Compu-Sexe, although if I ever managed to get on to that system, I cannot recall the shocking depravities that were visited upon me. I was probably too chicken to call, since I was under 18 at the time and never knew when my parents would walk in.

There was also a service available in Montreal called Datapac, which allowed users to dial in to a single local number and then be routed over a network to other computers that were also connected to Datapac, or to Tymnet, the U.S. equivalent. This was similar to calling an ISP today (Datapac was a commercial service and had multiple phone lines coming in). However, there was no equivalent to Web pages; you would use Datapac to connect to a given computer that you had an account on, or perhaps, to connect to a computer that you were trying to break into. The computers were identified by numeric sequences, similar to phone numbers, which were assigned by Datapac. Almost all computers that you would connect to required accounts because they would charge people for

time connected; Datapac also charged people for the time they were connected over Datapac.

The local BBSs were small operations run out of homes, using a single phone line and computer. Not much of a computer either; a typical
system was an Apple II (or clone) with 64K and two floppy disk drives.
Although BBS operators (who were known as "sysops," for "system
operators") would occasionally ask for donations, BBSs were basically
free, the main benefit of running one being that it made you a hep cat
in the local BBS scene. Some of the BBSs were not even available 24
hours a day. Some were only available during non-work hours, presumably because they were being run on someone's desk at work. Some
were unavailable during the evenings, when the owner of the phone
line was using it to connect to other BBSs; and some were unavailable
during the night, when the other inhabitants of the house didn't want
the phone to ring.

One way that BBSs tried to distinguish themselves and attract more
users was by putting up their own content. So in addition to the universal
S, P, and E choices, the sysop might add J for jokes, or K for his analysis of
Kierkegaard. One of the more impressive examples was a game called
Genocide II. Since anyone could play fairly slick games on their home
computer, the challenge for a BBS game was to take advantage of the
multi-user aspect of the BBS, without being hampered by the fact that
only one person was connected at a time and the entire interface was line-
terminal based.

Genocide II consisted of a world where every player had a spaceship,
which was at a certain location in a galaxy. Each day, every player could
enter four moves, where a move was a single operation such as changing
course, changing speed, firing torpedoes at other ships, or reallocating
energy to shields (the terminology for the game was based on "Star
Trek"—there has always been significant overlay between the worlds of
computer mavens and serious Star Trek fans). At a specified time of day,
let's say midnight, all the moves that all the players had entered that day

would be processed simultaneously by the computer the BBS was running on. Any time in the next 24 hours, you could connect to the BBS, see the results of the previous day's moves, and enter your four new moves. If you could not sign on in a given 24-hour period, you would effectively forfeit your move, giving the other players an advantage. The object, as you would expect, was to be the last ship left, at which point the game would start over.

There were also games played among users via email; an occasional game of (very slow) chess would break out, and I recall an attempt to organize a game of the strategy board game Diplomacy on a BBS, although I don't think it ever worked out.

I turned my friends Avi Belinsky and Val Bercovici on to these bulletin boards. Val had an Apple II clone in his room, something called a Golden II+, which was so junky we had to insert Lego pieces under the keyboard to make the keys function—but it worked. By the summer of 1984, right after we all graduated from high school, Val's father had gotten tired of us monopolizing the phone, and had a second phone line installed for Val's personal use. The three of us decided to run our own BBS on Val's computer. The only hardware change we had to make was to have a chip on his modem updated so it would support answering the phone (most modems at the time only supported calling out). We got this done through someone a year ahead of us in high school, who was a known figure in the Montreal BBS scene. The rest of Val's hardware, although basic, was adequate for the task—in the world of Apple II computers, the gap between a low-end system and a souped-up one wasn't that great. In any case, the fact that conversations would be limited to 300 baud would hide the limitations of the hardware.

We needed BBS software also, but that was easy to get. The source code to a standard BBS program called "Networks II" was floating around; most of the BBSs in Montreal were based on it (it originated the well-known choices of S for scan, P for post, and E for email).

Networks II was written in Apple Basic. It was a fairly trivial matter to modify the program so it welcomed callers with whatever name you chose to give your BBS. We called ours Transylvania, because Val was Romanian. We decided to go a bit further and add on some features not included in the basic Networks II code we received. These "features" were things that today it would seem laughable not to support: being able to email the author of a bulletin you had just read with one command (as opposed to remembering who wrote it, exiting the scan mode, and going into email mode), or remembering which bulletins each caller had read, so the next time they could be given the option to scan only unread bulletins (without this, they would have to remember on their own). In fact those features were then in vogue among Montreal BBSs, and most sysops had added them already, each presumably making his own separate modifications to the source code. In retrospect this situation was crying out for something like the open source community of today. The Networks II source code was freely available. I have no idea who originally wrote it, or what the royalty arrangements, if any, were supposed to be, but back then nobody worried too much about things like that. Everyone was busy hacking it up to improve it—what was missing was some way to fold those changes back into a common source code base that could then be redistributed. This wasn't due to any sense of intellectual property or not wanting to share your work, the idea simply never occurred to people, probably because there was no easy way to manage such a project and transfer the code around. With no Web pages and everything happening at 300 baud, it would have been too difficult to stay up to date.

Eventually we got all our improvements working and fired up Transylvania, but it never got very popular. We had to limit the hours it was open, to give us some time to call BBSs ourselves. In any case the BBS market was fairly saturated, given the small number that any one user could "stick" to, and the cool features we had added only brought us up to par with the other systems. Our most ardent user was someone who claimed he could crash our BBS at will. Unfortunately, when we dared him it turned out he was right.

There wasn't a lot a high school student in Montreal in 1984 could do to prepare for a career as a programmer. Our high school offered one class with the grandiose title of "Introduction to Computer Science," but it involved writing BASIC programs to do things like sort numbers—the kind of thing I had taught myself by logging on to the McGill mainframe. The only computer this class had access to was the central school board computer, dialed in to with a terminal sitting in the classroom. Each student would enter his or her program on punch cards, filling in little bubbles like an SAT answer sheet. The student would hand the cards to the teacher, who would scan them in on a punch card reader connected to the terminal. The teacher would run the program; if there were any errors, the student would make note of them, then go off and fix up the punch cards and wait for another turn to run the improved program. The reason for the punch cards was that the class was not allowed to use any storage on the school board computer, and the terminal itself had no storage. So scanning in the punch cards allowed each student to repeatedly simulate typing in the program really fast; after it was run each time, it was deleted from the system before the next program was scanned in. Occasionally, if there was only a small error preventing the program from running, the teacher would make the correction right away and re-run it, rather than sending the student away to fix the cards and wait for another cycle through the class.

During the spring of my senior year in high school, we got the chance to go on "work study" programs to investigate careers. I signed up for one in computers. It turned out to be at a phone company. I was apprenticed, such as it was, to a tape operator, working in the room where the mainframe computer's tape drives were—those large reel-to-reel tape machines that you see whirring in computer rooms shown in any movie made between 1960 and about 1987. The mainframe did not have much hard drive storage; instead, user data was almost all stored on tapes, which were stored on reels. Someone logged into the mainframe from a terminal elsewhere in the building would decide they needed the data that was on a specific tape. They would send a message that would show up on a display where the tape dudes (and their apprentice tape dude) were sitting, and we would scurry off, find the tape (they were all identified by numbers), mount it on one of the tape drives, and hit a key indicating the tape was ready. It's funny because when Avi and I were about twelve we would tell people that we wanted to be "computer operators" when we grew up. I think we had something a bit more glamorous in mind. Luckily, I already knew there was a bit more to a career in computers than what I had seen there, and I got to escape after a few days when my work study time was up.

The work we did on Transylvania that summer is a lot closer to what I did at Microsoft than anything I learned in school, even in college. You have some piece of existing code whose author is unknown; you and a few other people have to figure out how it works on your own and add some features on a deadline. The result may not be the most elegant code, but it works. In the end, you throw it all away after a few months.

If I had decided to punt college, I could likely have gone to Microsoft in 1984, shown my work on Transylvania and the games I had written for the IBM PC, and gotten a job as a developer. How many people in 1984 could say they had over two years of programming experience on an IBM PC?

Instead, I went away to college at Princeton. My first week there, I was talking to someone I had met and he mentioned he had just gotten a job at the computer center. I had been assigned a work-study job working in food services, but the computer center sounded a little more fun. After dazzling them with my years of IBM PC experience, I got a job as a "consultant," which meant I sat in a room on the ground floor of the computer center and answered questions from people who wandered in.

Most of the questions involved the mainframe computer, a large IBM system that was accessed via terminals scattered around campus. When I started in 1984 this was the main system available to students to write term papers on, although clusters of Macintosh and IBM PCs were slowly appearing. The terminals were not graphical; unlike today's word processing programs, which let you see fonts, boldfacing, underlining, superscripts, and so on right on the screen in a close approximation of what they will look like when printed, the terminals displayed characters in only one size and font; a term paper was sprinkled with special two-character codes indicating all the other fancy stuff. If you have ever written a Web page in HTML, it looked a lot like that. (In fact the language used was an early cousin of HTML.) However you could not see the result on the screen; you had to send it to a printer, and wait and see if it printed correctly.

It was even worse than that. Like most mainframe systems, the Princeton computer charged for use; a certain amount for every minute you used it, an amount for storage, and (especially) an amount to print. You could select either a line printer or a laser printer. The line printer was cheaper, but it couldn't do all the formatting that a laser printer could.

Every student was given, at no cost, $500 in a mainframe account at the start of the year. This slowly dwindled down as they logged on, edited, printed, and whatnot. If the balance dropped to nothing, the student was shut out from the mainframe for the rest of the year, unless he or she could convince the department to pony up real money. The $500 was an amount that would last you a year, as long as you saved laser printing for the final versions of your papers, and used the line printer for everything else. One of the benefits of working as a consultant at the computer center was that you could have unlimited computer money. This was legitimate, since we often used our account when helping other users, but it also meant that we could laser print whatever we wanted—a true guilty pleasure back then. I easily plowed through $2,000 of this fake money every year.

In the computer center there was also a line terminal that mostly sat there, but which was rigged up so any user on the mainframe could send a question to it—a primitive version of email support. Whenever this thing sprang to life (with an unholy racket), someone would have to wander over and read what the user had sent, then type back a reply. Luckily, it is much easier to say, "I don't know, go away" when the user is not physically present.

Princeton was connected to a wide-area computer network called Bitnet, which mostly linked universities. There was no Web browsing back then, but it did support email. After some nagging by my father and me, McGill also joined Bitnet, allowing me to start emailing to my father and saving me oodles of money on my phone bill.

In the spring of 1986, a consultant at the computer center wrote some software allowing us to read Usenet newsgroups on the main-frame. Newsgroups are still around today—alt.sex and its ilk. This was a great advance. The computer center was staffed with consultants until 11 o'clock at night, and those late nights got pretty dull. With Usenet now available, instead of sitting around at night submitting unnecessary laser printer jobs, we could sit around at night reading unnecessary newsgroups.

One summer I got a job at McGill, working on their mainframe. The unsubstantiated rumor was that my boss had been impressed with Left, Right, and Fire, my IBM PC game masterpiece. During that summer I discovered chat groups, ancestors to the present-day Internet Relay Chat and America Online Instant Messenger. A chat group consisted of a machine somewhere on the network (in those days, Bitnet), which was set up so that every message sent to it was echoed back to everyone who was currently subscribed to it. So you would come in during the morning and tell the central machine to subscribe you. From then on, anything you (or anyone else subscribed) typed would appear on your screen. The level of discourse was about the same as a chat room on AOL today. I spent the summer (when I wasn't doing my nominal job, whose purpose I forget) scamming on Bitnet women—all five of them. I had one interested until I told her I was 18 (that was too young for those who are curious). I "met" another woman named Katie who was working at Brown University that summer. Eventually she sent me a package of Orange Milano cookies in the mail, after I had mooned over how much I missed them (they were not available in Montreal at the time). That early experiment in e-commerce was the high point of our courtship, and I never met her in person.

Many people today view the Internet as a drastic change from what went before, and therefore assume that it will revolutionize everything. Certainly things are more connected than they used to be—when I went to work for Dendrite in 1988, it was not connected to any external networks, so I lost the access to email and newsgroups that I had enjoyed at Princeton. I had to resort to calling home from work to keep in touch with my family! Of course that would be unthinkable today. Still, online communities have existed for decades, and have followed much the same rules, on a smaller scale, that they do today.

Widespread access to the Internet has allowed people to form online communities that would never exist in real life, because the common interests that they embrace are so rare. Now anybody with an unusual hobby or interest can chat with people all around the world who share the same hobby or interest. The fact that occasionally those interests involve hurting people in a variety of ways should not detract from the huge benefit this has been to so many others.

Yet, when it comes down to it, you cannot borrow a cup of sugar on the Internet. Chatting with people in a foreign country is fascinating, but if it replaces a visit to that country, are people better off? The expression "It takes a village to raise a child" refers to a real-world community, not an online one. The real world is not neat and classified like the Internet, but it is the world that people ultimately have to live in. People who view the Internet as a dramatic new thing, and embrace it wholeheartedly, would be wise to learn some history. This stuff didn't arrive overnight. If people realize that the Internet is an evolution rather than a revolution, they will gain a healthy perspective about its potential to change the world.

15

Next

A question on the minds of many, both inside and outside the company, is whether Microsoft will continue its amazing run into the next millennium or begin the decline that seems inevitable for any company so successful.

The press is always looking for a good "death of Microsoft" story, and the current candidates for dealing the death blow are Linux, Java, and the Internet in general. But going back through the years, there has always been some company that was going to slay Microsoft: Lotus, WordPerfect, Novell, IBM, Oracle, Sun, or even smaller, since-forgotten companies like GO.

Will Microsoft be defeated by one of these external forces? Or will it continue to be able to create and evangelize the standard platforms for the industry?

Back in the 1980s, Microsoft was dominant only in operating systems. In applications—which, at the time, meant DOS applications—Lotus was ahead in spreadsheets, WordPerfect in word processors, and Borland in development tools. Although these companies made occasional sallies against one another (for example, Lotus bought a company called Samna, makers of a word processor called Ami Pro, to try to compete with

WordPerfect), they mostly stayed home and guarded their fortresses. The exception was Microsoft, which, while defending its operating system turf, was also trying to horn in on all the others' territories. Nobody talked about these battles being critical to Microsoft; when they failed (and they did regularly fail for a few years), it didn't hurt Microsoft's operating system safe harbor.

Microsoft kept hammering away, and with the giant boost it got from the shift to Windows as the standard operating system and Win16 as the standard API, it eventually came to dominate all these application areas. At the same time, the OS/2 work gave Microsoft a platform on which to go after a whole new tier of competitors, which until then it had been unable to threaten—Novell in networking, Sun in workstations, Oracle in databases. That work has now shifted to NT, but Microsoft is still chipping away at those markets. In the competition with Lotus, WordPerfect, and Borland, Microsoft went from a standing start to market dominance in less than a decade. It is not unreasonable, though scarcely a sure thing, to predict similar success against its new competitors.

The rise of the Internet has had many people predicting doom for Microsoft, but it seems astonishingly early to predict that. The Internet became significant in 1995. Think of what Microsoft's position was in spreadsheets five years after Lotus shipped 1-2-3, or in word processing five years after WordPerfect shipped its word processor. Microsoft had virtually *no* mind or market share back then.

The arrival of the Internet has caused a change in the kind of companies that are viewed as the main threat to Microsoft. Back in the early 1990s, it was operating system companies, such as IBM. By 1995, the main threat was seen as coming from browser companies, in particular Netscape. By the end of the decade, the battle was viewed as being between Microsoft and portal companies, such as Yahoo or America Online. One thing jumps out: The amount of work required to enter the fray, the amount of evangelism involved, and the degree to which third-party companies are locked into a platform (what I have referred to previously as weight), have all decreased significantly at each stage.

An operating system takes years to develop and entails diverting a considerable amount of company effort to evangelism to convince software developers to write software for, and therefore create weight for, the platform—something IBM did not successfully accomplish with OS/2.

A browser such as Netscape's Navigator takes months to develop, and the evangelism is not particularly hard—you add HTML tags that only your browser supports, document them, then show Web page designers why they are worth using. One step beyond that is defining an architecture for plug-ins, such as Java or ActiveX, and evangelizing that. This is still much easier than evangelizing an entire operating system's worth of APIs.

For a portal, the initial development time can be measured in weeks. A *Seattle Times* article on November 22, 1998, about Go2Net, a Web startup in Seattle, mentioned that some of the developers "have been assembling, testing, and debugging the company's 'portal'—a comprehensive site that serves as an index to other links. The site, a top Go2Net project that required several weeks' work from three developers, is to debut tomorrow." At the time of the article, Go2Net's stock was trading at $8 13/16. Thanks to its portal, its stock was soon being talked up as a hot Internet investment. Four months later Paul Allen, one of Microsoft's co-founders, announced he would invest up to $750 million in the company, pushing the stock price from $43 1/2 to $69 3/8 in the last two weeks of March 1999 (all these prices have been adjusted to reflect the fact the stock split 2 for 1 twice, in February 1999 and June 1999). The company was making plans to move to a new headquarters in the waterfront building where MTV's show *The Real World* was filmed. Does it get any better than that? On July 26, 2000, Go2Net announced a merger with InfoSpace, another Seattle Internet startup, which valued Go2Net at over $2.5 billion. Not bad for several weeks' works from three developers.

Evangelism for a portal is somewhat different than for a platform such as an operating system or a browser, at least as it currently works. A portal may have deals with a dozen or a hundred other sites to offer content and reciprocal links, but that will mean 100 business deals that are personally managed and often involve money flowing from the portal to the content providers. If the portal company decides to change something in the interface, it can notify the hundred other companies it has deals with and coordinate the update. There is no equivalent to this for an operating system or a browser, where you produce an SDK detailing how to write applications for your platform that is then sold or given away to third parties with which you do not necessarily have any further contact, and in particular which you are not paying to develop on your platform. In the future, portals may provide environments in which applications written by their users can be run, but at the moment this hosting functionality is either provided by the browser or operating system that the user is running, or in the case of applications hosted on the portal, is done only for applications that are explicitly approved and tested by the portal site.

This trend shows maturation in the industry, where the technology becomes less significant and business partnerships become more significant. For Microsoft, which is coming into this market from behind, the fact there is relatively little weight in the portals is a good thing, and makes it much less likely that America Online or Yahoo will dominate the market because they got there first.

People say that Microsoft "missed" the Internet. Certainly in 1995 it may have looked that way, but now it is like saying that General Motors "missed" the auto industry because it was not around in its earliest days. However the future development of the Internet plays out, what happened in the period from 1993 to 1995 won't have much impact on who eventually dominates the market.

In fact, the Internet should serve as a cautionary tale for Microsoft's competitors, because it shows how fast Microsoft can respond to a competitive threat. Within a year, in 1995, Microsoft's top management went from being mostly ignorant of the Internet, to viewing it as a threat that could be contained, to completely turning the ship to embrace it.

First of all, in 1995 almost all of Microsoft was consumed with the shift to Windows 95—writing the operating system or applications for it or testing, marketing, or evangelizing it. There was a feeling that a paradigm shift was occurring, but it was to Windows 95, and Microsoft was riding the top of the wave. There was no time or energy left over to focus on a second paradigm shift to the Internet.

Second, there were certainly parts of Microsoft that were already very aware of the Internet. Microsoft began working on including TCP/IP in its operating systems back in 1991. In the summer of 1994, I was working in the NT development group trying to decide what we would work on after NT 3.5 shipped. The project we selected was an Internet proxy/firewall. At the time we viewed HTTP network traffic—which is how Web pages are sent around the Internet—as just another type of traffic, along with that used by older Internet technologies such as FTP and gopher. But we had Internet taps in the hallways, and were surfing the Web (with the Mosaic browser, one of the first ones) and taking notes on it even way back then. This was a few months after Netscape had been founded, and months before it released the first public beta version of its browser.

I left the NT team in September 1994, opting to work on an interactive television project (one of several false starts Microsoft made in this area). I spent three months in the summer of 1995 working on a browser for a set-top box—the interactive television equivalent of a cable box. I am pretty proud of that work. It was based on the same source code, licensed from a company called Spyglass, that was used for the browser included in the first version of Windows 95. I added the ability to navigate using a television remote control instead of a keyboard, and to display streaming video inside a Web page. Rick Rashid, who was vice president of Microsoft Research and also was supervising the interactive television project, saw a demo of my browser and asked why we couldn't run all of the set-top box applications inside the browser. This predated the extremely similar Network Computer strategy by several years (the premise that the NC would take over computing is one that I personally don't support, as I'll explain later, but many people at the time did). Unfortunately that work went nowhere: I left the group to go work for Softimage in Montreal, the browser project foundered, and eventually that whole attempt at interactive television was scrapped. But the Internet was certainly in people's minds.

The rise and fall of Netscape is another example of how simplistic it is to attribute Microsoft's success to the company's luck in having been picked by IBM back in 1981 as the main operating system vendor for the original IBM PC. In 1995 Netscape had a huge lead in goodwill among Web users. People would put links to Netscape installation points on their Web pages, just because they wanted people to run a better browser—and also because some of their pages were best viewed with Netscape. Netscape seemed to have learned the lesson of Microsoft, and was actively extending the standard HTML tags with Netscape-only extensions—evangelizing an API and creating weight for its browser. Around this time I asked J Allard, Microsoft Internet guru, whether Microsoft could beat Netscape, and he said, "Nah, they're too entrenched." But despite this huge lead, Netscape stumbled badly. It used an enormous amount of resources trying to rewrite its browser in Java, before abandoning the effort completely. In November 1998, just three years after Netscape's IPO, America Online acquired the company (one of the main things AOL wanted was Netcenter, Netscape's portal—I suppose AOL didn't have three developers with a few weeks to spare). The browser was much less important to Netscape-within-AOL than it had been to Netscape as a separate company, and it showed. On October 12, 1999, the magazine *PC Week* began an evaluation of Netscape's latest browser, Communicator 4.7, with the following: "Pop quiz: Is Communicator 4.7 the latest hot version of the popular browser, or the final nail in the coffin for good commercial browsers from Netscape Communications Corp.? If you chose the latter, pat yourself on the back and start evaluating other browsers." Given how quickly Netscape lost its lead, Microsoft's 20-year run seems much more attributable to hard work and good decisions (and bad decisions by its competitors) than to mere luck.

*   *   *

Related to the Internet phenomenon is the alleged trend away from PCs as the main device for personal and business computing, to a "post-PC" world where PCs share networks with "appliances"—small devices that do only a few things, for example wireless phones that can also surf the Web. In a world like this, "on-the-wire" compatibility—the ability of devices to communicate using the same network protocol—becomes much more important than having all the parts come from one vendor. Such a market does not naturally tend towards a single software platform from one big company, the way the PC market did. Certainly, to dominate this market, Microsoft will need to work much harder than it did in the 1990s. Microsoft's response has indeed been to work harder—to try to dominate the set-top box platform market and the wireless phone platform market and the game system platform market and the hand-held device platform market and the smart card platform market and whatever other software platforms come along.

Why is Microsoft trying to stretch itself so thin rather than concentrating on its core PC business? The Microsoft way of approaching a situation like this is called "embrace and extend." What this means in the PC world is that when you put a PC running Microsoft software into an existing environment of heterogeneous machines—some Unix machines, some Macintoshes, and so on—it can communicate with them all reasonably well. However, it can communicate with other PCs even better—say, it can transfer files a little faster, or setup is easier. And if you switch your entire network over to be all PCs, they can all communicate even better.

How is this done? First is the "embrace" part—Microsoft's software can communicate using the same network protocols as the non-Microsoft systems it is "talking" to. Then comes the "extend" part—if a machine running Windows discovers that the other machine it is talking to is also running Windows, it will start using Microsoft-specific extensions to the protocols—or, more often, an entirely different protocol that unlocks more powerful features. So when two Windows machines talk to each other, they magically become more than the sum of their parts.

This all sounds nifty, and has worked well in the past. The problem is that it takes a lot of development work to do this, and even more testing work, as the number of possible machine pairs grows. What you need is to rather quickly—within a few releases—go to a model where the proprietary protocol is your main focus, and the standard one is the weak sister: sure it works, you can tell customers, but did we mention that if you go to an all-Microsoft network you get all these other benefits too? Then maybe one of your competitors reverse-engineers the proprietary protocol, or perhaps you publish the specs for it once you have some experience in using it. You have now migrated the whole industry off a standard protocol and onto a proprietary one that you control. This is the culmination of the embrace-and-extend strategy.

In a world where you are supporting not just a few operating systems but half a dozen or more, the result is an exponential increase in the size of the test matrix—the number of pairs of systems that you have to test to make sure they can communicate together. Imagine having all those operating systems—for set-top boxes and wireless phones and game systems and hand-held devices and smart cards and whatnot—and trying to maintain both a standard protocol and a proprietary one, and to test them all in every possible combination. If the standard protocol does not quickly disappear, or at least diminish in importance, you are in trouble. It is similar to the situation IBM faced with OS/2, where OS/2 supported both the Presentation Manager API and the Windows API, and Windows supported only the Windows API. In this comparison, your proprietary protocol is playing the role of Presentation Manager, the possibly better solution that has no reason to survive because everything is written to support its competition.

Worse, supporting so many operating systems means that you need to evangelize all of them to software developers. Microsoft has succeeded in the past by heavily evangelizing a very limited number of platforms—with the emphasis on very limited. As the company tries to branch out from the core Windows 98 and Windows 2000 platforms to included Windows CE for hand-held devices, the Xbox for games, and who knows what else for future hardware, the message to developers about which platform to write for becomes more and more confused, hurting Microsoft's key strength in the industry.

When Gordon Bell spoke to the NT team in early 1994, he discussed his vision of a worldwide computer network that was as universally easy to plug into as the phone system—the Internet, of course, although back then few people thought of it that way. But contrary to the current thought that the Internet will allow a huge variety of devices to thrive, Bell felt that it was important that the same system be running everywhere, to keep the network from getting bogged down with small incompatibilities between the machines, and to allow the same applications to run on all systems without getting bogged down in layers of middleware. Bell proposed that NT was the great hope to become this universal system.

I agree with Bell. I think Microsoft should stay home and defend the PC franchise, rather than try to cover all the bases and risk losing everything. A few years ago, a new class of machine came along that was dubbed the Network Computer, or NC. The big advantage of the NC was that it was simple: it had no local hard drive. The theory was that the less there was to it, the less could go wrong, both in terms of components breaking, and in terms of the user playing around with the software that was on the machine. The NC would only do Web browsing and run Java applets. The big backers of the NC were companies like Oracle and Sun, which were concerned about competition from Microsoft.

The NC was a throwback to the old days of computing, where people had terminals on their desks that connected to a mainframe on which their data was stored. The NC was announced with huge hype, but that has died away. First, it was not that much cheaper to build an NC than a real PC; you still needed a monitor, keyboard, mouse, memory—all you saved was the cost of a hard drive. Second, you lost the ability to expand the hardware—to add a printer or a scanner or a camera. If you added all that, you moved away from the simplicity that was at the core of the NC argument. It also turned out that people like to have control of their own machines and didn't want to go back to the old days.

When I was working on networking for NT back in the early 1990s, the main competition was Novell. One of Novell's main advantages was speed; its Netware server was faster than NT at performing many common network operations, especially as the number of clients grew. We eventually discovered that one of the keys to this was that Novell had designed its server to be dumb and its clients to be smart. Any time it was possible, work had been moved from the server to the client. As an example, in any network protocol there has to be some code that determines whether a packet that was sent by one machine was lost on the network before it reached the other machine. This typically involves starting an internal timer when the packet is sent, and if the expected response packet has not arrived by the time the timer expires, it is sent again. In Novell's architecture this was all the client's responsibility, which meant that the server had less code to run each time it sent a packet. As more clients were added, the load on the server grew more slowly. The NC design reverses this, putting all the intelligence on the server, and therefore making it harder to scale the server up to handle more clients. Of course, in an environment for Internet startup companies where venture capital money is essentially free, having to pay top dollar for a souped-up server is not a deterrent to using such a design.

Most important, Microsoft was able to respond to the NC with better software for the PC. The mantra used to defend the NC was Total Cost of Ownership, or TCO. The theory was that the physical cost of the hardware was only a fraction of the real costs, which included time spent setting up the systems, time spent fixing them when they broke, time the user lost while the machines were being fixed, and the "futz factor," time the user spent playing with their background colors, installing new software, and other unproductive tasks. Fine, said Microsoft, if you are worried about TCO, we have our own acronym for you—ZAW, or Zero Administration Windows. Zero administration by the user, that is. ZAW lets a central administrator set up a machine so that users cannot change the background colors or install new software unless they are permitted to—or, if the administrator chooses, forced to do so. If this sounds vaguely Orwellian to you, you are not alone. An early ZAW specification that I saw had on its cover a takeoff of the "Intel Inside" logo that read "Big Brother Inside."

Microsoft should be able to produce software that combines the best of both the PC and NC designs. The system could be simple to set up and use but also take advantage of the processing power and expandability of the PC. The fact that the NC stores data on the server makes backup easy, but means that it can take longer to store and retrieve your data, and if you cannot connect to the server, you can't work at all. A PC could store data in both places, allowing you to work if the server is down, but also automatically saving your changes to the server. More generally, if Microsoft keeps focused on the PC, it should be able to continue extending the platform, and maintain the functionality lead it has over dedicated devices, while copying their ease of use.

It should also be pointed out that the folks who are beating the drum about the future world of wireless Internet devices—the engineers, analysts, venture capitalists, bankers, and journalists who constitute the geek royalty of the moment—are also the ones who could actually envision using this kind of technology. Does the general populace really need to check their stock quotes or answer email while waiting in an airport lounge?

This kind of thinking is out of fashion at the moment, and its proponents are accused of not "getting" the Internet, but I think the real courage right now would be to stand up and defend the old model. This should ensure that the PC remains the central device in the new era of computing. Those other devices are, in a sense, like the hardware equivalent of middleware. They are an attempt to abstract out what are felt to be the important aspects of a PC, but they suffer from lower performance and the same lack of flexibility that middleware does for software: the designers have to take a snapshot of the industry and decide which technologies to include—USB no, PCCard yes, and so on. If they miss something, there is a delay before they can incorporate it into their products.

The PC should continue to be the hardware on which new technologies occur first. Other devices should be viewed as reduced versions of PCs, for use when you are in the field or don't have room for a keyboard or are in your living room rather than your den, with the understanding that you are temporarily trading off functionality for convenience. For the bulk of your tasks you will return to the one true computing device, the PC. Networking protocols will be evaluated in terms of how well they allow other devices to connect to a PC; the PC will remain the sun around which all the other devices revolve. Failure to bring this about will be a resounding indictment of the way in which Microsoft designs and develops software, and any resulting loss of market share will be well deserved.

16

Twenty-First Century Company

Despite Microsoft's past success against its competitors, I do not think the company's future is unremittingly bright. But the real problems will come from within. Microsoft is not a company with a firm set of procedures in place; it depends almost entirely on having exceptional employees. And I believe that in the near future, Microsoft is going to have trouble both in hiring more exceptional employees and in keeping the ones it has.

The most painful thing for Microsoft employees about all the legal issues swirling around is not so much the fear that Microsoft will be proven "wrong" in some sense of the word. It sounds trite, but the worst thing is that there has been a sense of innocence lost. In years past I went about my workday at Microsoft feeling upright, honest, noble, and true, and I assume other employees did also. Now Microsoft, because it is being sued by the attorneys general of multiple states, is being compared to tobacco companies. Once upon a time employees expected that Microsoft would be able to go about its business unencumbered by political concerns, buoyed by the power and popularity of its products. But in the past few years Microsoft has had to hire lobbyists, just like everyone else. I would remember stories of American companies trying to win contracts in countries where bribery is rampant and having to pay bribes of their own. I would wonder, would Microsoft be able to stay above all that in such a situation? Would its competitors allow it to? The notion is out there among Microsoft employees that when things get political, they don't always stay fair. Companies like Netscape that are losing on the technical battlefield can easily switch over to the political arena. Microsoft can win the business battles, and may win the current Justice Department case on appeal, but *someday* Microsoft is going to lose one of the political battles. As has already happened when the antitrust verdict was announced, these setbacks hurt something that people care a lot about—the price of Microsoft stock.

Ever since the Apple lawsuit ruling in 1992, people at Microsoft have been incredibly focused on the price of the stock. One reason is that the connection between hard work and the stock price is mentioned frequently: "Let's ship this and get the stock price up!" This has always been true: people have continued to work hard at Microsoft, and the stock price has continued to go up. It is an over-simplification, certainly. At many companies, people work hard and the stock price goes down, or the company gets bought out, or goes out of business. And as Microsoft becomes more and more of a bellwether stock for the entire technology sector of the stock market, or even the whole stock market itself, the price of Microsoft stock is more and more tied to general market conditions, as opposed to anything that Microsoft specifically does or is going to do. To employees this can be somewhat mysterious—on a day when the company doesn't announce anything, get sued by anybody, or have its stock downgraded by any analysts, the stock will drop 3%. Closer investigation will reveal that the whole market dropped, and Microsoft went along for the ride. As computers become more widespread and the computer market becomes increasingly saturated, Microsoft's ability to grow becomes more tied to the overall growth rate of the economy. As Microsoft becomes more and more of an international company, events overseas have more potential to affect earnings. So events like inflation fears or the Asian financial crisis of 1998 can create sudden downward pressure on the stock price, leaving puzzled Microsoft employees wondering, "What did I do?"

Why are employees so focused on the price of the stock? Two words that I have mentioned before—stock options.

Stock options are granted to certain categories of employees (such as developers) as a sign-on bonus. An option allows you to buy the stock at a specified price, known as the "strike price." For a new hire, that price is set at the lowest closing value of the stock in the first 30 days of employment. You cannot exercise the options right away; they become available ("vested") gradually, starting on the one-year anniversary of your grant date, and become fully vested 4 1/2 years after the grant date.

Let's say you were granted 200 options when you started, and the low stock price in your first 30 days was $50 per share. A year later, when the first eighth of your options vests, the stock is at $80 per share. So you can take that eighth of your options—25 shares—and immediately earn $30 per share on them, or $750. That $750 is free money, which you earned with no risk to yourself. And you still have 175 more options that will vest gradually over the next 3 1/2 years.

Now, $750 may not seem like much, but that's merely the tip of the iceberg. At the start of the 1990s the stock was around $100 a share, and at the end of the decade, it was also around $100 a share—but taking into account stock splits that have happened in the interim adds up to a 72-for-1 split. Thus, the stock was effectively trading at $7,200 a share in 1990 terms. So those 175 remaining options granted back in 1990, if you still had them, were worth well over $1 million before taxes.

Furthermore, every July employees are granted more stock options, which also vest over 4 1/2 years from when they are granted. The "golden handcuffs" of stock options will exist for employees as long as the price of the stock continues to go up.

Back when I started, few people expected to get rich from their stock options. One person who started just before I did said he thought they might be worth a few thousand dollars. I do recall one supervisor of mine who came to Microsoft from Apple in 1987 expressly because he thought the Microsoft options would be worth money. When he signed on, he bargained for a lower salary and more options, which Microsoft at the time was happy to grant him. Needless to say, he is now retired and living in a lovely lakefront home. With the various stories about Microsoft millionaires, and the rise of companies like Netscape, people starting now are much more aware of the value of options. As a result, Microsoft now rarely bargains with stock options when hiring people.

This wealth can have a strange effect on people. One employee with a few more stock options than he knew what to do with bought a car as a gift for a receptionist he was enamored of. Some employees treat the money as a gift, a rainy-day fund, but don't change their lifestyle much. My friend Avi Belinsky, former co-sysop of the Transylvania BBS who eventually also worked at Microsoft, once called me up to ask if I thought it was okay for him to buy a Mazda Miata and pay cash for it. He wasn't worried about the cost of the car—he was worried that by buying it he would be crossing some invisible line that changed who he was in some fundamental way. We had grown up in similar circumstances—both our fathers were college professors, we had lived a few blocks apart, and we attended the same grade school and high school, and he wanted to use me as a barometer to verify that paying cash for a Miata was not morally wrong and ridiculous in some way. I told him to buy the damned car.

*   *   *

One interesting effect of Microsoft stock's growth in the 1990s is that people got wealthy from options who never planned to. In Silicon Valley today, employees who get rich from options are the ones who took the risk of going to work at a startup company that had yet to make a public stock offering. People who joined Microsoft in 1990 were joining a company that was 15 years old, employed 5,000 people, had been publicly traded for four years, and had already seen its stock rise by a factor of ten. Yet this large, established company still earned them piles of cash. Perhaps this explains why people who strike it rich in Silicon Valley tend to immediately want to use the money to fund their own startup companies, while many of those at Microsoft want to take it easy for a while.

Some people do view options as their chance to get rich, and the richer the better. If Microsoft stock ever peaks, it will be visible only in retrospect. Often the stock has appeared to peak—when a recent spate of good news has driven it up, and bad news appears to be lurking on the horizon—and this has caused people to cash in large portions of their options. But the stock has so far always continued to rise, leading to anguished games of "what if" as people calculate how much they lost out on by exercising their options when they did. By the time I left Microsoft my initial grant had long since been exercised and the proceeds converted into other investments, and it could be momentarily depressing to calculate how much they would have been worth if I had had the foresight (and the intestinal fortitude) to hang on to them until the end.

In fact the stock dropped in the last few months I worked at Microsoft, so if I had really held my options to the end, I would have been depressed for holding on too long. Many employees are playing a nervous game of chicken with their options, hanging on to them, holding their breath through each drop in the price, and hoping that they have not already missed the peak. If this group, as a whole, ever decides that the peak has been reached, or has just passed, they may exercise their options en masse. Once people have no more options left, they have much less incentive to stay at Microsoft. They will have July-granted options continuing to trickle in every six months or so, but once they have the big stash in the bank, it becomes harder and harder for them to convince themselves to work for each extra six months just to earn a little bit more. The current antitrust situation is making people a little more nervous than usual, but it seems at the moment people are still holding out hope that the stock will rebound.

Thus, it becomes imperative for Microsoft to keep the stock price rising, or more specifically, to keep alive optimism that the stock price will continue to rise. Microsoft has historically had low turnover among its employees and, as I have said, relies much more on individual talent than on carefully thought out and documented processes for its continued success. At the current turnover rates the company is able to assimilate new employees effectively, but if ever the turnover rate tips beyond the point where the assimilation works, the company could suffer a rather drastic impairment of its ability to ship software.

For this reason, I think that Microsoft should consider splitting the company in two. The split would not be the one between the "systems" and "applications" groups that has been mandated in the Justice Department lawsuit ruling; instead, it would be between the old software business and the new Internet content business. Internet content firms are all losing money. Microsoft is no exception, except that the losses are all rolled together into corporate earnings, where they pale next to the massive profits generated by the desktop software groups. If the company were split, shareholders would be left holding shares in two companies: the old software Microsoft, which would now be more profitable than it used to be, and therefore would presumably see its stock price rise somewhat; and a new money-losing Internet content company, which would then be valued by the stock market at the same inflated price as all the other money-losing Internet content companies.

Bill Gates would presumably stay with the old software Microsoft, where he has shown over 25 years that he has an excellent knack for steering the company. It is *not* clear that he has the same knack for Internet content; he certainly is not a typical user, and there is no particular reason why he would have an innate feel for what the average Joe Internet wants. Splitting that off would allow him to devote all of his time to his core competence, the software side of the company.

*   *   *

A question looming over Microsoft is whether it will be able to support long-term careers. The company is only 25 years old; nobody except Bill has worked there for more than 20 years, and only around a thousand employees have been there for 10. Will Microsoft eventually become a place where people work all their lives and then retire at 65? Will Microsoft ever be able to support an employee who works 9 to 5, five days a week, for 40 years? If there is one thing that people associate with Microsoft, it is working long hours. Whenever my father told someone that I worked there, invariably the first thing they said was, "He must work a lot of hours." If Microsoft ever wants to endorse a product for profit, it should pick No-Doz—imagine an ad with Bill saying, "This is the stuff our guys use!"

Consider this description of Microsoft from a former intern quoted in Hadi Partovi's memo about campus recruiting, back in 1994: "The perception is that Microsoft is no longer an exciting place to work, that it has lost the small startup excitement that it had even five years ago....I would much rather work at a small startup, with lots of responsibility and a real sense of excitement in the air than at MS where the median age seems to have risen, and everyone seems to have a kid between the ages of 2 and 5."

When I first started working at Microsoft I had read *The Soul of a New Machine* and wanted to earn my own wings as much as that former intern obviously did, and I was single, so I worked all the time. Once I had entered the "kid between the ages of 2 and 5" phase, I scaled back my hours dramatically. At the same time, toward the end of my Microsoft career I felt as though I was gradually drifting away. My opinion wasn't as important as it once had been, even though I had much more experience to bring to bear. There was little chance of my being asked to manage a large team, because becoming a manager requires showing extra initiative, which means extra hours. In the book *Microsoft Secrets*, there is a quote about how potential managers are identified: "We'd like to believe that the team lead can do...at least as much as the other members of his team and his other stuff. In other words, I've got some solid good programmers on my team. If I'm really qualified to be the lead, I should be able to do as much in a week as he can do. But I really do it in three days…and spend the other two doing my other duties." That sounds great, but when the lead is making his schedule, will his boss let him say, "I am only scheduling myself for three days of development work each week"? Highly doubtful. Instead, that extra works winds up being done in extra hours each day. I was very leery of being a manager, because it puts even more pressure on you to work more hours.

Why do employees need to work so many hours? The key is that management does not view employee time as a scarce resource. Even if employees have spent time doing non-scheduled things at management's behest, they are still expected to attempt to meet their original schedule. Extra time worked by employees is a tool that can be used to whitewash any number of bad decisions made by management.

Will Microsoft go stale if people aren't working like crazy? Does the company need to keep people in a panic so it won't appear ponderous to college seniors it is trying to hire? I have often heard the comment that if a Microsoft employee is committed to a project, he or she will want to work the extra hours, or conversely, that people would not want to work on a project where people weren't excited enough to work a lot. I think this attitude (which I once shared) is wrong. Work may be important, but people may have outside commitments that are just as real, even if they are not reflected in an employment contract or a paycheck. Employees should not be marginalized due to a perceived lack of commitment.

The current discussion about employees leaving Microsoft is focusing on those who leave because they think Microsoft isn't stressful enough—people who want to start their own company. I think a greater concern as Microsoft matures, especially as experienced employees grow rich through stock options, is a brain drain of employees leaving because they want *less* stress. Six to ten years after college is one of the most demanding times at work, as people make the transition to middle-level management.

Unfortunately it can also be one of the most demanding times outside of work, as many people have several preschool-aged children at home. At a company like IBM, employees may work for 40 years—from right after graduation, through marriage and young children, on to having older children at home, and then having the children move out. This career path has been followed over and over. At Microsoft, just 25 years old, nobody knows whether this career path even exists.

The current Microsoft attitude is that if an employee cannot put in the time during a crunch, he or she should step aside and let someone else take the job. A new hire working 80 hours a week is viewed as more valuable than an experienced person working 50 hours a week. When employees are ranked during performance reviews, one test used to determine the ranking is to imagine that the company is on a boat that is sinking and consider which person you would throw overboard first. I always thought this nicely summed up Microsoft's attitude towards employees viewed as non-performing.

A friend of mine once asked Mike Murray, the vice president of Human Resources, if he was worried about experienced employees leaving. Mike said that he was more worried about experienced employees who were stagnating and preventing newer employees from moving up. In the current environment, that kind of thinking is risky. Microsoft has many jobs open and has lost some of its "coolness" factor to other companies. The replacement for that experienced person working 50 hours a week might not be an 80-hour-a-week hotshot, but instead a position that sits open for a year. Or a new-hire who works 80 hours, but gets much less accomplished than an experienced employee would in 50 hours. I must have been in the "deadwood" category that Mike was talking about, because when I announced I was leaving the company nobody made any attempt to convince me to stay. I got no going-away party, or gift, or even a firm handshake. I doubt the response would have been so tepid if I had been working 80-hour weeks.

Once when I was working on shipping a beta version of NT, I had planned to go away for a weekend white-water rafting with some other members of the NT team. I made the mistake of mentioning this to my boss. He told me to cancel the trip, to be around in case something broke. I did, and it still annoys me. This wasn't a vacation during a weekday—only taking Saturday and Sunday off! The other people didn't say anything and just went. So I hung around all weekend, and the only bug I investigated all weekend was in the code of one of the other people who had gone on the trip. At that moment I vowed never again to change my vacation plans for work.

There are other stories like this. It is notoriously difficult to plan vacations in advance because of schedules slipping. One person I know planned a six-week vacation a year in advance, in careful consultation with his manager. As you might expect, the six weeks wound up coming right in the middle of a ship crunch. He ended up leaving his family for part of the vacation and coming back to work. Since he was technically on vacation, he was paid as a consultant. And since he had rented out his house for the six weeks, Microsoft put him up in a hotel.

Months before Windows 2000 shipped, it was announced that the project would be going into "seven-day-a-week" mode, in which the results of overnight stress tests on the product would be reported seven days a week, bugs would be approved seven days a week, and code check-ins would be accepted seven days a week. The implied assumption was that people would also work seven days a week, although this was never explicitly stated. Working every weekend day for three months is the same as working five extra weeks at normal five-day-a-week hours, assuming that as much work gets done on weekend days as on weekdays (and that people's productivity doesn't decline as a result of burnout). Is five extra weeks on a project that took over three years really crucial? It seems hard to believe. What nobody has tried is assuming that you *don't* have the weekend days available for use. Count five days per week until the ship date, see what that allows you to accomplish, and do it. If you can't get it done in time working like that, either do less, or move the ship date back.

Microsoft has grown enough that it now has some real corporate knowledge about how things should be done. In the old days, Microsoft paid little attention to such things, reckoning that smart people would eventually do good things. As projects have gotten bigger, it has become more important to develop an established methodology. Although Microsoft is still lacking in this respect, there have been some real advances, such as the generalized awareness of the features-versus-date rule: you can aim for a feature set or aim for a ship date, but not both at once. Each time an experienced employee leaves he or she takes a little bit of that institutional memory along.

About four months before Windows 2000 shipped, there was a build break at midnight. Why were the builders working at midnight? Well, the previous build had been late getting out, and they had not started until then. And builders, being low on the totem pole, tend to listen when someone asks them to start a build at midnight. In response to this build break, the builders, as they had been ordered, began calling people, starting with the person who had checked in the broken code. When he didn't answer, they called his boss, who told them to jump in a lake. So the builders called *his* boss, who told them to call the first person again. He eventually answered, and wound up spending an hour and a half, from 12:30 to 2 a.m., fixing the break. It turned out the problem was not even in his code, but in some code from another company that he had been asked to check in.

This wasn't the day before the product was shipping; this was months before shipping. Waiting until the next morning to fix the problem would have been highly unlikely to delay the product. The whole situation upset me enough to send nasty email to the NT management team. To a man they all replied echoing the company line: if you broke the build you would get called, no matter when. You could feel the smugness oozing out of the email—"We showed 'em what happens when you break the build."

*   *   *

Microsoft sends out an annual survey to its employees. One of the questions presents two hypothetical people, A and B, and asks you which one you feel closer to. Person A says, "I am fully committed to my work and often do more than I have to do. My job is important to me and I am willing to give a lot for it." Person B says, "At my job, I do what I have to and no one can complain about my work. I don't see any point in doing more than I am required to." Another pair of people is quoted. A says, "I have a great deal at Microsoft. I work hard to make Microsoft successful, and Microsoft lavishly rewards me and gives me a great work environment in return. There is no place I'd rather work." B says, "I have an OK deal at Microsoft. I work hard to make Microsoft successful, but I often feel I give Microsoft more than I get in return. Microsoft is a good place to work, but there are lots of other companies that are just as good or better to their employees." In a third question, A says, "I never even think about leaving. I love working here—I wouldn't think about working anywhere else. As long as Microsoft continues to be a great place to work, I intend to stay here." B says, "I think quite a bit about leaving. I have a timeframe and/or stock price in mind. There are things happening here at Microsoft and/or in my personal life that are making me think hard about how long I'm going to continue here."

The challenge for Microsoft management, if it chooses to accept it, is to reorient itself to rescue those B employees. Development tasks would have to be prioritized correctly. Meetings would be kept to a minimum. Builds would not be scheduled to be released to testing at 9 p.m. It would be understood that the bug not fixed today would likely be fixed tomorrow. Management would have to be able to say "NO" to their bosses, to Bill, to the trade press, to customers. Projects that slipped would be accepted as such, with the pledge to do better next time—not by having employees work more hours than they did, but by considering how the entire team could have better anticipated and handled the slip.

Does Microsoft see any value in accepting this challenge? That remains to be seen.

*   *   *

In late 1998, a marketing decision was made to change the name of the Windows NT operating system. The team that had been working on what it thought would be NT version 5 now found itself working on a product called Windows 2000 (subtitled "powered by NT technology").

Some NT veterans decided to hold a "Windows NT wake." The email invitation read: "Come and help us celebrate 10 years of the greatest OS on earth. Come and help us mourn the passing of the 'NT' moniker, the one that shook the industry. We are having a private gathering of all the old timers to remember NT, NT the way it used to be. Let us remember friends gone by, buildings left behind, and roosters laid to rest. Let's drink beer, retell old stories, and bask in the memories of the greatest team EVER." (At some point in the early development of NT, a rooster took up residence for a while on the shore of the small lake next to the building where the team was located, eventually disappearing as mysteriously as it had come.)

At the wake, T-shirts were handed out with "Windows NT: 1988–1998" inscribed on them. From all over the company, people who had worked on the early versions came together in the cafeteria of Building 26 to drink free beer and rehash old times. The team had almost all stuck together up until the shipment of the second version, in 1994, but since then it had fragmented; some of those assembled hadn't seen each other in four years.

There were a couple of televisions set up, showing various videos that had been made back then. I got sentimental watching this, and not just because everyone looked so young. Someone said, semi-seriously, "Give me a hug!"

One of the videos was a "day in the life of the NT team," showing team members working (and occasionally playing) in Building 2, the old home of NT. It was shot back in 1992. The building was much smaller; the team was much smaller. The build lab had three people working in it; the other labs looked ridiculously small.

In one segment, Dave Cutler, gruff as ever, sat on his chair in his office and talked about the team at the time, how they had grown together, and how great a team it was. He said, "Someday we're going to look back and realize that these are the good old days."

Watching it, six years later, I knew he was right. I had changed, and Microsoft had changed, and for better or worse, the good old days were gone.

About the Author

Adam Barr grew up in Mount Royal, a suburb of Montreal. He received a Bachelor of Science in Engineering degree in Computer Science and Electrical Engineering from Princeton University in 1988. After graduation he worked as a software developer, first at a small company called Dendrite Americas, then at Microsoft. At Microsoft he worked on several software projects, including the first two versions of Windows NT, interactive television, Softimage, and the fifth version of Windows NT, known as Windows 2000. He left Microsoft in April 2000 to take a break and work on this book. He lives in Redmond, Washington with his wife and three children. This is his first book.

Glossary

Application. A computer program that runs on top of an operating system and generally interacts with the user to perform a particular set of tasks on the user's behalf, for example, a word processor. What precisely causes a program to be called an "application" is the subject of some debate.

Application Programming Interface (API). A well-defined interface between two layers of software. The layer on top is said to call the API; the layer on the bottom is said to export the API.

Assembly language. A low-level computer language that is closely tied to the machine language of a specific microprocessor. Assembly language is human-readable, but whereas one line of code in a higher-level language may correspond to many lines of machine language, one line of assembly language usually corresponds to one line of machine language.

Assembler. A program that translates assembly language to machine language. The term is also used to mean assembly language itself.

Beta. An early test version of a piece of software that is sent outside the company for others to use. Betas can be used to test the features of a piece of software, or to test it for stability, or to give users a chance to prepare for migrating to the final version when it is released.

Binary. A compiled program, so-called because it is represented in binary notation, where every digit is a one or a zero.

BIOS. Acronym for Basic Input/Output System. The lowest level of software on a computer, layered between the operating system and the hardware. BIOSes are sometimes referred to as "firmware."

Bit. Contraction of "binary digit;" a bit can hold either a one or a zero.

Bug. A flaw in a piece of software.

Build. As a verb, to compile a program. As a noun, can mean either the process of compiling a program or the resulting compiled program.

Build break. A syntax error in the source code that prevents a build from completing successfully.

Bus. Electronic circuitry within a computer that is used to move data between different parts of the computer, such as the memory, the hard drive, and the video screen. Expansion cards will be designed to fit a specific bus, such as EISA, ISA, PCI, or VESA.

Byte. 8 bits of data, which is enough to hold approximately one character.

C. A programming language, in which most of Microsoft's operating system code is written.

Check in. As a verb, to copy source code from a developer's machine to a central source control server. The noun "checkin" refers to a set of source code that is checked in together.

Code. As a verb, to write software. As a noun, a computer program, generally used when referring to it in source form.

Compile. To convert source code into machine language.

Compiler. A program that compiles software.

Debugging. Determining why a bug occurred, in particular what specific part of the source code is at fault.

Developer. A programmer. At Microsoft this is the most common term used, abbreviated to "dev."

DOS. Acronym for Disk Operating System. Microsoft's first operating system, designed for the original IBM PC. IBM referred to it as DOS; the press usually referred to the version specifically made for the IBM PC as PC-DOS; Microsoft, which initially supported it on other platforms besides the IBM PC, called it MS-DOS.

Driver. A low-level piece of software that usually talks directly to hardware at the driver's bottom layer.

EISA. Acronym for Extended ISA (see ISA). A faster version of the ISA bus, designed by IBM's competitors as competition for MCA.

Execute. To run a piece of software. In a sentence, "execute" isn't used when a person is the subject, so you could say "the computer executed the program," but not "Joe executed the program." (see "run" for comparison).

Evangelism. The process of convincing other software developers to write software that interfaces with your software in some way, especially to convince them to call your exported APIs in their code.

Evangelist. A Microsoft job title, for someone responsible for evangelism.

Flyback. An on-campus interview candidate deemed worthy of being flown back to Microsoft's main campus in Redmond, Washington for further interviews.

Function. A piece of code that is grouped together to perform a specific operation each time it is executed.

Graphical User Interface (GUI). A computer program or programs that display to the user a look that is similar to that of Microsoft Windows or the Macintosh OS: windows, icons, mouse control, and so on.

ISA. Acronym for Industry Standard Architecture. The bus design included with the first versions of the IBM PC.

Java. A programming language developed by Sun, which is designed to allow programs to run unchanged on any computer.

Linux. An independently-written version of the Unix operating system, developed using the open source development model, available for free to anyone.

Machine language. The sequence of ones and zeroes that the microprocessor on a computer understands and can execute.

MCA. Acronym for MicroChannel Architecture. A bus designed by IBM for inclusion with PS/2 machines, designed to replace ISA and give IBM strict control of expansion cards for the PS/2.

Middleware. A layer of software that generally runs between an application and an operating system, and is meant to hide the details of the operating system from the application.

Open Source. A system for developing software in which the source code is freely shared along with the binaries, and all users are encouraged to read it and suggest changes.

Operating System. The lower levels of software that run on a computer, which hide the details of the hardware and provide a platform on which applications can run.

Original Equipment Manufacturer (OEM). Maker of complete computers, such as Compaq and Dell. The term is particularly used at Microsoft to describe those who include software bundled with computers they sell.

OS/2. An operating system, initially worked on by IBM and Microsoft and later by IBM alone, designed to replace DOS.

PCI. The current standard personal computer bus.

Porting. Modifying a program to allow it to run in a different environment from the one it was initially designed for; in particular, modifying an application written to run on one operating system to enable it to run on a different operating system.

Program. A piece of software that accomplishes a task. Can refer to the source code or the compiled binary.

Program Manager (PM). A Microsoft job title, referring to someone who is responsible for the design of software and also for ensuring that all other work required to ship the software is completed, without having those responsible for that other work actually report to him or her on the organizational chart.

Programmer. Someone who writes software.

PS/2. Acronym for Personal System/2. A line of machines designed by IBM in the late 1980s to replace the IBM PC, aimed (unsuccessfully) at restoring IBM's control of the personal computer industry.

Run. To execute a program. Unlike "execute," "run" can be used either in a sentence like "The computer ran the program" or in one like "Joe ran the program." The second case really means, "Joe caused the computer to run the program."

Software Design Engineer (SDE). A Microsoft job title, referring to developers, a.k.a. programmers. Sometimes mistakenly called Software Development Engineers because of the use of the term "developer."

Software Development Kit (SDK). A package of documentation, sample code, libraries, and so on that is made available to programmers who want to write applications that run on a given platform.

Software Test Engineer (STE). A Microsoft job title, referring to people who test the software to ensure that it is ready to ship. Universally referred to as "testers."

Source Code. The computer instructions that a programmer writes when creating a program.

Source Control Server. A central computer that holds the master copy of all the source code for a project.

TCP/IP. A piece of software, the core network protocol that controls transmission of data over the Internet. A given implementation will have several parts, supporting TCP (Transmission Control Protocol), IP (Internet Protocol), and several other protocols.

Test. A specific task done to check that a piece of software functions as it should. Also used at Microsoft to refer to a testing organization as a whole (as in, "We need to make sure test has signed off on this.").

Unix. An operating system first written at AT&T, known for its stability.

User interface (UI). The top level of software, which the user interacts with.

VESA. A bus that evolved in the early 1990s as a faster replacement for EISA, but which itself was made obsolete by PCI.

Weight. What is created when an application is written to use the API of a specific operating system.

Windows. Microsoft's graphical operating system. There are two main versions of Windows: a mainstream one which has evolved over time from Windows 3.0 to Windows for Workgroups to Windows 95 to Windows 98 to Windows Me; and a more powerful one, which started as Windows NT 3.1 and became Windows NT 3.5, Windows NT 3.51, Windows NT 4.0, and now Windows 2000.

Winsock. An API, created by a committee with members from Microsoft and other companies, that is used to communicate over a network, including the Internet.